Peaceful Selves

PEACEFUL SELVES

*Personhood, Nationhood, and the
Post-Conflict Moment in Rwanda*

Laura Eramian

berghahn
NEW YORK · OXFORD
www.berghahnbooks.com

First published in 2018 by
Berghahn Books
www.berghahnbooks.com

© 2018, 2019 Laura Eramian
First paperback edition published in 2019

Library of Congress Cataloging-in-Publication Data
A C.I.P. cataloging record is available from the Library of Congress

British Library Cataloguing in Publication Data
A catalogue record for this book is available from the British Library

ISBN 978-1-78533-711-6 hardback
ISBN 978-1-78920-493-3 paperback
ISBN 978-1-78533-712-3 ebook

CONTENTS

ILLUSTRATIONS

ACKNOWLEDGMENTS

Ethnographers are always something of a burdensome presence in the lives of our research participants: we need guidance to accomplish basic tasks in cultural settings unfamiliar to us, we ask tedious questions about why people are doing what they're doing, and we're always watching and listening. In other words, we ethnographers ask a lot of our research participants, and I am infinitely grateful to everyone in Rwanda who gave generously of their time, energy, and perspectives. I am especially indebted to my host family, since the presence of a *muzungu* in their household complicated their lives to some degree. Particular thanks also go out to the people I call Charles, Bernadette, Simbi, Rose, Odette, and Pauline, who were extraordinarily patient and helpful throughout my fieldwork. They helped me make connections, talked to me about their lives, and even assisted me in navigating the opaque government bureaucracy of visa applications and research permits. I would also like to thank the National University of Rwanda for providing me with logistical support and a base of operations, as well as the peace-building organizations and student genocide survivors' association whose members were central to the progress of my research. To all of you, *murakozi cyane.*

To my mentors and colleagues who offered support—intellectual and moral—throughout this process, my deepest gratitude. For guidance and comments on various versions of this work, I thank Malcolm Blincow, Carlota McAllister, Lindsay DuBois, Martha Radice, Paul Antze, Susan Thomson, and Dan Yon. I would also like to thank the peer reviewers whose constructive suggestions helped to strengthen this book.

Thanks to my colleagues in the Department of Sociology and Social Anthropology at Dalhousie University for providing me with an intellectually stimulating and warmly collegial environment in which to write this manuscript. From informal conversations in the hallway to feedback on an early version of Chapter 2 that I presented at the Department Speakers Series in 2012, I am grateful for your support.

I would like to acknowledge the support of the Social Sciences and Humanities Research Council of Canada and its Doctoral Canada Graduate

Scholarship, which supported the fieldwork on which most of this book is based. Dalhousie University's Academic Innovation Funding supported the fieldwork I conducted in 2014. Parts of Chapter 2 have been previously published in two journal articles, "Ethnicity without Labels? Ambiguity and Excess in Postethnic Rwanda," which appeared in *Focaal: Journal of Global and Historical Anthropology* Volume 70 and "Ethnic Boundaries in Contemporary Rwanda: Fixity, Flexibility, and Their Limits," which appeared in *Anthropologica* Volume 57, Issue 1. An earlier version of Chapter 3 was published in an article, "Personhood, Violence, and the Moral Work of Memory in Contemporary Rwanda," in the *International Journal of Conflict and Violence* Volume 8, Issue 1.

My thanks go out to the editorial staff at Berghahn Books for shepherding this project through to completion. I have greatly appreciated their careful, timely management of all aspects of the editorial and production process.

To my family, who spurred me on from fieldwork to finished manuscript, I am deeply appreciative. To my spouse and partner in life, Peter Mallory, it is hard to overstate what you did to make this book possible. From your long-distance moral support during my many months of fieldwork, to your careful readings and thoughtful feedback on every single chapter at every single stage of their development, to your sweetly uninhibited enthusiasm for this project, you saw it through with me from start to finish. Finally, to my parents, thank you for the love of learning and curiosity about the world you instilled in me all my life. This book is dedicated to my dad, Gregory Eramian, and to the loving memory of my mom, Linda Eramian.

ABBREVIATIONS

ARPR	Association rwandaise pour la paix et la réconciliation (Rwandan Association for Peace and Reconciliation; a pseudonym)
ICPD	Institut pour la construction de la paix durable (Institute for Sustainable Peace Building; a pseudonym)
IRSAC	Institut pour la recherche scientifique en Afrique central (Institute for Scientific Research in Central Africa)
MRND	Mouvement révolutionnaire national pour le développement (National Revolutionary Movement for Development)
NGO	Non-governmental organization
NUR	National University of Rwanda
NURC	National Unity and Reconciliation Commission
PARMEHUTU	Parti du mouvement de l'émancipation Hutu (Hutu Emancipation Movement Party)
RPF	Rwandan Patriotic Front
RWF	Rwandan Franc, the local currency
SORWAL	Société rwandaise d'allumettes (Rwandan Match Company, a match factory in Butare)
UNAMIR	United Nations Mission for Rwanda
UNAR	Union nationale rwandaise (National Union of Rwanda)

Introduction

PERSON, NATION, AND VIOLENCE IN RWANDA

❧

> A human being is only human. You can change at
> any moment. We are conditioned by our lives, by our
> entourage. No one is stable.
> —Thomas, Butare, February 2009

Butare[1] residents are vigilant people. Very little escapes their notice, and from the countless vantage points in the town's hilly terrain, there always seems to be someone watching. When they spot the professor from up the road wearing a suit in the morning, they speculate that he must be on his way to the capital, Kigali. They wonder what takes him there so often and who pays for his travels. One person might tell another that he saw his car parked at an upscale hotel restaurant, a characteristically indirect way of commenting on the driver's extravagant consumption choice. Local authorities call on the population to be on the lookout for former *génocidaires* (those who committed genocide) returned from neighboring Burundi or Congo to finish what they started in 1994. Door locking is practiced compulsively, and razor wire and broken glass line the brick walls that transform wealthy people's homes into miniature compounds. And with a very different kind of vigilance—one that indicates the magnitude of devastation that befell Rwanda two decades ago and the moral imperative to remember—long-time town residents are capable of naming precisely how many and what kinds of relations even their relatively distant acquaintances lost in the 1994 genocide.

Perhaps it should come as no surprise that people monitor each other and remember losses carefully in a social world still marred by the violence of 1994. The Rwandan genocide captivated and horrified the world not only because so few outsiders to the region knew anything about this tiny, landlocked central African country, but also because of the unnervingly intimate way in which the massacres unfolded. On orders from the government led by the Mouvement révolutionnaire national pour le développement (MRND),[2] the military, youth militias, and ordinary citizens took up arms against their Tutsi compatriots and "moderate" Hutu opponents of the genocidal campaign. Subsistence farmers, laborers, schoolteachers, fishermen, and university students alike joined in the massacres and looted victims' belongings. The Hutu-led government of the 1990s had painted all Rwandan Tutsi as complicit with the Rwandan Patriotic Front (RPF), a Tutsi-led invading force from neighboring Uganda that sparked a civil war in October 1990. In the end, analysts estimate that 800,000[3] people were killed between April and July of 1994, an endpoint marked by the RPF taking control of Kigali and forming a transitional government. Tutsi genocide survivors describe the genocide as a time of chaos when they did not know who was a protector and who was an executioner, or which of their family members were dead or alive. Today, survivors muse in private moments about how tranquil Butare felt in the months leading up to the violence. "It was so calm, just like it is now," Hélèna,[4] a genocide survivor, remarked ominously one evening as dusk fell on the town. "We didn't know what they were planning. We didn't see it coming." And so, Butare residents search for signs. They keep their eyes and ears open for signs of danger in the habits of neighbors and strangers alike, and they wonder what warning signs they missed in 1994 and whether things could have been otherwise.

Two decades after the genocide, Rwandans are still grappling with vexing questions of how an ordinary population could be mobilized to kill their neighbors, colleagues, and friends and what this means for their collective futures. What kinds of persons were capable of making or letting the genocide happen? And most pressing of all, how can Rwandans know that it will not happen again? Vigilance over home security or returning *génocidaires* might seem like very different practices from everyday scrutiny of which neighbors are going to Kigali or where they go to eat or drink. But in Butare, it is precisely these observations, interpretations, accountings, and evaluations that expose the inseparability of concerns about outbreaks of violence and attentiveness to the moral status of one's co-residents. It is *through* everyday evaluations—of what is good versus contemptible, of why some prosper while most struggle, of what people owe to each other, and of the basis of social belonging—that Butaréens[5] puzzle through those bigger questions about what made the violence possible. What I suggest in this book is that

Rwandans' understandings of post-genocide social life and their efforts to make sense of the violent past converge on the predicaments of personhood and self-making.

Anthropology, Personhood, and the Post-Conflict Moment in Rwanda

This book tells a story of how Rwandan visions of peace and modern nationhood find expression not just in the political, legal, administrative, economic, ideological, citizenship, and even architectural reforms that other authors have analyzed (e.g. Doughty 2014; Newbury 2011; Pottier 2002; Purdeková 2015; Reyntjens 2015a). My ethnographic findings show that such visions also depend crucially on the production of new kinds of persons in the quest for modern nationhood, since both state leaders and the population at large envision the causes of violence and possibilities for peace largely through the capacities of persons. The intersection of persons with politics is especially palpable in Butare, the "intellectual capital," from which dominant ideas about ethnic difference and the legitimating fictions of government regimes have long been disseminated. By personhood, I mean not a psychological, biological, or even legal property of human beings, but rather the fundamentally social and cultural nature of the *category* of the person and the modes by which people enact it through concrete practices (Lester 2017). It is the sociocultural basis of personhood that places it squarely within the purview of the anthropologist's ethnographic sensibility.[6] Personhood is a cornerstone of classic and contemporary social anthropology, and especially debates about whether persons are best understood as bounded, cohesive, and autonomous versus porous, composite, and comprised of relationships with others (e.g. Battaglia 1995; Carrithers, Collins, and Lukes 1985; Carsten 2004; Comaroff and Comaroff 2001; Dieterlen 1973; Dumont 1992; Ferguson 2013; Fortes [1973] 1987; Jackson and Karp 1990; Lambek 2015; Marriott 1976; Mauss [1938] 1985; Piot 1993; Riesman 1986; Strathern 1988; Wagner 1991). It is a conceptual category situated at the nexus of the self[7] and the collective, and it informs the obligations people have to particular others—both living and dead. Indeed, we cannot ask what a person is without asking how people respond to the question, "Who are you?" Whether the answer is a surname and given name, only a given name, or a relational identifier (e.g. "I am the son of A"), it communicates cultural principles for how to locate others and how people belong to and with each other. Any given view of the person necessarily implies a view of how people can and should connect to and detach from each other (Hickman 2014: 317). It raises nothing less than the very condition of possibility for groupness and the basis on which collective life is sustained (Cohen 1994: 8, 22), both of which have been profoundly called into question in Rwanda by the history of violence.

The personhood concept is analytically powerful because it captures the fundamental tension between who we are versus who we think we ought to be or could become (Jacobson-Widding 1990: 31). Indeed, personhood demands a view of life as intrinsically problematic (Jackson and Karp 1990: 28): those "oughts" are never singular or consistent, and people can and do feel that they are simultaneously supposed to be very different kinds of persons. This is more than a problem of role conflict. These tensions are located in the fundamental nature of the self—a never static or uncontested abstraction that underlies how people draw on shared yet contested values to make and remake their social worlds (ibid.). In this sense, personhood is an inescapably normative element of social life. In Mauss's terminology, it is shared expectations of *la personne* against which *le moi*[8] or actual selves and the things they say and do are measured. People are never simply "passive bearers" of personhood (Fortes [1973] 1987: 251). Their appropriations of the norms that govern it and the practices through which they enact it (Lester 2017) are precisely what preoccupy the ethnographer. Hence, while formalized ideas about the nature of persons should not be conflated with experiences of *being* a self, they should not be dichotomized either.

The normative element of personhood raises the kinds of things of which people are, could be, or should be capable. As Talal Asad (1993: 13) writes, personhood cannot be teased apart from the *capacities* attributed to "normal persons"—and, by extension, extraordinary persons. In the post-genocide moment in Butare, people's evaluations of each other revolve around discerning capacities for autonomy or dependency, solidarity or exclusion, meeting or breaking obligations, and most crucially perhaps, capacities for violence or for resisting calls to commit it. The question of capacities is shot through with popular Tutsi and Hutu[9] stereotypes, because in Rwanda, different ways of getting things done are ethnically marked, although often indeterminately so. Ethnicity in Rwanda constitutes the core idioms in which unfold state formation struggles and debates about what a modern, independent Rwandan nation ought to look like. But at the level of everyday practice, ethnicity also informs shared expectations around personal capacities (Eramian 2015). Since Tutsi and Hutu stereotypes remain linked with the nature of work, social relations, hierarchy, and equality (Doughty 2015: 431; Eramian 2014), the possibility is always open for remarks about someone's capacities for honesty, treachery, dependency, or autonomy to be received as "ethnic" commentaries. Even more troublesome, social actors appear to have contradictory capacities—for both meeting and breaching obligations, for both aiding and exploiting others, or for both violence and empathy, having killed a neighbor but saved a friend. As Thomas elucidated in the epigraph, it is the changeability of what people appear to be capable of and what those shifts might mean that Butare residents watch over so carefully.

The basic moral questions of human social life that the personhood concept asks us to consider are in no way limited to the Rwandan context or "post-conflict"[10] societies more generally. Indeed, languages and practices of selfhood are "cultural resources" through which all social actors evaluate what constitutes a good life (Illouz 2008: 20). However, the scale of the violence of 1994 and the way it was perpetrated—by neighbors against neighbors, colleagues against colleagues, and friends against friends[11]—render questions about the capacities of persons and the nature of social belonging all the more pressing. How do social actors navigate the competing demands of remembering those whom they lost and orienting to a future no longer marred by the past? What is owed to those who died so violently? What is a "good life" in the wake of genocide? What of a "good person"? And how do people who suddenly and violently lost so many others experience belonging and dislocation in their social worlds? The argument of this book is that moral and practical dilemmas around what makes for "good" post-conflict persons in Rwanda intersect with debates about how the 1994 genocide was possible and what modern nationhood and a future unencumbered by violence could look like. The ethnographic perspective uncovers how Butaréens are people caught in contradictory moral frameworks of individuated and composite personhood as they try to manage obligations to remember victims, cultural expectations of sociality, and state directives to prosper and develop. Yet this book does not simply tell a story about Butare. Through this Rwandan context, it tells a broader story of the subtle, yet burdensome demands placed on selves and social relationships by global post-conflict imperatives to remember, forget, develop, or reconcile. It is a case for attention to social practices and configurations of personhood for understanding how and why post-conflict reconstruction agendas succeed and fail, and the unevenness with which they do so.

Configuring Personhood in Rwanda

A central question that underpins anthropological debates on personhood is the degree of universality of the dominant model of the person in Western thought, namely the person as isolated, cohesive, autonomous individual (e.g. Carsten 2000, 2003; Douglas and Ney 1998; Dumont 1992; Ferguson 2013; Geertz 1973; Goffman 1959; Mauss [1938] 1985; Mead 1913; Strathern 1988; Charles Taylor 1985, 1989; Christopher C. Taylor 1992). Out of these debates emerge two classic ideal types of personhood, and it is the practical tension between them in Butaréens' self-making practices that animates this book. On the one hand is the "egocentric," individuated, possessive, rights-bearing subject of (neo)liberal thought who aspires to self-mastery and freely associates with and dissociates from others. This subject seeks self-knowledge and discovery, as though a "core self" is contained within, waiting to be revealed and developed (Taylor 1989). On the other hand is the relational, porous person of the anthropological literature who is never a complete, discrete entity, but is always in the process of being built out of relations with others.[12] This composite, "socio-centric" person is not a bounded and autonomous agent who *has* relations, but rather a "node in a network of social relationships" contingently *constituted by* relationships (Ferguson 2013: 226). But in practice, these types are never mutually exclusive (Carsten 2004; Ewing 1990; Hollan 1992; Lambek 2015). Like all ideal types, they are confounded by the complexities of the world as it actually is, so they are difficult to parse in practical terms. These formalized views of the person are unstable, yet overlapping moral reference points that articulate aspirations, ideals, and evaluations of self and other, the good and the contemptible. Indeed, some argue that the egocentric liberal subject is merely a "folk model" of a self that is always in practice socio-centric and reliant on relations to know who one is (e.g. Douglas and Ney 1998: 8; Smith 2012: 61; Strathern 1992). Smith (2012: 51), drawing on Englund and Leach (2000), even suggests that at least since the turn of the century, anthropologists have taken for granted that all persons are both relational and individual.

For these reasons, I do not argue that Butare residents idealize either bounded individual or relational selves or that they simply "are" one or the other. Nor is my point that the Rwandan state aims to impose liberal, individuated personhood on a population that still values "traditional" relational forms. Rather, I ask how the analytical distinction between relational and individuated personhood—and its confounding in practical, lived moments—can elucidate what it means to live in a post-conflict moment. My analysis foregrounds how *both* state projects and Rwandans' everyday practices are caught—and sometimes caught out—in irresolvable tensions and moral ambiguity over what makes for "good persons." By "good persons," I do not simply mean people with good intentions; moreover, I mean that they strive to live up to post-conflict ideals for what a person is and ought to be. The trouble is that no single set of values can eliminate the dissonance produced by the intersection of relational and individuated moral reference points in people's relationships with both the living and the dead. Indeed, "*[w]ho we are* is something larger than can be described or circumscribed by any single hierarchy of value or set of commensurable values" (Lambek 2008: 151, emphasis in original).

In Butare, a liberal, individuated view of the self is closely linked with "modern" personhood. *Pace* Bauman (1989), town residents condemn the genocide as premodern, a product of the condition of postcoloniality rather than modernity. The value placed on the ideals of individuated personhood is evident in the growing tendency for town residents to configure the self as a project on which to work, which theorists argue is a defining feature of modern liberal selfhood (Foucault et al. 1988; Giddens 1991; Illouz 2008; Rose 1996). In the Rwandan context, this way of configuring the self is starkly embodied by President Paul Kagame, who has styled himself as not just a political leader, but also a (controversial) modern visionary and moral compass for the nation, or the "New Rwanda." This latter term captures a vast array of post-genocide reforms, including de-ethnicization, government decentralization, economic development, shifting diplomatic alliances, and judicial, educational, and land reform (see Pottier 2002; Straus and Waldorf 2011). In his public addresses, Kagame adopts the persona of a demanding corporate manager of the New Rwanda as he extolls the virtues of dignity through self-reliance and individual freedom of choice guided by an inner moral core (e.g. Kagame 2013). While we might be tempted to dismiss this as the rhetoric of political elites out of touch with what matters to "the people," this way of orienting to the self nonetheless resonates both among the prosperous and the disenfranchised in Butare. In their strivings for higher education to develop personal capacities and skills, for start-up capital for an entrepreneurial venture, or for modern housing, clothing, and other possessions, Butare residents struggle to fulfill a vision of modern selfhood, to become persons who take purposeful action to affect their life circumstances rather than leaving it to chance (Bauman and Raud 2015: 9). They articulate these aspirations in their yearnings to be "not just anyone" or "to find their creativity" in order to "start something up" and become a "self-made man [*sic*]." Through these idioms, they invoke not just individualism in the sense of privileging the bounded, autonomous subject, but also individuality in the sense of remarkableness or distinctiveness (Cohen 1992: 181). They stake claims to capacities beyond the expectations of "normal personhood" in Rwanda. In so doing, they reject self-definition as tokens of a type or through status and role obligations. People articulate the failure to "become someone" in the idiom of fading into the undifferentiated mass of unilingual Kinyarwanda speakers. Should a university graduate or failed entrepreneur be forced to return to the hills[13] to take up cultivating again, he will "forget every word of French and English that he learned," as one worried soon-to-be graduate put it.[14]

What of the relational self in Rwanda? The ethnographic record emphasizes a relational, composite, or context-dependent Rwandan person. Like many an African configuration of self (e.g. Comaroff and Comaroff

2001; Dieterlen 1973; Lienhardt 1985; Riesman 1986), ethnographers have represented the Rwandese social person as never complete and as always being built out of relations with others, including kin, friends, patrons, and clients (e.g. Taylor 1992, 2005; Vidal [1985] 1999). Exchange of social fluids, especially beer, creates and maintains relationships that constitute persons, and the exchange of sexual fluids through the fusion of each parent's "gift of self" explains how a child is produced (Taylor 1992: 45). De Lame (2005) demonstrates how practices of beer sharing and other exchange relations are central to forging belonging and consubstantiality among neighbors on the rural hill of Murundi. During my fieldwork,[15] I found that beer sharing was equally important in Butare as a way of binding people in self-constituting relationships of friendship, kinship, or clientship, as "people *produce each other* through the gift of things that they consume" (Taylor 1992: 6, my emphasis). I also found a relational configuration of personhood in Butare residents' tendency to refer to others by kinship statuses more often than by their names, which indicates that who one is is deeply connected to one's relations.[16] A friend or acquaintance with children is called *la maman* or *le papa* more often than by name, and modifiers for age or other characteristics are used to distinguish people from each other, for example *le vieux papa* (the elderly father). Teknonymy, a practice by which parents are referred to by the names of their children, is also prominent in Butare. For example, a married couple, Ferdinand and Josephine, are usually called by the teknonyms they acquired after the birth of their son, Kalisa: Mama-Kalisa and Papa-Kalisa. Naming practices like these lay bare how the self is situated relative to others and never distinguishable from them.

As much as ideas about personal development and "becoming someone" align with the values that accompany the contemporary transformations of late capitalism and neoliberalization, it would be a mistake to see these "individuated" formal views of the person as purely imported, post-genocide social forms that are replacing "traditional," relational understandings of the self. Indeed, Taylor (1992: 187) found a longstanding Rwandan belief in individual responsibility in that people are thought to bring misfortune on themselves through their transgressions. He also recognized an ethic of personal independence and individual enterprise among the popular healers with whom he did fieldwork in the 1980s (Taylor 1992: 21–22). Finally, Catholicism in Rwanda has for the past century added layers of complexity to the duality of the person: while the relational Rwandan self and its capacities are changeable and never definitively knowable, Catholicism preaches introspection and discovery of the inner self through confession and conversion (cf. Simpson 2003). Competing voices of conservative and progressive Catholicism also produced views of the person as bound by status and role obligations and as autonomous agents of change, respectively (Gifford

1998; Longman 2001: 182). In light of these longstanding contradictions, my point is not that Rwandan configurations of the person have changed significantly in the post-genocide moment. Rather, this book shows how the enduring tension between personal autonomy and relational compositeness in Rwandan selfhood takes on a new moral weight and redoubled significance in light of post-genocide debates about the path to peace, development, and modern nationhood.

Peaceful Selves

Neither the category of "peaceful self" nor those of relational and individuated personhood are ones that Butare residents would ever use. Peaceful selfhood is my way of trying to capture the range of dispositions, capacities, values, and interests—by no means all compatible—to which town residents aspire in their quest to be "good persons," or those "capable of peace" in the New Rwanda. The term is not meant to suggest that Rwandans *feel* "at peace"— quite the contrary, as this book draws out how they are perennially caught in the paradoxes of their post-conflict aspirations. Indeed, I inflect the term "peaceful self" with a marked sense of irony because the post-genocide moment leaves Butare residents decidedly *unsettled* and beset with imperatives to pursue hopelessly contradictory enactments of their personhood.

Even though composite and bounded views of the person have long coexisted in Rwandan thought, and even as Rwanda is by no means the only place where they coincide, the contradictions between them carry especially high stakes in relation to the violent past. Both state rhetoric and everyday talk link features of relational personhood to the history of violence, and "Western-style" individual personhood to the possibility of more peaceful futures. These ideas find expression in Butare residents' characterizations of "the West" (*l'Occident*) where they say people respect each other's rights to pursue prosperity, independent thought, and personal development. But at the same time, there are dangers associated with persons who are excessively atomized and self-interested, and the relational view of the person still informs what it means to live well with others and to realize modern, peaceful selfhood and nationhood. Each ideal type has its duality, and each can both bolster and threaten possibilities for peace; hence the practical indeterminacy of just what a "peaceful self" is or could be.

Popular explanations for the 1994 genocide blame persons who were so enmeshed in social hierarchies that they were unable to resist the influences of superiors to commit violence. In this popular narrative, the Hutu political elite of the 1990s exploited its patronage networks down through local officials to ordinary Rwandans to set the massacres in motion—an account supported by the findings of scholars like Fujii (2009) who examine the everyday social relationships through which the genocide was organized. To explain people's acceptance of those orders, Butaréens point to "typically Rwandan" qualities of excessive deference to superiors, obedience, and an overall "poverty of the mind" (*pauvreté d'esprit*). The crucial linkage to relational personhood is what Fujii calls the Rwandan "logic of contamination" (2009: 99–101). It is common to hear Butare residents—both Tutsi and Hutu—speak about positive and negative emotions or ideas being contagious. They say it is hard, but essential to steel oneself against the "negativity" of those who cannot move past the genocide, either because they harbor anti-Tutsi sentiment or because they are mired in grief. This logic of contagion is based on the idea that the person is inherently porous; it supposes that it is natural and inevitable that people take on the prevailing outlook(s) of those around them (ibid.). Thus, to explain why so many of their compatriots followed orders to join the massacres in 1994, Butare residents rely on the notion that exposure to the ideas of proximate others means that a person will eventually absorb and act on those influences.

The "contagion" explanation for the genocide casts a long shadow over established modes of sociality, selfhood, and the ways people are connected to each other in Rwanda. When they indict webs of hierarchy and people's inability to withstand proximate influences to explain the genocide, Butaréens implicitly indict the kinds of persons who are permeable and who are by extension accused of lacking autonomy and the capacity for independent thought. In other words, the same networks of hierarchy, reciprocity, and relatedness through which Rwandan personhood is built took on dangerous new contours in 1994 when they were mobilized to commit massacres. Today, talk about causes of the genocide easily slips into talk about what makes for modern, moral social relationships and the kinds of persons who are capable of them. Reciprocally, talk about moral qualities and good versus bad social relations can quickly turn to talk about what made the genocide possible. Such a remark came from Simbi, an ex-RPF soldier and intermittently employed university graduate. One day, he complained to me about an altercation between two of his subordinate employees who had asked him to solve their dispute rather than working it out themselves:

> You know what the problem is here? If given the choice between someone else solving their problems for them versus looking after their own affairs, everyone prefers the first option. They'd rather have someone else take care of their problems even if that means they have to obey orders. It's always been like this here in Rwanda. It's the source of so many of the problems we see here. You know, sometimes I think that if people here weren't so quick to follow orders, we wouldn't have seen the problems of the 1990s. (Butare, March 2009)

In light of the history of violence, these are not just critiques of the perceived shortcomings of dependent relationships, but are also efforts to distance the self from the moral failings by which people typically explain the genocide. While scholars have noted that educated urban dwellers in many postcolonial settings invoke the virtues of individualism to justify cutting off patronage obligations (Carrier 1999), popular explanations for the genocide provide an additional rationale for doing so. During my fieldwork, educated Butare residents routinely claimed the kinds of liberal, autonomous personhood that one might expect any postcolonial elite to assert. Butaréens like Simbi talked about how dependent relations of patron–client bonds that have long characterized Rwandan forms of sociality produce people who are unable or unwilling to think for themselves. Another typical expression came from Viateur, a university graduate and computer technician, who drew an uncomfortable connection between "Western" selfhood and being more "advanced" and therefore more capable of peace during an informal conversation in his repair shop. When I pressed him about what he meant by this, he explained that Westerners do not become embroiled in violence because they do not blindly obey superiors and they have an inner moral compass that lets them resist negative influences. Viateur asserted that voluntary social relationships rather than obligatory ones make peace possible, and he suggested that patron–client bonds are dangerous because they draw people into hierarchies of command. As he explained, Westerners enter freely into relations of equality based on mutual liking rather than instrumentality and dependency, which they associate with "premodern" life (see Carrier 1999; Silver 1990). The glaring paradox in all of this, and one certainly not lost on all Butare residents, is that those who expound on the linkage between "Western" personhood and peace do so even as it was a Western-educated political and intellectual elite[17] that was the driving force behind the 1994 genocide.

At the same time, peaceful selfhood necessitates living up to ideals of the relational, composite selfhood that Butaréens are at times so quick to disparage. The current government, led by the Rwandan Patriotic Front and President Paul Kagame, may call on Rwandans to develop individual capacities for autonomy and dignity through self-reliance, but the moral worlds of Butare residents are much more complex than this. More than anything, it is the hardships of living in the absence of those killed in the genocide that lay bare the composite dimensions of selfhood even for those Butaréens who claim autonomy. For those who suffered losses of family and other significant others in 1994—so especially for Tutsi whose family members were the primary targets of the genocide—the devastating effects of violence on how personhood is constituted are palpable in their informal recollections of deceased victims. A central finding of my fieldwork was that genocide survivors in Butare practice informal remembering and maintain relational exchange ties to the dead to mitigate the sense of social dislocation they experience in the post-genocide period (Chapter 3). These kinds of suffering suggest that, when the self is built out of relations with others, to lose those relations is to lose a part of one's own person and one's place in the world. The problem is compounded by the awkward position that postcolonial urban dwellers occupy, the position that Cohn (1996) describes whereby they appear to have one foot in the world of the local and one in the world beyond (often the country of the former colonizer), which makes claiming belonging difficult under the best of conditions. Herein lie the moral dangers that Butaréens tend to associate with the autonomous individual who is no longer sufficiently "of" the local and who cultivates selfhood from an "inner core" rather than composite sources. So while they do strive to set themselves apart from the kinds of persons built out of social relations, at other times they extoll the virtues of being "of" Rwanda and "of" Rwandans. The excessively individualistic person who lacks a sense of sociality, who refuses mutual constitution with others by withholding shared substances like beer, is ultimately just as incapable of living well with others—of peaceful selfhood—as the blindly deferential, composite person. Hence, post-genocide self-making projects also respond to demands to enact longstanding forms of sociality in which persons are relationally constituted through exchange. But it is not only these everyday practices that drive the persistence of relational views of the person. Both state and non-governmental organization (NGO)-driven processes of transitional justice and reconciliation use practices like the sharing of banana beer or other drinks to reaffirm victims' and perpetrators' mutual constitution through shared substance. Such rituals can follow both the local level gacaca[18] tribunals and peace-building workshops that aim to provide reparations from perpetrators to survivors (Dominus 2014; Longman 2010b). In the moral order of Rwanda, the composite features of persons figure prominently into dispute resolution mechanisms and reconciliation strategies, like shared agricultural work (see Chapter 5), that aim to promote convivial social relations between those pitted against each other in 1994.

The "peaceful" self, then, is one fashioned neither strictly according to the logic of individuality nor relationality. For Butare residents, each carries its own possibilities for forging good post-genocide social relations and dangers for producing renewed violence. Different configurations of the person catch people in different moral orders. For this reason—and for the same reason it is hard to fully separate Mauss's la personne from le moi—formalized notions of personhood are never simply abstract. People experience them as thoroughly practical problems of everyday life, which pull them in different directions. And as they work to manage these competing pulls and strive to close the gap between what they think they are and ought to be, they both engage in social practices of distinction (Bourdieu 1984) and participate in a form of symbolic violence (Bourdieu and Wacquant 1992) to which they and others are subject. This symbolic violence emerges when impossibly contradictory standards of "good" post-conflict persons— rooted in the irresolvable tension between two configurations of the self—are misrecognized as the personal failings of individuals to adequately reconcile them. The ethnographic question is how these ostensibly incommensurable understandings of the person are played out in practical situations (Lambek 2015: 400). As Lienhardt (1985) warns, we can exaggerate the relational African person, and in Butare, to do so is to miss some of the most striking practices of self-making and self-understanding in which residents engage— ones that I will suggest open up jarring contradictions in what it means to have lived through political violence.

Recovering the Person in Post-Conflict Studies

Attention to the self is a latent theme in studies that rely on life histories to draw out experiences of post-conflict social life (Burnet 2012; McLean Hilker 2014; Sommers 2012). It also emerges in studies of trauma and self-making (Abramowitz 2014) and in studies of care and mutuality under conditions of violence (Bolten 2012). Yet scholars still understand little about how figurations of personhood play out in concrete practices that shape post-conflict agendas and interventions. Explicit attention to these questions is crucial, however, because as Lester (2017: 2) notes, the conceptual foci of anthropological study, like power, identity, violence, and agency, always imply some working understanding of how people configure the self and relationships to others. If not carefully theorized, an unmarked, liberal model of the self often finds its way into the analysis (Douglas and Ney 1998; Lester 2011) such that those whom post-conflict interventions aim to reconcile, develop, punish, or "heal" are represented as individual, bounded, rights-bearing subjects who voluntarily connect with and disconnect from others. By unsettling self-making practices in a post-conflict setting, I aim to raise questions about what concepts like peace, justice, reconciliation, and repair can mean and what kinds of projects—political or personal—are realized in and through them.

In the Rwandan context, two transitional justice frameworks have dominated analysis of the hardships of social life after violence and normative approaches to redressing them: first, judicial processes to try perpetrators of violence, and second, post-conflict reconciliation. This book is not a sustained critique of either these mechanisms or scholars' analyses of them, and my purpose in delineating them is not to suggest that they get it all wrong. Rather, I do so strictly to draw out how these two modes of doing transitional justice might be caught in complex, yet often overlooked sets of expectations of what persons are and how people configure belonging, distress, or aspirations for the future in post-conflict settings. An ethnographic approach to personhood in post-conflict social life can shift the kinds of questions we ask about Rwanda and other post-conflict societies by untangling assumptions about what kinds of subjects transitional justice mechanisms aim to embrace and produce.

There is no shortage of critical literature that analyzes post-conflict social life through debates about the potential of perpetrator trials to overcome the legacies of mass violence. Scholars debate the possibilities and limits of trials to "do justice" in the sense of redressing harms, and they ask how judicial processes can promote or undermine possibilities for reconciliation between victims and perpetrators. In other words, they take up the relationship between retributive and restorative justice approaches (Biggar 2001; Booth 2001; Borneman 1997; Felman 2002; Minow 1998; Roht-Arriaza 2006; Stover and Weinstein 2004). However, my interest is in the view of the person contained in these ways of apprehending or bringing about the post-conflict moment. In both the trials themselves and the scholarly debates about them, the rights-bearing qualities of the liberal subject are paramount. Punishment of perpetrators through retributive transitional justice mechanisms is directed at redressing rights violations against victims or, in the case of crimes against humanity, a broader, abstract human collective. In a thoroughly Durkheimian style, restoration of human dignity is equated with restoration and reaffirmation of human rights through the ritual of punishment at trial (Borneman 1997). Here, justice is less about punishing the perpetrator than it is about vindicating the victim (Biggar 2001: 10). Leaving aside the important question of whether trials effectively restore rights or do anything else besides render judgments and punishments (Arendt 1963; Stover and Weinstein 2004), it is worth asking, does this ritual reaffirmation of human dignity interrupt the persistence of the violent past in the present? In what ways do the personhood concepts of those on trial and those whom trials aim to vindicate bear on how we understand post-conflict judicial processes? If Rwandans configure persons not only as bounded, autonomous subjects, but also as relationally constituted "members of one another" (Rivière, quoted in Lambek 2015: 395), to what extent can debates about punishment and its social benefits square with their suffering in the wake of the 1994 genocide, so much of which is brought about by a sense of dislocation in the absence of others who constitute the self? In what ways might trials and the testimony provided at them point also to the impossibility of restoring selves (cf. Booth 2001: 778; Chakravarti 2014; Hamber and Wilson 2002: 47)?

Similarly, a vast critical literature delves into what post-conflict reconciliation means and to whom, what political agendas it might conceal, the burden it places on victims and survivors to forgive, and the mismatch between state-driven reconciliation campaigns and the daily concerns of those who have lived through violence (e.g. Gibson 2004; Rettig 2008; Ross 2003; Shaw 2007; Thomson 2013; Wilson 2001; Zorbas 2009). In the case of Rwanda, much of this work aims to debunk the RPF's claims to promote reconciliation, which many scholars argue is a thin veil for victors' justice and the repression of democratic freedoms. As important as those analyses are, I bracket them to draw out how conversations about the nature of the person are absent from both critical and laudatory work on post-conflict reconciliation, and why they matter.

Reconciliation discourse and practice are caught in the logic of dual moral orders and dual expectations of good Rwandans. On the one hand, reconciliation universalizes the commonsense Euro-American category of the liberal individual person, so that bounded, choice-making subjects precede the transactions into which they enter (Ferguson 2013: 226). The idea of reconciliation supposes that conflicts leave in their wake (at least) two sides to be brought together, each composed of autonomous, individual subjects who choose to make or break bonds with each other. This notion of reconciliation is rooted in a long tradition of social theory that sees the absence of social integration as a modern affliction whose solution is the forging of social bonds (e.g. Durkheim 1997; Mazlish 1989). As Chapter 5 elicits in greater depth, local peace-building experts are quick to read avoidance of social contact between Tutsi survivors and Hutu perpetrators as the absence of a relationship between them and a sign that people need to be educated, coached, and counseled into choosing to re-enter each other's lives. On the other hand, if we think in terms of the relationality of the person, "reconciliation" (if this term retains any sense at all) might be something other than a deliberate act by autonomous persons to reconstitute a broken bond. Butaréens cannot "be someone" unless entangled in reciprocal relations with others that make them members of their social worlds. But there is a double edge to these relations in the wake of violence, and the sources of post-genocide hardship are often not the *absence* of relationships, but rather all of the ways in which victims, perpetrators, and bystanders are *already* enmeshed in relationships (Doughty 2015). Hence, reconciliation as both analytical lens and institutional practice runs up against the ambiguity of how the moral order of reconciliation is conceived and what kinds of subjects it seeks to act on and produce. From a relational perspective on the self, reconciliation tries to re-establish relations in which people are already entangled, and not always by choice. What does it mean to "reconcile" if people conceive of themselves as comprised of relations with others, including with the dead who cannot be brought back and with perpetrators who, having taken those lives, sit as unwelcome mediators between survivors and their dead? And what kinds of self-claims are advanced when people *do* mobilize the moral language of reconciliation and embrace a choice to actively work on how they feel about those who harmed them or whom they harmed? Far from being a simple matter of bringing divided ethnic groups back together, reconciliation as both state project and everyday practice presupposes particular kinds of persons, but never consistently or unproblematically.

Attending to the self-concepts caught up in and produced by post-conflict strategies of redress draws out the cracks, ambiguities, and paradoxes in both state-level and ordinary people's strategies of managing the challenges raised by legacies of violence. Nonetheless, my foray into personhood in Rwanda's post-conflict moment is not intended as the "missing piece" that renders our understandings of what it means to live through violence complete. Our analytical concepts and categories are always exceeded by the complexities of the social worlds they aim to capture (Bauman and Raud 2015: viii–ix), and the possibilities for how we interpret our findings are always multiple. In this book, I aim to elicit the uncertainties and excesses of self-making in post-genocide Rwanda and the unsettling ways Butaréens experience them. Projects of remaking selves are never merely private, personal matters tangential to state-driven projects to effect the post-conflict moment. Instead, it is in and through self-making that these projects unfold and find expression—projects that are never strictly imposed from above, but that are also embraced by Rwandans, albeit in ambivalent, uneven, and contradictory ways.

Ethnography in/of Butare: Who, What, and How

By now, it might be apparent to the reader that my fieldwork took place with a very particular subset of Rwandans. I worked with Butare residents who constitute an urban, educated elite of the country. My findings are based primarily on long-term participant observation, including living with Butare residents, taking part in their daily lives, and informal conversation. I supplemented this approach with semi-structured interviews, which afforded the opportunity to ask questions that may not come up in everyday talk—not necessarily because they are sensitive, but because social situations powerfully shape appropriate topics of conversation. As concerns the particular individuals whose stories and experiences populate these pages, I tried to build connections with people who were linked to (or felt excluded from) the prominent institutions of Butare life, including the Catholic Church, the National University, and local organizations linked to the post-genocide moment, including survivors' associations and peace-building organizations.

In the end, though, and as is common in ethnographic fieldwork, I am not sure if it was always I who chose my participants or they who chose me.

Almost all of my research participants spoke the colonial language of French fluently or competently, and the handful who did not were proficient English speakers who had lived as refugees in neighboring Uganda or Tanzania. It was in French that the vast majority of my conversations and interviews took place. All of my participants had completed some secondary school, and a number of them had attended university. This is a small fragment of the population, to be sure. Though Kinyarwanda, English, and French are all official languages, 90 percent of the population speaks strictly Kinyarwanda, the Bantu vernacular that is unique to Rwandans.[19] Only 8 percent speak French, and only 4 percent speak English (Steflja 2012).[20] While their education and linguistic competencies set my research participants apart from the majority, they were nonetheless a more diverse group than first meets the eye. Some were very much among the socioeconomic elite, including associate and full professors, clergy, successful business owners, civil servants, and doctors. There were others, however, whose "elite" status was more equivocal. New, less-established professors were paid so poorly that, like so many underemployed Rwandans, they were unable to provide three meals a day for their families. I also worked with many low-skill, but not necessarily uneducated workers, including restaurant servers, motel cleaners, and groundskeepers, as well as the unemployed. A number of them were university educated, and they faced difficulty in reconciling the ambitions they had harbored as students with the disappointments of their lives following graduation. Still others worked in high-status, yet precarious positions, especially short-term contracts with foreign NGOs that produced patterns of cash windfalls followed by periods of idleness and penury. Yet even as the intersections of education, occupation, income, and social status are hardly straightforward in Butare (cf. Williams 2015), that does not mean that the challenges town residents face are the same as those of the rural population either. Indeed, from the perspective of the rural majority of subsistence farmers and laborers, even these marginal urban residents lived in a different world characterized by modern privilege.

To work with urban people who have an interest in English and French language politics at all, some of whom benefit disproportionately from and provide ideological support for the RPF's drive for urban development and modernization, might seem to reproduce uncritically the idea purveyed by government officials that there is nothing to learn about contemporary Rwanda from "peasants" (Thomson 2010). Parallel to the moral imperatives that Williams (2015: 25) notes for anthropologists working in South Africa to study the "poorest of the poor," so among Rwanda scholars there is an ethic of responsibility to make heard the voices of the poorest and most marginalized by RPF development policy and standards of legitimate victimhood (e.g. Sommers 2012; Thomson 2013). My intention is not to question other scholars' laudable commitment to studying marginalized Rwandans or to debate the relative legitimacy of different categories of research subjects (cf. Williams 2015: 25). My ethnographic interest in Butare is borne of the central place of this town and its residents—from the colonial period up to the present day—in giving shape to debates about what Rwanda and Rwandans ought to be. Butare is an old colonial seat of power, stronghold of the Catholic Church, and home to the National University. My aim is to provide insight into how the people on whom state aspirations to remake Rwanda depend make sense of the tensions, contradictions, and competing moral demands they face in the wake of 1994. While the social worlds of educated urban dwellers are not representative of Rwanda's rural majority, it is precisely their exceptional social and political location that sheds light on the contradictions at the very core of post-conflict "improvement" schemes in Rwanda. As Englund (2006: 38) cautions, even when social actors embrace the rhetoric of the powerful—in this case, entrepreneurship, development, and individual autonomy—they do not spontaneously become the kinds of subjects that rhetoric aims to produce. What is striking about educated Butaréens' invocations of RPF development rhetoric is not only that it indicates constraints on what is sayable in the "New Rwanda," but also that it belies a deep ambivalence about the visions of a good society behind this rhetoric. For so many aspiring elites in Butare, there is a yawning chasm between the types of persons whom they say they should become and what they think they actually are. In other words, elites have contradictory "lived experiences" too—ones that may alternately prop up or undermine the projects of the most powerful. But they nonetheless offer understandings of what it means to dwell in a post-genocide society, and working with this social category affords novel ethnographic perspectives on the intersections of state agendas, moral regulation, and everyday conundrums linked to selfhood, belonging, and exclusion.

As many others have noted, doing fieldwork in Rwanda is not without its perils. Most problematic are the tight state controls on what researchers are permitted to study and RPF suppression of critical perspectives on their approaches to governance, a point I elaborate in Chapter 1 (see also Thomson 2010). Researchers, just like Rwandans, must be careful about what they say and to whom about the country's past and the direction of government-driven change. Another challenge is that Rwanda has been inundated with foreign researchers seeking to understand social life in the wake of 1994. Perhaps nowhere is this the case as much as in Butare, since many researchers rely on the National University for support ranging from visa invitation letters, library resources, and research assistants, to the expertise of Rwandan scholars. Many Butare residents are wary and weary of the presence of foreign researchers in their lives. Thomas was a university student in agronomy and executive member of a genocide survivors' association when I met him in 2008. A tall and slender young man, he joked that he has the look of a "typical Tutsi" and that his friends even tease him for bearing a striking resemblance to President Paul Kagame. As a prominent member of his association, he bore the burden of handling the large volume of researchers who came looking for interviews, connections to other survivors, or logistical support. "There were two Americans here not long before you came," he remarked to me one day. "They swooped in for two days, and they asked me terrible questions about the genocide. And then they left—poof!" (Butare, January 2009). He went on to commend me for not asking anyone to recount their experiences in 1994, but for letting them talk about it how and when they wished to. I could not help but wonder if his praise was a strategy of ensuring I did not get any ideas about asking those "terrible questions" now that he and I had known each other for nearly a year and had an established rapport. My choice not to ask people direct questions about the genocide was as much methodologically as ethically informed, since my interest lay in how and when talk turns to the genocide (and other pasts) in everyday talk and how and when people avoid raising it. Understanding life in post-genocide Rwanda necessitates learning to listen for both speech and silence and knowing when not to ask questions (Burnet 2012).

Since Butare is a hotspot for foreign researchers, it takes time and patience to cultivate productive working relationships. Not only are residents cautious of newcomer researchers, researchers are also easily inundated with offers from actual or aspiring "professional stranger handlers" (Agar [1996] 2008: 135) who purvey services as drivers, translators, tour guides, research assistants, or brokers. Following common practice in Butare, I relied on my existing networks for finding local assistance where necessary. I occasionally required a Kinyarwanda translator, notably for the official genocide commemorations and *gacaca* tribunals I attended in 2008, and later in my 2014 fieldwork, for workshops held by local peace-building organizations. I have employed the same translator throughout my fieldwork, a trusted friend I have known since 2004.

Throughout my fieldwork, I lived with a professor and his family, who resided in the mixed-income neighborhood of Tumba-Cyarwa near the university. While their house stood out from many of the neighbors' with its walled compound, spacious flower and vegetable gardens, indoor plumbing, and electricity, living with them nonetheless earned me the credibility of someone willing to live in a modest *quartier populaire*, not *en ville* or in the affluent neighborhood of Taba where most foreigners reside. Living with a Rwandan professor also provided me with insights into the social networks and private lives of these prominent residents. My hosts relied on me for routine favors, like picking up packages, and in emergencies, as when I was called to the hospital to care for my "host mother" after she was badly injured in a fall from a motorcycle taxi.

Nevertheless, I was not treated as an ordinary member of the household. My comings and goings were closely monitored, and as a young woman, my occasional absence from the house after dark raised the curiosity of my hosts. I typically used evenings to write up field notes and to converse with my host family, especially during power cuts when there is little to do except talk. Simultaneously, though, my foreignness and my status as an academic meant that I was treated with prestige usually accorded only to Rwandan men. In the evenings, my hosts expected me to drink beer in the living room with the men instead of helping the women in the outdoor kitchen. When I offered to assist with meal preparation, the reaction was a combination of dismay and amusement no matter how much I assured them that I routinely prepare food at home. One household resident openly worried that I would lose a finger if entrusted with a kitchen knife.

Living in Tumba-Cyarwa allowed me to do a lot of walking, which made me a visible figure in Butare. Town residents harbor not only suspicion but also curiosity about foreigners and are not shy about seeking a relation of patronage in the first moments of a meeting. It was not unusual for a complete stranger to sidle up to me during the roughly twenty-five-minute walk from Tumba to the town center. He or she (but usually he) would ask where I was from, where I was walking to, what I was doing in Butare, and finally, how we might stay in touch. I found these encounters difficult to manage because of their intensity and the pressure to establish a relationship and exchange mobile phone numbers with someone I had just met. Still, they were useful ways of meeting people, especially university students, who often wanted to practice speaking English with me. By contrast, I got to know older adult Butare residents through the networks of my initial contacts at the university. Over time they introduced me to their friends and associates on campus, including library staff and administrative assistants. Several of my initial contacts were also close with local small business owners, so they introduced me to members of the local commercial elite. The commercial center of Butare is concentrated in a small area, so I would then cross paths with the same people regularly.

With students and faculty, participant observation, informal conversations, and interviews usually took place on campus. A key part of this work involved volunteering and collaborating on projects with a student genocide survivors' association. The association's projects aimed to raise money to purchase basic items, like school supplies or toiletries, for its members. With small business owners, participant observation, interviews, and informal conversations took place in their homes and places of business. I would provide small services to them, like translating their signage from French to English to help them attract the growing numbers of Anglophone visitors to Butare (see note 20). Butaréens also liked to take me on long walks around the town and its outlying areas, because it was a way for them to demonstrate (both to me and to themselves) their rootedness and knowledge of the region. These excursions would always feature narratives of what happened in different places (sometimes during the genocide, but also other pasts), when and by whom each house was built, and the good and bad behavior of the inhabitants. I visited museums and genocide memorials. I attended the commemorations for the annual week of mourning for the genocide in April, as well as ten *gacaca* tribunals for genocide suspects held in Butare town. I accompanied people on trips to the countryside to visit family members, and I went with my host family to Sunday mass every week at the cathedral. I was invited to thesis defenses and celebrations for the birth of a child. I attended parties, sometimes in people's homes, sometimes at a church hall or a private school's anniversary party. For mundane tasks, too, I joined friends and acquaintances, including trips to the market or hardware store. I participated in *umuganda*, the day of community work carried out across the country on the last Saturday of each month. Finally, in 2014, I did participant observation in the offices of two Butare peace-building organizations, attended peace-building workshops, and conducted interviews with organization personnel about their work. Through it all, I listened carefully and asked questions about people's worries, aspirations, successes, and frustrations, what is admirable or discrediting, and what is a good life worth living or one simply lived by necessity. I listened for the topics that people tried to avoid, be it ethnicity, the genocide, their income sources, or the activities and associations they preferred to keep private (or at least that they wanted to keep from me). I learned to map the relationships that Butaréens form with kin, neighbors, friends, co-workers, employees, patrons, and clients, what is exchanged between them, and the meanings they attach to these relationships. In sum, I learned to track the relationships that constitute the social person and the connections people draw between the nature of those relationships, the history of violence, and visions for the future.

The chapters of this book are organized around four politically charged loci of post-genocide social life. They are ethnicity (Chapter 2), memory practices (Chapter 3), work and entrepreneurship (Chapter 4), and civil society-level peace building (Chapter 5). While they seem disparate in their range, what unites them is that each is a flashpoint in which post-conflict expectations of personhood are enacted, contested, and interpreted in everyday life in Butare. Likewise, each draws out a central facet of the relationship between violence, peace, and the capacities of persons, because each is linked into key structural reforms that characterize the "New Rwanda." Chapter 1 acts as an anchor for the four subsequent chapters with its foundational discussion of the post-conflict moment in Butare and the central place of the town in Rwanda's history and (post)colonial political struggles. As the story of personhood in Butare unfolds, a jarring contrast in the subjectivity of town residents emerges: on the one hand, they come across as deftly strategic in the social relationships they form and the modes of self-making in which they engage. But on the other hand, they emerge as devastated and socially dislocated as they struggle with the weight of the violent past and the losses of significant others in their lives. How can we make sense of these two images of Butare residents? As this book will show, this dissonance reveals much about what it means to inhabit a post-genocide social world.

Notes

1. On the new 2006 administrative map that divides Rwanda's twelve former provinces (*intara*) into only four (plus the city of Kigali), Butare is known as Huye. Nonetheless, I retain place names from the pre-2006 map throughout this book, since Rwandans still used them at the time of my fieldwork.
2. In 1991, the MRND party was renamed. It retained its acronym, but was re-baptized as the Mouvement républicain national pour la démocratie et le développement (National Republican Movement for Democracy and Development).
3. While 800, 000 is a generally accepted figure for the number of dead, these counts are controversial and political. They range from early estimates of 500,000 (des Forges 1995) to over one million according to the Government of Rwanda.
4. All names used are pseudonyms, and other details have been changed to protect people's identities. As is common practice in ethnography focused on small communities of people who are largely known to each other, some of the Butare residents I describe are composite characters. This is a further measure to protect people's identities while also ensuring that their perspectives and experiences come out.
5. This is a term for Butare residents commonly used by local people and in French-language scholarship on Rwanda.
6. It should be noted that anthropologists have debated whether the self can be studied ethnographically; see Lester 2017 for one account of these debates.
7. Although some theorists of the category of the person, particularly Mauss ([1938] 1985), conceptually distinguish self from person, I use them somewhat interchangeably here. For Mauss, human history unfolded a story in which people went from thinking of themselves as "personas" or "masks" to individual selves and role performers (Hickman 2014: 320). My interest, following Battaglia (1995), is not either the experience of self or cultural frameworks of selfhood alone, but rather "problematics of self-action" and how people enact personhood through concrete practices (Lester 2017).
8. In the essay that inaugurated a sustained anthropological interest in personhood, Mauss ([1938] 1985) conceptually distinguished between *le moi* (the experience of being a self, of having a life trajectory, and the ability to generate a narrative of one's life) and *la personne* (shared, culturally conditioned social expectations of human beings). However, Carrithers (1985: 234) argues that by the end of the essay, Mauss himself has slipped

from a focus on *la personne* to a focus on *le moi*, which suggests they cannot be easily held apart, even for analytical purposes.

9. Since the Tutsi–Hutu opposition has primarily animated Rwanda's political struggles, I bracket the third ethnic category, the Twa, who comprise 1 percent of the population.

10. I place this term in quotation marks to indicate its fundamentally problematic nature, although I continue to use it since it is a conventional term in the scholarship. The notion of "post-conflict" implies a linear transition from violence, to "post-conflict," and back to peace, a formulation that rarely captures how people experience conflict and its aftermath. Further, the very idea that there can be a "post-conflict" seems to suggest that there is such a thing as a society free of conflict, a proposition that evokes functionalist perspectives that see "equilibrium" and absence of conflict as the "normal" state of societies.

11. Hatzfeld (2005), through interviews with incarcerated *génocidaires*, found that they framed the act of killing a friend as an act of mercy. Prisoners explained that it was better that they kill a friend quickly and painlessly than let a stranger needlessly draw out the death. These kinds of justifications for killing add layers of moral complexity to the nature of the massacres and the motivations behind them.

12. There are variants of the general type of the relational person, including the "dividual" or "partible" person (Strathern 1988), the "joined up" person (Carsten 2004: 83), and the "fractal" person (Wagner 1991), but all were formulated as ways of probing the cross-cultural relevance and analytical utility of the bounded, atomized individual.

13. Even though the entire country, urban and rural, is built on the rolling hills for which Rwanda is famous—it is commonly called the "Land of a Thousand Hills"—when Rwandans talk about "the hills" (*les collines* [French]; *imisozi* [Kinyarwanda]), they are always referring to rural regions rather than towns.

14. There are no figures available for how many university graduates in Rwanda find work for which their degrees prepared them and how many return to rural subsistence farming. Anecdotally, however, I can attest that I have lost touch with most of the university students with whom I worked in 2008–2009 because they have returned to their rural hills of origin where they no longer retain their mobile phone numbers and where they have little to no access to email. Of the six university students with whom I spent substantial time during my doctoral fieldwork, I remain in contact with only two who did find work in urban centers.

15. My fieldwork in Rwanda began in 2004, followed by two extended stays from 2008 to 2009. Most recently, I returned between May and July of 2014. This book is based on a total of eighteen months of fieldwork.

16. Butare residents also explain this reluctance to use proper names as a symptom of mistrust and secretiveness. It is not unusual for a new acquaintance to avoid giving her or his name upon meeting. I have heard people who have lived in Euro-American contexts where first names are freely disclosed joke about how "Rwandan" it is not to introduce oneself by name.

17. For example, the infamous propagandist of the 1990s, Léon Mugesera, completed his doctoral studies from 1982 to 1987 at Université Laval in Quebec City, Canada.

18. The *gacaca* courts are loosely based on precolonial Rwandan dispute resolution mechanisms, but unlike their predecessor, sentences handed down at the "new" *gacaca* carry legal weight. Because of the volume of suspects who allegedly killed or looted property during the genocide, the new *gacaca* was controversially implemented nationwide in the early 2000s to relieve pressure on the regular court system. See Corey and Joireman (2004) for a review of the controversies surrounding *gacaca*.

19. Kinyarwanda is mutually intelligible with Kirundi, the language of Burundi.
20. Contentious language politics characterize post-genocide Rwanda. In a rejection of its former Belgian colonizers and the French allies of the genocidal regime, Rwanda made a sudden legislative change in December 2008, which saw English, not French, become the language of instruction after the first three years of primary education in Kinyarwanda. In 2009, Rwanda's application to join the Commonwealth was approved, which further cemented English as the new language of power. Fluent French speakers in Butare resented that they were unable to communicate meaningfully with the new crop of Euro-American Anglophone ex-pats who increasingly replace Rwanda's longstanding French and Belgian ex-pat population. For both practical and political reasons, I found it useful to assume people spoke French rather than English throughout my fieldwork. Most were pleasantly surprised when they discovered I speak French, and doing so set me apart from unilingual Anglophone newcomers, whom Butare residents dismissed as understanding very little about Rwanda.

Chapter 1

THE POST-CONFLICT MOMENT IN BUTARE
AND ITS ANTECEDENTS

∞

"If it weren't for the university, Butare wouldn't even exist anymore," Charles, a professor at the National University of Rwanda (NUR), remarked as we made our way into town in his car from a gas station just outside the university campus. It was January 2008, and I had just returned to Butare for the first time in four years. Charles's car, a European model from the mid 1980s, was having mechanical problems, so we were on our way to his local garage. The laboring car slowed our progress to a putter on what was ordinarily a stretch that took less than five minutes to traverse by car. As Charles was commenting on Butare's reliance on the university, we passed the campus genocide memorial, an open pavilion displaying photos of student, staff, and faculty victims of the 1994 genocide. With the car windows open and at our slow pace, we could hear the unsettling swishing sound of groundskeepers cutting grass around the memorial with rhythmic swings of machetes. On our left was a heavily forested area where public toilets were under construction in a dubious attempt to curb the rampant public urination opposite the memorial. As Charles noted, no one will pay 100 RWF (US$0.14) to a latrine attendant when they can go to the forest for free.

We continued along the main road through town, the same paved highway that connects Butare to Kigali to the north and the Burundi border to the south. It was morning, and people were on the move. Traffic was sparse, but the road was lined with flocks of children in school uniforms and *paysans*—"peasants" (*abaturage* or *abahinzi*; *umuturage* or *umuhinzi*, sing.; distinguished from "urban people," *abanyamujyi*, or *umunyamujyi* sing.) as Butare residents call rural people—transporting chickens, hay, goats, plantains, manioc, and other goods to their buyers. Also in the bustle of foot traffic were university students walking in pairs or small groups. Each one clutched a mobile phone in her or his hand—a practice Charles characterized as pointless, since so few students can afford a prepaid airtime card. A pair of police officers, one stationed on each side of the road to monitor traffic, gave friendly waves to Charles as we passed. "All the police know me," he explained. "They don't make much money, so they often ask me for a lift when I see them on the side of the road." Pedestrians peered at us since private cars—even older models in poor repair like Charles's—are relatively few in number in Butare. Most traffic in the town consists of the taxis and buses belonging to the five local intercity transportation companies, motorcycle taxis, and the slow-moving, overloaded transport trucks on which this landlocked country with no rail system relies for the movement of goods. Just past the main gates of the university, a lavish new hotel was under construction, its elaborate architecture incongruous against the low sheet metal structures surrounding it. Charles commented that the builder could be in for an unpleasant surprise, since he predicted that few visitors to Butare would be able to afford premium room rates.

As we arrived in the town center, we passed the dirt road that turns off to the enormous Butare cathedral built by the Belgians in 1936–37 and the Groupe Scolaire, Rwanda's oldest secondary school and an institution whose history is steeped in the production of rigid inequalities between Tutsi and Hutu. Commercial buildings that house hair salons (almost all of which are labeled "hair saloons" in a common translation error), hardware stores, and mobile phone dealers looked especially bright shades of orange, yellow, green, and blue in the morning sun and stood out against the reddish-brown soil characteristic of the region. The large veranda of the local landmark hotel, the Ibis, was quiet that morning, save for a small group of white people enjoying a leisurely al fresco breakfast. The two white 4x4 vehicles parked out front carrying the World Vision logo most certainly belonged to them. Also quiet were two small grocery stores stocking mostly dry goods and housewares, the internet cafes, and the print, copy, and photo shops. The ticket offices of the local bus companies, however, were buzzing with activity. Butare residents make frequent trips to Kigali for business, shopping, family visits, or to obtain documents from government offices in the capital.

Charles was skeptical that his local mechanic would be able to help. "Butare is too small," he explained. If he needed a new part, he would have to go to Kigali. We turned off the main highway at the stadium and continued onto a bumpy, winding unpaved back road. Plumes of smoke rose from behind private homes where cooking fires and waste heaps burned. Charles expertly weaved the car left and right around potholes and washed out tracts of road. We passed the SORWAL (Société rwandaise d'allumettes) match factory, the local prison, and an orphanage before we arrived at our destination. The garage was little more than an empty lot of packed soil scattered with gutted cars and trucks from which used parts were sourced. A white truck with a faded UNAMIR logo (United Nations Mission for Rwanda) was among the discarded vehicles. In its broken-down state, it struck me as an appropriate monument to the ill-fated mission so widely regarded as having failed to save lives during the genocide. After a short examination of the car, the mechanic confirmed Charles's suspicions. He would have to go to Kigali for a new part, and, as Charles added later once we were alone again, where the mechanics are more familiar with fixing European cars. "You see? Butare is still a long way from Kigali," he sighed in reference to their relative sizes and degrees of urbanization rather than the physical distance. "It's the university that keeps things going here, and nothing ever really changes."

The aim of this chapter is to locate the town of Butare, its history, and its place in the "New Rwanda." I argue that the social world of Butare has long been a nexus of debates about modern personhood and nationhood in Rwanda, debates whose roots reach back at least to the era of decolonization. The argument is built on the fundamental assumption that there is a value in seeing the town and its past through the eyes of residents themselves. Even as a convincing historical analysis must draw on existing scholarship, facts, and figures, strong ethnography must also explore historical contexts through people's perspectives and concerns in the contemporary moment. I begin with further reflections on Butare from town residents, like Charles's above, and my own observations of its spatial structure and its changing features over the ten years I have come and gone from it. Second, I provide a narrative of how the genocide unfolded in Butare, the town's contradictory reputations, and how they figure into Butaréens' key concerns about what kinds of persons they ought to be in the post-conflict moment. Finally, I show how contemporary contradictions of personhood are by no means purely new, post-genocide phenomena. I trace out the historical antecedents to modern Butare through a discussion of state formation and the political struggles shaping longstanding debates in Rwanda about modern nationhood.

A Crossroads of the Modern and the Parochial: Butare in the "New Rwanda"

Being in Butare is a little like being in a "single resource town"[1] in decline, yet struggling for renewal. It has been known for decades as the "intellectual capital," with its NUR campus established upon independence in 1962, its ethnographic museum, Catholic seminaries, and its prestigious secondary schools established during the colonial period. But by 2013, there were thirty-one universities officially recognized in the country (seventeen public and fourteen private), an explosion that has challenged Butare's monopoly on the production of the local elite.[2] These changes have had rapid effects on residents' perceptions of their town. Whereas in 2008, Charles complained about the personal inconveniences of trying to get his car fixed in Butare, by 2014, town residents framed slow urban development as something of a collective embarrassment—a reflection on the kinds of persons who reside there.

"Butare is for the peasants now," Odette, a Tutsi genocide survivor declared one morning as I sat in her comfortable, but sparsely furnished living room in the neighborhood of Tumba. Although it was a bright, sunny day, the room was dimly lit with curtains drawn to keep out the already blazing equatorial sun. It was *umuganda* Saturday, the monthly day of compulsory community work in Rwanda. An industrious woman who had recently turned sixty, Odette had no qualms about non-attendance at *umuganda*, even though those who fail to show up are subject to a fine. As a restaurant owner and taxpayer, she said that she does her part to rebuild Rwanda every day. She continued, "Butare hasn't changed like other small towns—like Gitarama, like Gisenyi. There you see real changes—tall new buildings, new paved roads. When they started the *imihigo*,[3] Butare scored the lowest of any region. It used to be the second most prosperous center after Kigali." I asked Odette why she thought that development in Butare was lagging behind that of other urban centers.

> It's two things, I think. First, with the university, Butare attracts a lot of young people, and it's they who are most likely to be unemployed. Students are here to study, not to build the local economy. But second, and maybe this is the more important problem, it's the consequences of the genocide. Butare accounted for such a high proportion of the victims—it was the intellectual center. But most of those intellectuals were killed in 1994, so now it's a different story. And as you know, so many intellectuals today live in Kigali instead of Butare. (Butare, June 2014)

What Odette suggested was that, in the absence of intellectuals killed in 1994, there are few people left in Butare with the vision and means to maintain or enhance the prosperity of the town and region. For her, with a dwindling population of intellectuals, Butare is no longer a center of progress, but is now "for the peasants."

Odette's disparagement of her town might be dismissed as an off-hand, elitist remark, but it is significant in light of the government's vision for post-genocide Rwanda. Following the genocide, the RPF leadership crafted an image for themselves as liberators who stopped the massacres and inaugurated a new era of peace, order, economic growth, and national unity—the fundamental pillars of the "New Rwanda." Popular non-fiction celebrates the rise of President Paul Kagame, who is characterized as a visionary leader and architect of unprecedented recovery from postcolonial civil conflict (e.g. Kinzer 2008). The high-modernist ambitions of Kagame and the RPF aim to make the New Rwanda a middle-income country that is not dependent on foreign aid and that is driven by innovation, entrepreneurship, and integration into regional and international commerce (Straus and Waldorf 2011). International observers praise Rwanda's GDP growth under Kagame, which averaged 9 percent each year between 2001 and 2014 (World Bank 2015). Visitors marvel at the explosion of cosmopolitan growth in Kigali, where upscale cafes, twenty-four-hour grocery stores, and sushi restaurants are popping up in the commercial core, where city streets are kept immaculate and carefully landscaped, and where construction cranes transform the landscape with avant-garde hotels, commercial buildings, and conference centers.

By the time I returned to Rwanda in the spring of 2014, the RPF's campaign for the New Rwanda was in full swing, but just as Odette suggested, it was a slow and uneven process in Butare. New building regulations required that all commercial structures stand at least two stories tall, a change that resulted in the reconstruction of the Hotel Ibis into a multi-story structure housing shops that flank its veranda on the main level and a restaurant and newly renovated rooms up above. The market had been transformed into a four-story building from the old, sprawling outdoor square that I remember from previous field stays. I heard one town resident disparagingly joke that the "*petits paysans*" [little peasants] must tremble in the face of the new structure and probably do not even know how to navigate staircases with their goats. Whole commercial areas of Butare housed in old single-level buildings had been closed down to make way for new developments, most notably the formerly bustling commercial district near the market known as the *quartier arabe* (Arab Quarter). But because no developers had come forward to raze the buildings, they remained standing but condemned, and the *quartier arabe* had the feel of a frontier ghost town (Illustration 1.1). The landscape of the entire town was dotted with partially built multi-story structures that stood idle, construction stalled, as the bank loans ran out and entrepreneurs were unable to complete their projects (Illustration 1.2). Town residents would narrate to me the story of each failed or stalled project and their theories for why each person had failed. At times, they would blame the entrepreneur's "lack of discipline" or "poor planning." By contrast, in the case of a hotel in the neighborhood of Taba that was tantalizingly close to completion, the builder's neighbor, Rose, herself a small business owner, explained that this diligent man simply ran out of money before he could

Illustration 1.1 The abandoned *quartier arabe* (Arab Quarter) of Butare condemned for demolition (photo by author).

Illustration 1.2 In the foreground, a stalled commercial construction project in central Butare (photo by author).

make the hotel operational: "He never even took a drink—not even a Fanta. I would see him at the site all day every day to supervise. And still he's left with nothing." Among all of these monuments to stalled and/or failed entrepreneurial dreams, there is the odd tall, gleaming construction that protrudes from among the characteristically simple architecture of Butare, for example the recently completed addition to the Hotel Credo (Illustration 1.3). Structures like this one stand as markers of what builders aspire to, but few achieve.

Signs of new investment in public infrastructure in Butare also greeted me in 2014. New streetlights had been installed along the main road, the lamps painted in the blue, green, and yellow shades of the Rwandan flag—a detail I could not help but interpret as a not so subtle symbol of the government "bringing light" to the people, with all the paternalism this implies. A central bus terminal was under construction next to the National Museum. It is designed to be a smaller-scale version of the Kigali bus terminal, Nyabugogo, a loud square churning with commuters near the edge of the capital. Some who lived near the construction site worried about the noise the new terminal might bring, since at Nyabugogo, music blares from the shops that form its perimeter and informal sellers of candy, drinks, and tissues crowd around buses and thrust their wares through windows at captive passengers awaiting

Illustration 1.3 In the background, a new addition to the Hotel Credo amid a series of traditional built structures (photo by author).

departures. The Butare stadium had also been razed and was undergoing reconstruction into what appeared to be a mammoth structure of concrete bleachers—a sharp contrast to the old stadium with its worn brick walls and narrow rows of dilapidated wood and steel benches. But while change is afoot, its benefits are hardly distributed evenly, and beneath the veneer of a few new constructions lurks deep socioeconomic disparity. In 2011, 47 percent of Huye district residents[4] still lived in poverty or extreme poverty. Only 20 percent of residents' homes had concrete floors, the rest made of simple packed earth. Less than half of town residents used electricity as their main source of lighting, and 76 percent made their living from agriculture. And in spite of the RPF's bombastic claims about turning Rwanda into a regional technology hub, only 4 percent of district residents have used a computer before and report feeling confident to use one again (National Institute of Statistics of Rwanda n.d.).

The RPF's program of economic growth and development is a curious study in neoliberal reform. On the one hand, it embraces classic neoliberalization principles, especially faith in enterprising activities to maximize national and personal wellbeing (Rose 1992: 145) and the priority placed on encouraging foreign investment. Government development rhetoric is part of a forward-looking project for remaking both Rwanda and Rwandans to forge a modern, orderly, and disciplined nation. Indeed, President Kagame encourages educated youth in particular to "use [their] youthful energy" to strive for innovation and entrepreneurial ventures in order to become self-reliant (Kagame 2015). In true neoliberal fashion, Kagame frames the aggregate effect of these individual strivings in terms of national development and prosperity.

On the other hand, the RPF is a thoroughly paternalistic regime, and there is an ever-present subtext in all of their engagements with the population that "the RPF knows best." Through its "decentralization" initiatives, the Government of Rwanda aims to micromanage all spheres of Rwandan society, and in principle, this broad, interventionist approach is precisely what most neoliberal regimes do *not* aspire to (Rose 1992: 146). RPF officials frame decentralization as a strategy for dismantling the apparatus through which the genocide was organized, but it also makes it possible for the party to install its cadres in all regions at all levels of government (Reyntjens 2011: 14; Thomson 2013: 51–52). In this way, the chain of command remains thoroughly centralized, and local-level civil servants are expected to report to higher-ups about any sign of insurgency or non-compliance with RPF ideology and policy (Reyntjens 2011: 16). Indeed, the RPF's tight controls on freedom of speech in the "New Rwanda" are well documented, especially the restrictions on freedom of the press and the conflation of any criticism of government policy with the crime of "divisionism"[5] (Human Rights Watch

2008; Pottier 2002). Critics argue that this sweeping, vaguely defined offense stifles meaningful debate and coerces the local media, would-be political rivals, and ordinary citizens into complying with government policy and ideology (Reyntjens 2011: 8–18). The RPF imposes strict barriers to the formation of competing political parties, and contenders have faced intimidation and arrest. One such challenger was Victoire Ingabire Umuhoza, who in 2010 attempted to form a coalition to compete with the RPF and its allies[6] but was ultimately prevented from running and imprisoned for threatening national security.

Furthermore, under the guise of security, development, and efficiency, the Government of Rwanda dictates who lives where through their campaign of "forced villagization" that aims to settle all Rwandans in *imidugudu* (Newbury 2011) instead of the traditional pattern of dispersed housing. A closely related government intervention in housing decisions is the "Bye Bye Nyakatsi" campaign that forced rural Rwandans to destroy their "embarrassing" thatched roof huts and build structures using roof tiles instead. Authorities mandate which cash crops farmers in each region must grow, which means they are dependent on their earnings, not their products, for food. Strict regulations prevent people from selling street food, and it is illegal to walk barefoot in Kigali. Finally, the government keeps tabs on who has contributed to the national Agaciro Development Fund. Agaciro is known as a "solidarity fund," and it calls on ordinary citizens to help decrease and eventually eliminate Rwanda's dependency on foreign aid. Agaciro translates roughly as "dignity" or "self-worth" in Kinyarwanda—a sign of the times and the kinds of persons state leaders wish to produce. As Butare residents characterized it, the contribution is voluntary in principle, but the social pressure to donate is high. Hence, the "New Rwanda" is characterized by a peculiar alchemy of state exhortations to citizens to become autonomous economic agents, coupled with the expectation that they never tread on the tightly circumscribed limits to just what kinds of autonomy they ought to cultivate.

The RPF's atypical approach to neoliberalization is not the only dissonance in post-genocide government interventions. The forward-looking project of forging the New Rwanda rubs up uneasily against the state-sponsored imperative to remember the genocide and its victims. Annual commemorations at the national level are carefully orchestrated each April during the official week of mourning.[7] District leaders, schools, universities, and religious leaders are also expected to organize local ceremonies to honor victims in their own communities. National genocide memorials, like the Murambi technical school and the Nyamata church, display the remains of victims as a testament to the scale and the horror of the genocide and the failure of international actors to intervene (Eltringham 2014). There are re-interment projects under way in which bodies are exhumed from mass graves and reburied in dignified sites with markers and monuments. What is jarring and incongruous about the RPF's New Rwanda is the exaggerated upbeatness of the government's forward-looking vision alongside the solemn weight of the past. This dissonance is not lost on President Kagame, who aims to resolve it by turning remembering into a ritual of group reaffirmation and renewed collective energy to build better futures. As he put it in a 2015 speech at the university in Butare:

> Today we are remembering our loved ones killed here at the university and the residents around here who were killed elsewhere but buried in the university forest. What happened here represents what happened in other parts of the country. Remembering this genocide is not a waste of time because it provides new energy to stand and address the challenges brought by our history. This also helps build a foundation for our future and the wellbeing of Rwandans. (Kagame 2015)

Genocide in Butare: Contradictions, Past and Present

Paradoxes arise in the reputation and characteristics of Butare in the local lore around the genocide. A popular narrative circulates about what happened there in 1994, and while it is corroborated by historical analyses, its content must also be contextualized in the current moment with the government's emphasis on the illusoriness of ethnicity. Rather than presenting several similar accounts from different Butaréens, I borrow Liisa Malkki's (1995) strategy of the narrative panel, a composite of accounts from Butare residents of how the 1994 genocide unfolded there. It is worth noting that this composite comprises the words of both Tutsi and Hutu residents.

> Here in Butare, we were always integrated—Tutsi, Hutu, and Twa. We intermarried; we lived together with no problems. It's the southern culture (*la culture du sud*), the intellectual culture—here, we always thought of ourselves as the same people. Yes, we had rich and we had poor, but in the *culture du sud*, we really did live well together. Even when the genocide started in the rest of the country, things stayed calm here in Butare. People from other regions came here because they had heard that Butare was safe. We had a Tutsi *préfet* [prefect], and he held off the massacres. The Hutu of Butare, many of them were also moderate, and they didn't want to kill their neighbors. The government had to bring in outsiders to kill and to spur the population to do it. So it wasn't until about 21 April that the killing began in Butare. They brought the *interahamwe* [youth militias mobilized for the massacres] to stir things up, and it worked. People started to turn. They set up roadblocks everywhere, just like in the rest of the country. They had roadblocks at intersections in town, at the university gates. We would hear screams at night in the *quartiers* [residential

neighborhoods], and we knew what was happening. Tutsi started to flee. Even at the university—the students and professors killed. They would hunt Tutsi in the dormitories and chase them into the forest [Ruhande Arboretum on campus]. Doctors at the hospital were killing Tutsi patients. The priests turned on their followers. But you have to remember that a lot of Hutu were killed here, too, because the *interahamwe* thought, "if these Hutu are so content to live with the Tutsi, they must be against us." Our southern culture turned out to be why the *génocidaires* came after the people of Butare the most.

This narrative constitutes a curious blend of support for the RPF view that unity is the "natural" state of Rwandan society until outsiders disrupted it, coupled with an acknowledgment of Hutu victimhood that is at best downplayed, at worst outright denied by the government. In part, this narrative must be read as an assertion of the moral superiority of southerners in contrast to the stereotypically anti-Tutsi stance of northern Rwanda, the historically Hutu-dominated Kiga territory that was conquered in the late 1800s by the Tutsi *mwami* Rwabugiri. This north–south opposition only grew more pronounced with the politics of the genocide. The inner circle of President Juvénal Habyarimana's party, the Mouvement révolutionnaire national pour le développement (MRND) that launched the genocide, were northerners. Habyarimana was known for implementing policies that favored his northern stronghold of support (Longman 2010a: 138). Prior to the genocide, 25 percent of the population of Butare province was Tutsi— the highest of any of the former twelve provinces of the old administrative map. This, coupled with the fact that so many eventual victims fled to Butare province when massacres began in their home regions, meant that Butare suffered the highest proportion of deaths of any single province, with 20 percent of all killings during the genocide (Guichaoua 2005: 25). Nonetheless, it would be a mistake to think that little support existed for the Habyarimana government in Butare. The MRND held a majority there, and in the early 1990s, key local figures were party followers. These included the NUR rector and vice rectors, the deans of arts, agronomy, sciences, and public administration, and a number of other high-ranking administrators. The director of the National Museum of Rwanda, an eventual massacre site, was likewise a Hutu MRND supporter from Gisenyi, as was the director of the SORWAL match factory, who played a key role in financing the *interahamwe* militias (Guichaoua 2005: 120–23).

Nonetheless, popular narratives of the genocide in Butare frame the town as a bastion of peaceful, harmonious culture in which the liberal intellectual influence kept people "above" such "parochial" concerns as ethnic rivalry. While Butaréens may idealize the harmony of the pre-genocide past, there is truth to the delay they report in the start of the massacres (Guichaoua 2005;

Jefremovas 1997). But simultaneously, its historical status of intellectual center means that Butare was where theories about Tutsi superiority and Hutu inferiority were formulated and disseminated to the rest of the country, from the late colonial period of elite ethnic rivalry through to the anti-Tutsi propaganda cooked up by the university intellectuals of the 1990s. It is the position of the town as both haven of peaceful ethnic coexistence steeped in modern intellectual culture *and* reviled cradle of "Tutsi privilege" and ethnic ideologies that sets the scene for understanding the tensions and competing demands to which Butare residents must face up at the level of everyday practice. Anthropologically speaking, then, the question is, how do Butare residents live out the contradictions of their past and present? I provide a series of framing vignettes to anchor some of Butaréens' most pressing concerns in the post-conflict moment and how the broader project of remaking Rwanda shapes life in this unevenly changing center. The first one acquaints us further with Charles and the situation of Butare's intellectuals in the "New Rwanda." The second introduces Bernadette, the wife of a local professor, and her struggle to become a "good Rwandan," both enterprising and humble. The third deals with how Butare residents are concerned to distinguish "real friendship" from instrumental relations of patronage and reciprocity, particularly how the former is regarded as a mark of modern selfhood. The final vignette concerns Pauline, a Tutsi genocide survivor, and the difficult ways the genocide makes itself felt in the present. Each one gets at tensions I rely on later in the book and each captures a central aspect of how people try to piece together their selfhood in the post-conflict moment, as they work to make sense of new configurations of power, economic development, and governance, all set against the legacy of a history of violence.

"I Like to Be Free"

A Hutu university professor in his late forties, Charles is a classic type of figure in Butare: member of the educated elite, fluent French speaker, and professional stranger handler who commonly receives new researchers when they arrive at the university. A serious and introspective man, he prides himself on being "well organized"—a good planner and budgeter who adheres to deadlines. He gets frustrated when others do not plan ahead, when they invite him to meetings at the last minute, or if they change plans without warning. Nonetheless, his quiet demeanor belies an assertive streak. Charles is known for being able to get things done that others cannot. Whether it is a matter of finagling an extension on tuition fee payments for a student, contending with cantankerous bureaucrats for my research permit, or tracking down a colleague's stolen car parts, Charles is the person to call.

Charles was fond of telling me how he "likes to be free," by which he meant that as a faculty member, he can set his own schedule, he does not have to report to a supervisor, and he can take on additional projects and consultancy work as he pleases. One evening, however, as we sat in his impeccably tidy living room furnished with comfortable plush armchairs and sofas, he explained that there are profound constraints on intellectuals in Rwanda—ones that arguably make Charles decidedly un-free in other ways. Charles, who was still wearing the tracksuit and sandals he favored for his evening walks, had invited me for dinner that evening. By chance, a power cut struck, one that persisted for three full days. We had been watching the national news station, Rwanda Television, which had been airing campy local music videos—ones that Charles disapproved of because they showed soldiers dancing with their rifles, which he interpreted as a glorification of war. When the power failed, Charles began asking me about academic life in Canada and eventually directed the conversation to the constraints he faces as a local intellectual. Each postcolonial regime in Rwanda has relied on intellectuals like Charles to produce the ideas that legitimate its rule. These legitimating ideas have each time been based in a particular understanding of the nature of ethnic difference, which is then linked to the question of who the rightful inhabitants of Rwanda are. Under the extremist Hutu-led government of the 1990s, these legitimating ideas came from intellectuals like Léon Mugesera, who famously exhorted the population to defend the Hutu nation against its Tutsi interlopers. Today, the legitimating narrative of Rwandan ethnicity is much more liberal in its content, but it is made to do political work that is decidedly authoritarian. The only acceptable view of ethnic difference in the RPF's "New Rwanda" is that it is illusory, a colonial (and anthropological) invention to divide Rwandans. Rwandans of all status levels are instructed in this story, be it through attendance at *ingando*[8] re-education camps, peace-building workshops, or speeches from government officials. "Many of our students are in the military, you know. You might have one who is a *maneko* [spy] instructed to report on professors who try to tell any different story about Rwandan history or politics. We have many important sources and stories about our past, but they are not appreciated today," Charles explained. His phrase, "not appreciated," was itself a carefully chosen euphemism to avoid overt criticism of the RPF's monopoly on the past. The absence of academic freedom means that scholars like Charles must produce publications that do not contradict its version of the past. The following, though not Charles's work, is a typical example:

> Up until the beginning of the [twentieth] century, in the popular Rwandan imaginary, "the country of a thousand hills" evoked a country where milk and honey flowed, a country where values like friendship, fraternity, solidarity,

love, bravery and patriotism constituted the foundations of education and the cement of social relations between all Rwandans. These Rwandans were proud to share the same history, to commune through the same culture, and to share the same language ... The history of Rwanda, like that of the Great Lakes region, was reconstituted through a vision characterized by racist ideology and by diffusionist theory developed near the end of the nineteenth and start of the twentieth century, respectively. Reconstituted in a vision marked by racism and the will to divide and conquer, the ancient history of Rwanda was reduced to migrations of the three components of Rwandan society: the Batwa, the Bahutu, the Batutsi. To these three groups, baptized Pygmoids, Bantu, and Hamite, were attributed different origins and racial identities. Moreover, colonial political policy, served by ethnologists and by missionaries, excelled at classifying, differentiating, and ranking them. (Kanimba 2005: 129–30, my translation from French)

In their attempt to erase ethnic categories from Rwandans' sense of self, RPF leaders revived a very old ethnic ideology based on the notion of unity of all Rwandans, one first promulgated by the Abbé Alexis Kagame, his protégé, the colonial anthropologist Jacques Maquet (1961), and other historians (Pottier 2002: 110). This is a story of precolonial ethnic unity based on innocuous "occupational" distinctions between Hutu cultivators and Tutsi pastoralists engaged in symbiotic relations of patronage and mutual aid. European colonizers, who pitted Tutsi against Hutu and polarized ethnic relations, shattered this harmonious equilibrium. Hence, the RPF is to be credited not only with stopping the genocide, but also with forging a renewed era of pan-Rwandan unity. To promote the idea that all citizens are simply "Rwandan," the government removed ethnic labels from national identity cards and outlawed ethnic self-identification. It would be impolitic for a Rwandan intellectual like Charles to draw on well-known sources that show ethnic relations were fraught even before they were hardened and consolidated by Europeans (e.g. Newbury 1988; Vansina 2004). Local scholars avoid writing about institutions that produced ethnic resentment, like the precolonial *ubureetwa* corvée, which obliged only Hutu men to perform the most humiliating forms of servitude for the Tutsi elite. Even marginal Tutsi were exempt from this labor of gathering and drying firewood, fetching water, and serving as night watchmen (Newbury 1988: 140–41), an ethnic status differential that calls into question the idyllic narrative of precolonial ethnic symbiosis. But while Rwandans might be constrained from openly debating the historical accuracy of RPF history, the interesting ethnographic question is what people actually *do* with that narrative and how it figures into aspirations for and evaluations of the kinds of selves Butare residents want to be. As critical as Charles was that night of the selective history to which he must adhere, at other times I heard him fervently insist on the importance of building pan-Rwandan unity if the country is to see a brighter future. Indeed, what is crucial is that people like Charles reproduce state narratives not only because of coercion, but also because it is the narrative by which one shows oneself to be a modern person not caught up in ethnic skirmishes. Being a member of the educated elite in Rwanda has always meant indoctrination into the ideology of ethnic difference of the day, and so even those who know and value other stories of Rwanda's past can nonetheless find it appealing to reproduce today's narrative of power. It is this interpretive dimension that is crucial for understanding why Rwandans acquiesce to their government's authoritarian directives beyond a simple dynamic of domination/oppression. Still, Charles's claims to being free and liking his autonomy sit at odds with the limitations he faces as a scholar in the "New Rwanda." Or perhaps this tension is not so difficult to resolve. After all, when could it be more important to assert one's autonomy than when it is so very limited?

Becoming Someone, Remaining Humble

Bernadette, a professor's wife, was feeling discouraged. We were seated in her backyard sharing grilled corncobs and watching the household chickens scurry around to compete for the occasional kernel we tossed in their direction. It was late Sunday afternoon, and Bernadette had changed out of her church clothes and was wearing an old sleeveless top and wrap skirt stained with soot from cooking fires. A Hutu woman who had grown up in a rural area near Butare, she got a degree from the NUR later in life, since she had to care for her children on her own from 1996 to 2000 when her husband was completing his PhD in Europe. Subsequently, she completed a Master's degree by distance studies at a Kenyan university, and by 2014 she was aspiring to pursue doctoral study. Nonetheless, Bernadette suffered from chronic unemployment and social isolation now that her children were at boarding school. A devout Catholic, she went to mass first thing each morning and again every evening, but I suspect she did this as much for an excuse to leave the house as to express her faith. She explained:

> It's hard for me to stay alone at home all day. I want so badly to find a job, but they are so few. I applied for one advertised at *The New Times* [the pro-state English-language newspaper], and there were thousands of applicants there. And when I talk to the neighbors about it, they say to me, "You? Why do you have to work? Leave the jobs for those who need them." But now that my children have grown up, I want to do something for me. I want to keep studying; I'd like to teach university. There is a new one in Taba, and I know the director… (Butare, June 2014)

Bernadette had more than one plan on the go to "do something" for herself. She had also embraced the spirit of entrepreneurship and opened a small kiosk that sold household basics, like cooking oil, soap, and sugar. She never talked much about her shop, and I had the distinct sense that it was struggling. Besides, her real passion was for an academic career, and a couple of weeks after our conversation in her yard, I saw her again, ecstatic to have just secured a course to teach at the new Taba university. There was a catch, though. She was not being paid, because the school had no budget for faculty, but she still saw this as a monumental opportunity. "If I can show that I'm good, then maybe when they do get the money they will give me a paid position. For now, I'm just so glad to have something—something to do." Bernadette embraced her unpaid position not because she was duped by her employer or by the broader rhetoric of self-improvement current in the post-genocide moment. Quite the opposite, in fact. In the privacy of her living room, Bernadette sharply criticized her government for placing responsibility on people to find or create work when there are no jobs. "How are people supposed to start something up when they have nothing?" she would rhetorically ask. Still, it is possible to be critical of a direction of change and to nonetheless desperately want it to work out. And so, diligently each evening, Bernadette prepared her lessons and corrected student work in the gloomy glow of a forty-watt lightbulb at the family dining table.

Still, for Bernadette, there was more to living a good life than just her modern career ambitions. Like many urban dwellers who have rural roots, Bernadette was proud of her gardens and her knowledge of and capacities for cultivating foods to save money at the market. In Butare, home agriculture is not only a subsistence strategy but also a form of moral agency. Even when it is not a primary mode of subsistence, to have a flourishing home garden plot shows that one still has a connection to rural life ways. Bernadette liked to show me around her vegetable garden and explain her knowledge of sowing and harvest cycles. The garden was a wild, unkempt hodgepodge of plantains, manioc, beans, carrots, squash, and corn, but she explained that a disorderly mixture of crop varieties was a good strategy to avoid exhausting soil nutrients. But simultaneously, Bernadette validated her socioeconomic status by dedicating her front yard almost entirely to decorative plants and flowers. In Butare, neatness and attention to detail in decorative gardens are correlated with the relative wealth and status of the property owner, since it shows an embrace of European aesthetics and standards of "good houses." Bernadette's ornamental gardens were maintained with great care. The domestic worker, the gardener/night watchman, and sometimes Bernadette herself ensured that dead leaves were swept away, grass was well manicured, and plants were pruned and trimmed. Retaining walls were kept clean of dirt and debris. Plants included varieties of low ground cover, creeping philodendron along the walls of the compound, rose bushes, and dieffenbachias. Shade trees provided comfortable seating in the garden for the occasional afternoon party that might be hosted there. Bernadette recounted to me what happened when they moved to Ngoma and how the neighborhood residents reacted to the improvements they made to their house.

> The people in the neighborhood don't understand how we even got this house because it was never advertised for sale. As soon as we bought it, I told my husband we had to put up a brick wall because people could see right in from the road. Before we lived in a house we rented from the university on the other side [of town], but we've been here now about four years. So all of a sudden, the wall went up around the house and we moved in and everyone in the neighborhood was asking, "Who lives there?" But our society is like that; here, everyone is jealous. *Je laisse ces gens* [I forget about these people; I leave these people alone]. You know, one time a peasant came here to do some work on the house, and he saw how the umbrella trees in our garden grow straight out, and do you know what he said? He said, "Oh, even the trees grow better *chez les riches* [at rich people's homes]. I tried to grow those but they just wouldn't grow right. *Chez les riches*, everything is better. Even the trees grow straighter." (Butare, February 2008)

For striving for a career and the outer trappings of modern living *and* seeking to remain connected to rural livelihood strategies, Bernadette was subject to contradictory and indeterminate evaluations. For maintaining a home garden, which is by no means a livelihood necessity for her household, neighbors praised her for her humble simplicity. On the other hand, she was subject to criticism for having built a walled compound and attractive decorative gardens in an area where not everyone shares her household's socioeconomic status. The structure next door was a crumbling, one-room house surrounded by a sorghum field, so Bernadette might be seen as flaunting her success in front of less fortunate others. Even more significant, Bernadette relied on hired help to perform most of the maintenance that goes into both her vegetable and ornamental gardens, even as she always called them "my gardens." The labor of the hired help in maintaining these gardens called into question Bernadette's connections to rural life ways and knowledge and suggested she might have an exploitative streak if she claimed the vitality of her gardens as her own.

"True" Friends and Modern Selves

Social relations are fraught for middle-class Butaréens. Invitations to drink in local bars are often pretenses for requesting a favor, be it to activate social connections to secure employment, a request to help finance a wedding, or to obtain a driver's license without passing the test. Beer sharing is among the most important practices by which social relations are sealed and reaffirmed in Rwanda (de Lame 2005: 307), and since invitations to drink often conceal ulterior motives, people are inherently suspicious of them. Town residents agonize over discerning who is a "true friend" (*vrai ami*) and who simply wants something from them. Since exchange relations are constitutive of the self in Rwanda, they affect people's reputations (de Lame 2005). Town residents try to distinguish gifts between *vrais amis* that are not thought to conceal ulterior motives and that they call *impano*, from "interested" gifts, known as *ruswa* (a neologism that derives from the French *reçois*, a form of the verb *recevoir*, to receive) or *inyoroshyo*, both of which translate as pot-de-vin, or bribe. Of course, conclusive judgments as to what are gifts and what are bribes are often confounded by the practical overlap of these categories (Werner 2000). Still, Léon, a local restaurateur, made the distinction between true and instrumental friendships forcefully and concluded that there are no true friends:

> I have no friends. Sure, there are people I spend time with, we chat, we maybe travel together. But I have no friends. I used to think I did, and then back in 2006 I was having a lot of problems and I discovered that people who I thought were friends were actually my enemies. I mistrust everyone now. I hold everyone at a distance. I watch them like this [crosses arms and narrows eyes]. Everyone I know is an acquaintance, not a friend. A friend, a true friend, is someone who shares your burdens, someone who treats your problems like their own. But I don't have anyone like that, someone who cares for me no matter what. Friendship is not about conditions, like the exchange of goods. You know, one time a guy came by here asking me for a monthly subscription card for the restaurant; he couldn't pay in advance like you're supposed to but I let him have it anyway. I did this for two months, and then I told him he needed to pay in advance like everyone else. He protested and he left without paying, so I kept the voltage regulator he lent me. But then he came back one day and told me that he only had one friend in Butare. I asked who, and he said it was me. Why me, I asked. "Because you helped me when I had nothing to eat." But you see, that's not friendship. He wouldn't have called me a friend if I hadn't done that; it was conditional on my help. Friendship is not about exchanging goods. (Butare, June 2008)

Charles made similar distinctions when he saw his wife ingratiating herself with their daughter's school headmistress after church, but he thought that true friends do exist:

> You know, my wife thinks that the reason to have friends is for what they can give you. This is a very bad way to be; friendships have nothing to do with money or favors. A real friendship is not about these things. It doesn't mean

you can't ever ask a friend for help, but it's not the basis of the relationship. You don't make friends for material gains first and foremost. My colleague, François, the Abbé Célestin, the doctor Grégoire, they are true friends of mine. We are friends not because of what we can do for each other, but we can call on each other sometimes if we need something. When we go out for beer, we split the bill, or we take turns, like you do in Canada. We do not try to profit from each other. (Butare, February 2009)

Here, Charles did not outright say what a "true friendship" is; rather, he characterized it by what it is not. On another occasion, however, Charles characterized his "true friends" as *imfura*, one of the highest compliments one can pay in Rwanda. *Imfura* means those of high status and moral standing and who have the qualities of *ubupfura*, meaning nobility of heart or dignity. In this instance, he explained that what draws him to his "true friends" is that he can trust their moral judgment, respect their opinions, and he can trust they are not out to profit from him.

In their characterization of true friendship as one not determined by exchange of goods or favors but by fondness for the other and the sharing of problems and challenges, Charles and Léon want to claim that "modern" social bonds decouple the instrumental from the affective. For them, the "lop-sided" friendship of patron–client exchange (Pitt-Rivers 1961: 140; see also Pitt-Rivers 2016: 447) is not friendship at all, because patrons and clients do not necessarily care for each other no matter the state of their exchanges. Strikingly, Léon and Charles see true friendship in the same way many classical social and political theorists did: as a modern bond par excellence, one that is chosen on the basis of mutual liking, that is not determined by circumstance, that is not formally institutionalized, and that people can make or break more or less as they please (Allan 1998; Silver 1990). Of course, in practice, usefulness and affection are not so clearly demarcated in modern Western friendship (Rawlins 2008). Still, the point is how Butare residents assign capacities for true friendships to modern persons—those who are bounded, autonomous, and who freely choose to connect and disconnect from others rather than being encumbered by relations of obligation—ones now besmirched by their harnessing in the organization of the massacres in 1994. In claiming to have "true" friends (or in Léon's case, in claiming to know the difference), Charles makes a claim to modern selfhood that he says most Rwandans lack, including his own spouse. Charles used his knowledge of Canadian beer-sharing practices—acquired while visiting Toronto and Ottawa for conferences—to assert the moral superiority of voluntary, affective relations between independent subjects over relations of mutual obligation determined by traditional forms of patronage and reciprocity. Sahlins' view (1972: 134) that "everywhere in the world the indigenous category for exploitation is 'reciprocity'" would resonate with Charles. The making and marking of modern, peaceful selfhood in Rwanda is always inseparable from the question of what kinds of relationships people ought to form, what (if anything) is owed to others, and the moral basis of connection and disconnection from others.

Genocide Is Always Between Us

"Whenever I have been away from Butare, as soon as the bus enters the town limits, I get a feeling of dread," Pauline, a widowed genocide survivor and small business owner in her fifties, mused after having returned a day earlier from visiting friends in Kigali. Since she resides only a few streets away from the house where she and her "old family" were attacked in 1994, the genocide haunts her daily life in the town. Pauline rarely spoke of that day, but she once told me how the *interahamwe* came and marched them out of the house. "I thought that was it for all of us. They killed my husband and one of my sons in front of me. But then they told me that my fate was to suffer without them. And so I am here, but sometimes I wonder, am I really living?" (Butare, July 2008). What she called her "old family" consisted of her husband and six children, but only two daughters survived. In 2008, she was informed that a prisoner had talked at *gacaca* and that the remains of two of her children had been found in a mass grave. Pauline struggled with this discovery and revealed a profound ambivalence about the practice of maintaining memorial sites and the duty to visit them. She refuses to visit the burial site and declined to collect clothing that belonged to them. "I try so hard to remember them alive," she explained. "Why would I want clothing to remind me of how they died?"

Pauline also faces difficulties reconciling the loss of her "old family" with the obligations she feels to her surviving children. She talked about how her daughters, both of whom were only babies in 1994, "have no history" because they do not know their family roots and have no discernible connection to their place of birth.

> Oh, it's difficult with the genocide. You avoid thinking about it, you flee from those thoughts. It's so exhausting to talk about that time. I need to go for a walk or put on music when things get hard. You can't fall back into those negative times. There was a time when we were all in it. This period of 1994… 1994 up to the present, the memories come every day. Even when you're talking to other people about something else, you're with others, but all it takes is seeing a girl the same age your daughter was when you lost her and immediately you think… the school uniform… ohhhhh. Me too, I had a little girl… you see? You go see a family and there is a couple. *Mon dieu*, you

can never forget, you see *le monsieur*, the children—you see? With me and my daughters, even up to now we don't know how to talk about their father, about their brothers and sister. The words don't come. It's something we always carry that weighs heavily on us. We can look at photos sometimes, but we don't talk. It's hard. I think they'd like to ask me questions, but they don't dare. And it's better that way. Sometimes I think, I'm the adult, I should find the courage to tell them, but I can't. Even now, it's so rare to hear one of my daughters speak the name of their brothers and sister. Their father, yes, very rarely. My oldest said to me once, "*Maman*, I had a dream last night." "What dream?" I asked her. "A good dream. Someone came to visit me in my dreams." I asked her who came. She said, "Ahhh, no, I'm not telling." It's like they're saying "papa." I think this might be a good thing, but we don't know how to talk about it.

It's like my daughters have no history. They don't dare ask about their father's death because they know their mother has never told a soul what exactly happened. They have trouble now in their relationships. They are ok in groups where they can talk about general things, but they can't open themselves to anyone so they won't talk about personal things. There are boys who are interested in them, but they always say, no, we don't need that. It's because they've never lived with a man before, since they hardly remember their father. There are entire parts of themselves they know nothing about— essentially the whole time they lived in Rwanda when they were small because they've been in Tanzania ever since primary school. When you meet people and you get to know them, you talk about your past and your childhood, your family. But they can't because they don't have anything to say. All people know about them is that their mother is Rwandan. They keep their vague knowledge of their own past hidden to avoid having to tell anyone—they don't want to talk about it because they actually don't know what to say—who was their father, what was he like, their siblings, where they grew up… all missing from their memories. The three of us keep this secret, this *mauvais secret* [terrible secret]. (Butare, May 2008)

In other words, survivors like Pauline underline how certain dimensions of social personhood, particularly the genealogies in which they are embedded, have been lost to youth in the years since the genocide. Pauline feels as if she has failed her children because they are incapable of answering the central questions of selfhood and its sources, "Who are you?", "Who are your parents?", or "Where are you from?" She takes personal responsibility for failing to keep her daughters sufficiently connected to Butare because of her own inability to talk about their missing relations. In the early years after the genocide, she explained, she felt that she needed to get them away from the "negativity" in Butare, and this is why she sent them to school in Tanzania at an early age. Similarly, Pauline confessed that she has sought out friendships with foreigners like me because it is easier than relationships with local people where, as she put it, "the genocide is always between us." But at the same time, her close ties to foreigners raise questions in other residents' minds about just how committed she is to Butare. Both she and I have heard people criticize her for forming too many relationships with wealthy outsiders, and they intimate that it is her own fault if she feels adrift from her local social world.

Antecedents to Post-Genocide Butare: Person, Nation, Modernity, and Equality

Clearly, there are contradictory currents shaping post-genocide forms of sociality, belonging, and exclusion in Butare, and these contradictions have a history that reaches far beyond the genocide itself. However, any foray into Rwandan history must be prefaced with some cautionary notes. In oral historian Jan Vansina's words (1998: 38), Rwanda's colonial and postcolonial historical sources are part of "an intense propaganda war." Indeed, the writings of Rwandan intellectuals, colonial historians, and anthropologists have for decades been at the center of Rwanda's political struggles. The histories they wrote shaped the terms of the discourse of ethnicity, and Tutsi and Hutu political leaders alike invoked them to assert their legitimacy and right to govern. Furthermore, the *ibiteekerezo*—oral tales about Rwanda's precolonial past—have been central tools in the battle over Rwandan history and historiography. They deal, among other things, with questions of settlement, changing rights to land or cattle, and genealogies (Vansina 2000: 381). The colonial-era Institut pour la recherche scientifique en Afrique central (IRSAC), located in Butare and reputed for the pro-Tutsi stance of its researchers, was the primary repository for the codified versions of the *ibiteekerezo*. Most of the tales recorded by the IRSAC come from the region around the Tutsi royal court, which has generated concerns that elite-centric versions were recorded (Vansina 2000: 375). Much of this research, writing, and recording of *ibiteekerezo* on the emergence of ethnic categories (e.g. Codère 1962; de Heusch 1966; D'Hertefelt 1964; Kagame 1972; Louis 1963; Maquet 1961; Vansina 1962) came with the heightened political consciousness of the 1950s and 1960s when the search for ethnic origins and historical ethnic hierarchies was explicitly linked in political ideologies to the question of who the rightful rulers were. It is not surprising that the resurgence of ethnic antagonism during the civil war of the early 1990s likewise brought on a renewed interest by Rwandan scholars in the historical roles of the Belgian colonial administration and the Catholic Church as allies or enemies of one ethnic faction or another (e.g. Kalibwami 1991; Rumiya 1992).

The sociopolitical significance of personhood, or ways that people fit in with each other, rise and decline with the forms that social and political struggles take in different times and places. Since ethnicity and other foundations of who people are emerge and are made relevant through everyday encounters and social situations (Eriksen 1993: 1), it is difficult to ascertain the character of those relations in the distant past. Nonetheless, scholars argue that especially in the northern regions of Rwanda, clan (*ubwoko*; pl. *ibwoko*) or lineage relationships were in precolonial times a much more significant component of personhood than ethnicity or political ties (Chrétien 2003: 254; Guichaoua 2005: 30; Newbury 1980; Rumiya 1992: 142). But by the late 1950s, at the center of decolonization struggles in Rwanda was the question of what modern personhood and nationhood ought to look like, debates that hinged on Tutsi and Hutu ethnicity and who had a legitimate claim to govern postcolonial Rwanda. Although it was not slated to become the national capital upon independence, Butare was a central site for the unfolding of these struggles. Together with Save—site of the first Catholic mission in Rwanda established in 1900—and Nyanza—the center of the precolonial court from which the *mwami* ruled—Butare was part of the colonial power nexus. It was there that the formal school system established by the Belgian colonial administration and the Catholic Church produced the local elite, and with it, new inequalities and social boundaries that permeate both the politics of the genocide and post-genocide social life.

State formation is never an event that produces a concrete, cohesive state structure, but is rather a claim to political legitimacy that is above all historically constructed (Abrams 1988: 80; see also Corrigan and Sayer 1985; DuBois 2005; Joseph and Nugent 1994; Roseberry 1994). As Corrigan and Sayer (1985) argue, state formation and cultural revolution are inseparable and must be apprehended together. In the case of postcolonial state formation processes in and around Butare, cultural revolution meant a radical rethinking of the longstanding ethnic hierarchy and the veritable Tutsi monopoly on social status and political power. It entailed an effort to reconfigure the meanings of ethnicity in a cultural struggle over what modern nationhood and equality should mean in the context of difference. Indeed, ethnicity became *the* site of struggle over meanings of equality and modernity in decolonizing Rwanda, and these struggles produced layered complexities in how personhood and nationhood are entangled. In the end, a cultural revolution in the meaning of modernity and equality reordered—but never definitively so—the relative worth of the qualities and capacities stereotypically associated with Hutuness and Tutsiness.[9] By legitimating their right to govern in ethnic terms, Rwanda's first indigenous politicians also delineated certain modes of belonging, exclusion, and individual conduct (cf. Corrigan and Sayer 1985: 6). Hence, questions of selfhood and questions of nationhood are never fully separate. By what processes were personhood and nationhood debated in postcolonial state formation processes in Butare, and how did competing ethnically based factions advance claims to be Rwanda's legitimate shepherds toward modern nationhood?

Producing the Local Elite of Butare

Postcolonial struggles over state formation in Rwanda cannot be apprehended apart from the processes by which Butare's tiny Tutsi and Hutu elites were produced. Other scholars have established the colonial exclusion of Hutu from schools and civil service posts as an early source of ethnic resentment that was carried forth in the anti-Tutsi ideology behind the 1994 genocide. As a result of colonial school segregation, posts in the government and church were virtually restricted to the Tutsi elite. Linden (1977: 163) quotes Monsignor Classe's edict to the Catholic missionaries in 1928, "You must choose the Batutsi because the government will probably refuse Bahutu teachers … In the government the positions in every branch of the administration, even the unimportant ones, will be reserved henceforth for young Batutsi." When the Catholic White Fathers opened their first school in Nyanza in 1905, it had twenty-six students, all sons of Tutsi chiefs (Mamdani 2001: 89). In the late 1940s and early 1950s, Tutsi enrollment at Butare's Groupe Scolaire ranged from sixty-three to eighty-five students compared to only thirteen to nineteen Hutu students each year (Lemarchand 1970: 138). But the ethnic composition of the student body was not the only problem. The colonial education system was instrumental in valorizing Tutsi at the expense of Hutu. As Semujanga notes, the Groupe Scolaire in Butare was where the myth of Tutsi-Hamite identification reached its pinnacle. This myth, which stated that the Hamitic Tutsi were a superior race who originated from Abyssinia and who conquered the Bantu Hutu—the "true" black men—was taught to the sons of Tutsi chiefs at the Groupe Scolaire as a factual, historical narrative (Semujanga 2003: 148; see also des Forges 1999: 34–35). The notion that "Tutsi is best for command" while "Hutu is best for agriculture" was the very foundation of the colonial education system (Semujanga 2003: 242) and ensured that virtually only Tutsi students secured employment and powerful positions in the colonial administration.

Colonial education had far-reaching implications beyond the overt production of ethnic inequality and ideology. The restriction of formal schooling to a tiny, primarily Tutsi elite also entangled ethnicity with other social boundaries around status, training, occupation, language capacities, conduct, and tastes. Cohn (1996) has shown that the production of an indigenous elite through colonial schooling results in a small group capable of moving between two worlds: the "parochial" world of home, and the "modern" world of the European metropole. Colonizers, having entered into new territories about which they knew little, required the services of local mediators and translators. These mediators, however, were not already waiting to serve the colonial powers; rather, they had to be produced and given a stake in colonial rule. The effect of conferring this privilege on a select few was to create a loyal, governing elite, a small group who had an interest in the maintenance of colonial authority (Anderson [1983] 1991: 126; Cohn 1996: 21). In Butare, the boarding school (*internat*) model of colonial education was instrumental in this process because it produced a new, primarily Tutsi elite who had one foot in the world of Rwandans and one in the world of Europeans. The idea was that, to become modern, students had to undergo physical separation from their Rwandan families to learn European habits, styles of reasoning, dress, and tastes (cf. Cohn 1996: 48). Perhaps more important, the close proximity to bearers of modern Western culture allowed Rwandan students to form face-to-face relationships with Europeans which conferred on them the power and prestige of the mediator role. In only a matter of decades, the colonial education system produced new boundaries of ethnic belonging and exclusion and new ways of getting things done for the educated Tutsi elite—in sum, new kinds of persons who wore European clothes, spoke and wrote European languages, but who were nonetheless still Rwandan and straddled two social worlds.

State Formation and Ethnic Difference in Postcolonial Rwanda

With formal independence on the horizon in the late 1950s, factions emerged along ethnic lines to deal with the pressing question of who has the right to govern postcolonial Rwanda. The "ethnic obsession" took hold primarily among the tiny, Western-educated elite who graduated from Butare's Groupe Scolaire and the nearby Nyakibanda seminary (Chrétien 2003: 300). At this point, Tutsi and Hutu elites in and around Butare were competing over nothing less than which of them was more modern. Tutsi and Hutu elites thus made parallel, but diametrically opposed claims in terms of ethnic difference in order to justify their struggles to govern post-independence Rwanda. The primary pro-Tutsi party in the first elections was the monarchist Union nationale rwandaise (National Union of Rwanda; UNAR), established in 1959, which aimed to preserve the rule of the *mwami*. In UNAR ideology, equality was the name given to the postcolonial re-entrenchment of the traditional hierarchy couched in terms of national unity. Somewhat ironically, UNAR's posturing around national unity and equality was intended to mitigate troublesome statements made by conservative members of the Tutsi elite. In 1958, a group of elderly Tutsi clients of the *mwami* issued a statement known as the *Premier écrit de Nyanza*, which asserted that "there could be no basis of brotherhood between Hutu and Tutsi … Since our king [*mwami*] conquered the country and the Hutu and killed their petty kings, how can they claim to be our brothers?" (quoted in Lemarchand 1970: 154). This statement invoked the inherent right of the Tutsi to rule based on the *mwami*'s court's interpretations of history and colonial racist theories about natural Tutsi superiority. By invoking historical claims to Tutsi superiority and ethnic difference, this statement put ethnicity out in the open in the political debates around postcolonial state formation.

Against these conservative Tutsi claims to superiority, UNAR sought a new ideology upon which to legitimate their candidacy. It was based on the idea that the decolonization and modernization processes require an educated elite to identify and seek solutions to emergent political, economic, and administrative challenges (cf. Alatas 1977; Shils 1961, [1960] 1972). In this vision of the "good postcolonial Rwandan," to be modern is to earn one's status from achieved rather than ascribed (ethnic) attributes, the latter being pejoratively associated with traditional social hierarchies. Indeed, UNAR used their level of attained education to advance their suitability for government office, not their ascribed Tutsiness, but the trouble, of course, was the very inseparability of these two things in most people's minds—an association that persists today. They claimed for themselves the personal attributes and cultural capital required to instill a sense of national identity, pride, and unity in the population. They staked Tutsi legitimacy on the promotion of equality in the sense of shared Banyarwanda (people of Rwanda) identity. UNAR propaganda promoted the virtues of the kingship and the *mwami* as a symbol of the unity of all Rwandans, and thus proclaimed that ethnic difference was illusory and a colonial invention. From this perspective, Rwandans were all the same people and the Belgians should be blamed for their internal divisions. UNAR accused its Hutu rivals of dividing the country with its open ideology of ethnic difference, and it claimed to unite Rwandans under the figure of the *mwami*. In a 1959 circular warning of the imminent formation of a pro-Hutu opposition party, UNAR exhorted the population,

> Rwandese! Children of Rwanda! Subjects of Kigeri,[10] rise up! Let us unite our strengths! Do not let the blood of Rwanda be spilled in vain. There are no Tutsi, Hutu, Twa. We are all brothers! We are all descendants of Kinyarwanda! (Quoted in Lemarchand 1970: 161)

But for UNAR opponents, its ideology of unity was merely a claim to the legitimacy of traditional instruments of Tutsi rule thinly veiled by an ideology of radical nationalism (Linden 1977: 260).

UNAR was defeated when its main rival, the Parti du mouvement de l'émancipation Hutu (Hutu Emancipation Movement Party; PARMEHUTU) won the 1961 legislative assembly elections by a landslide and held a referendum to abolish the mwamiship—the ultimate symbol of Tutsi rule.

What appealed to the population was not simply PARMEHUTU leaders' shared ethnicity with the majority. Indeed, even in the 1956 subcheiftancy elections, most Hutu were still voting for Tutsi representatives, since those elections resulted in only a 5 percent decline in Tutsi representatives (Linden 1977: 237).[11] Rather, PARMEHUTU's winning strategy was to mount a campaign that redefined the basis of modern nationhood, valorized longstanding stereotypical Hutu qualities, and disparaged Tutsi ones. For PARMEHUTU, equality was based on concerns about socioeconomic needs, social justice, and redressing the long history of oppression of the Hutu majority. Indeed, an equation quickly emerged by which Hutu = people = poor = majority (Ntakirutimana and Semujanga 2010: 49). Spurred by the social Catholicism of a new wave of missionaries of the 1940s and 1950s, PARMEHUTU laid its claim to legitimate rule on the ethnic dichotomy between the Hutu and Tutsi and put forth its mandate to defend the "humble folk" against abuse (Chrétien 2003: 302). PARMEHUTU drew ideological ammunition from the 1957 Manifesto of the Hutu (reproduced in Heremans 1973: 70–72). It cited the disproportionate power, status, and wealth held by the Tutsi minority, which comprised no more than 14 percent of the population. It called for a range of broad transformations in the order of things, including an end to the Tutsi monopoly on political power, social and economic assistance to the Hutu to bring them out of poverty, and access to education. In addition to these reforms aimed at transforming the material conditions of the Hutu, a cultural dimension was included which called for a change in attitude (*esprit*) concerning the idea that, in accordance with respect for Rwanda's culture and customs, elites belonged only to the "Hamitic" rank. In the political and cultural struggles over postcolonial state formation, the ideological project of the PARMEHUTU for the first time made Hutuness stand for qualities deemed worth upholding: equality based upon shared work and shared benefits in the modernization effort underpinning the decolonization process. Simultaneously, traditional forms of Tutsi eliteness took on contemptible contours and inverted the ethnic moral hierarchy that had characterized much of colonial Rwanda. But this, of course, cannot be read as a happy story of historical justice. Out of decolonization-era ethnic rivalries also grew the first outbreak of violence against Tutsi in the name of Hutu nationalism. In the 1959 peasant revolt that marked one of the first points at which ethnic consciousness took firm hold among ordinary Hutu (Newbury 1988: 195–96), the first waves of Tutsi refugees fled Rwanda in an ominous foreshadowing of what was to come in 1994.

The centrality of ethnicity to UNAR and PARMEHUTU state formation contests consolidated layered excesses and dissonances in the meanings of Tutsiness and Hutuness. In these stereotypes converged debates about both "good persons" and the basis of modern nationhood. Hutuness, associated with the peasantry and the subordinate position in patron–client exchange, has certain positive moral qualities and capacities, especially stamina for the hard work and physical labor of agriculture with which the Hutu have long been stereotypically associated. In large part, this reputation is linked to the phenotypic stereotype of the Hutu—short, sturdy, and dark-skinned Bantu (Maquet 1961). Humility, honesty, and good-naturedness are positive elements of the Hutu stereotype (Semujanga 2003: 114–17; des Forges 1995: 44). But in Hutuness are also embedded less praiseworthy traits that arise from the stereotypically subordinate position of the Hutu in the precolonial system of *ubuhake*[12] cattle clientship. These qualities include poverty, a desire for positions of servitude, and child-like dependency (Lemarchand 1970: 43). In other words, there are two main "Hutu" capacities or ways of getting things done: either through hard work and physical labor (an admirable trait) or by appealing to a potential patron for assistance and entering into a relationship of dependency (a less respected trait).

Tutsiness connotes a contrasting locus of traits because of colonial stereotyping of the Tutsi as superior political leaders and patrons to dependent clients. Phenotypic characteristics also form part of Tutsi stereotypes, including tallness and slenderness, light skin, and narrow facial features—qualities grounded in the putative Hamitic origins of the Tutsi. Catharine Newbury (1988: 12) notes that "Tutsi," as it was used in everyday talk, often referred not to descent, but to a social condition of wealth. Especially in the precolonial and colonial seats of power, like Nyanza and Butare, the term "Tutsi" was used by the powerful in a self-definition of their own eliteness (ibid.), a distinction that encompassed not only class, but also power and cultural features (D. Newbury 1998: 85). The largely positive characteristics associated with Tutsiness are independence of thought and action and the ability to look after oneself, instead of seeking the assistance or protection of a patron.[13] A person who demonstrates self-sufficiency is appreciated in Butare because, it goes without saying that, since 1994, everyone has had problems and so residents speak highly of those who do not burden others. However, these same traits can be inverted: the self-sufficient person is also un-neighborly and can lack a sense of sociality when it comes to assisting others. Furthermore, the stereotypical Tutsi is lazy and refuses to work hard, but instead makes wealth on the backs of the Hutu. Cleverness, trickery, and wiliness are also stereotypical Tutsi qualities (Lemarchand 1995: 9; C. Newbury 1998: 9) because it is said that the Tutsi tricked the Hutu into exploitative relations of servitude. "Tutsi" capacities or ways of getting things done are either using one's ingenuity to get by on one's own (an admirable trait) or by tricking others and putting them in positions of dependency (contemptible traits). In the post-genocide moment, however, trickery and dissimulation have taken on new contours and are no longer strictly

"Tutsi" traits. Tutsi survivors invoke these same qualities to characterize Hutu who, as one middle-aged male survivor put it, "went on pretending like everything was normal and then suddenly—*Pow! Ils nous ont génocidés* [they committed genocide against us]." These are, of course, stereotypes, and they do not contradict the reality that most Tutsi in Rwanda belong to the rural peasantry, that plenty of Hutu meet elite criteria, or that people of all ethnic descent categories can situationally exhibit honesty, trickery, dependency, or autonomy. Indeed, this is precisely the point, as postcolonial state formation produced cultural frameworks shot through with ethnic tones by which admirable and disparaged capacities of persons are produced, valued, and interpreted.

Conclusion

When struggles over modern nationhood emerged in Rwanda for the first time, they were fought in ethnic idioms. Hence, it is *through* ethnicity that personhood and nationhood were coproduced. The ethnic grounds on which UNAR and PARMEHUTU contested each other on the eve of decolonization laid foundations for debates about modern personhood and nationhood in Rwanda that still permeate contemporary politics and everyday evaluations of moral agency. UNAR state formation strategies show that there is nothing novel about the RPF's claims to promote pan-Rwandan unity and the idea that to be modern is to be above ethnicity. In the case of both UNAR and the RPF, critics have suggested that these claims are little more than strategies of disguising what is, in practical terms, Tutsi rule. We see Charles caught in the imperative to adhere to the RPF's narrative of precolonial unity both because he has little choice and to preserve his own elite status, while at the same time trying to assert traditional "Tutsi" elite qualities of independent thought and action. When Odette explains that Butare has declined in prosperity in the absence of (Tutsi) intellectuals killed in 1994, she echoes decolonization-era ethnic rivalries and the crucial linkage UNAR made between an educated elite and the path to modern nationhood. In Bernadette, we see a woman who on the one hand embraces traditional markers of eliteness through intellectual status and the "New Rwanda" edict that prosperity and peace will only come through individual ingenuity and enterprise, and on the other hand, whose moral world is grounded in an attachment to the rural life ways first valorized by PARMEHUTU, including a stance that sees a truly "modern" Rwanda as one in which all Rwandans could benefit from development. Finally, in Pauline's narrative of how the genocide is always between her and other survivors, she struggles over what it means to belong in Rwanda today, both for her and for her surviving children, as they live with the consequences of a campaign to purge Rwanda of Tutsi for the good of the "Hutu nation."

In a nexus of power relations characterized by both modern and parochial features, Butare residents have been at the heart of postcolonial debates about what Rwandans ought to be. They live with a peculiar legacy of the genocide and its politics, one rooted both in a history of ethnic integration and fierce ethnic competition for political and moral legitimacy. As educated urban dwellers both steeped in intellectual culture and distanced from the center of power and urban development in Kigali, Butare residents live out crucial contradictions in the post-genocide project of remaking personhood and nationhood. They face the imperative to remember the genocide and to be agents of change for the "New Rwanda," to "become someone" yet also remain humble and grounded. These tensions are not simply the product of RPF state formation strategies and the politics of the genocide, but are steeped in the colonial and postcolonial history of Butare, where debates about ethnic difference and the modern person and nation have powerfully shaped competing ideas about "the good." What this history shows is that even when successive regimes work to legitimate their rule through cultural revolution in the meaning of ethnic difference and modern nationhood, competing perspectives are never fully ruled out and continue to inform people's everyday evaluations of each other's conduct. Indeed, the RPF stakes its claim to political legitimacy on a cultural revolution in the meaning of ethnicity to break with the divisive ethnic ideology of the previous, genocidal regime. But in what ways do other ideas about ethnicity, including popular Tutsi and Hutu stereotypes, continue to inform people's understandings of what "kinds" of persons they are dealing with? It is to this question that the next chapter turns.

Notes

1. I am grateful to Malcolm Blincow for this analogy.
2. By 2014, the Rwandan government had amalgamated those new universities with the old National University, and united them under the singular name, the University of Rwanda. Each campus now houses a different college or faculty. As of 2014, Butare was home to the College of Arts, Media, and Social Sciences (CAMSS). However, I maintain the name, National University or NUR to refer to the Butare campus, because this is how Butare residents continued to refer to it during my fieldwork.
3. *Imihigo* is the Kinyarwanda term for performance contracts that translates as "promises to deliver." The contract is between the president and the district leaders, who compete for the highest ranking. Since 2006, each district of the country is measured and ranked according to a list of social, economic, and justice development indicators, including the percentage of people subscribed to the national health insurance plan, poverty reduction, number of school toilets built, number of women using family planning methods,

number of houses with electricity, and somewhat more vague indictors like "thinking big" (Institute of Policy Analysis and Research Rwanda 2014).

4. Statistics are only produced at the level of the district (*uturere*), so all statistics for Butare town are subsumed into those for Huye district, whose population is roughly 328,000 in an area of 580km².

5. Law no. 47/2001 and law no.18/2008 of 23 July 2014.

6. Even though the RPF is the governing party, the current regime is officially a coalition between it and the Christian Democratic Party, the Islamic Democratic Party, the Rwandan Socialist Party, the Democratic Union of the Rwandan People, and the Party for Progress and Concord.

7. In 2015, the government decided that national-level commemorations will now take place every five years, but local-level ceremonies to remember victims still take place annually.

8. *Ingando* camps are "solidarity camps" compulsory and/or encouraged for a number of different subsets of the population, including released prisoners, religious leaders, ex-combatants, teachers at all levels of education, and incoming university students. The camps are managed by the National Unity and Reconciliation Commission (NURC). Critics argue that their purpose is political indoctrination into RPF ideology rather than a good faith endeavor to promote peaceful social relations (Mgbako 2005).

9. These are abstractions commonly used in the literature (e.g. Burnet 2012; Fujii 2009; Lemarchand 2002) that refer to the shifting and hybrid loci of qualities (phenotypic, cultural, or moral) that people perceive "ethnically" (Lemarchand 2002). They are not strict, reified dichotomies, but conceptual tools for thinking about how everyday forms of social action are marked by ethnic stereotypes.

10. Kigeri was the last ruling *mwami* of Rwanda, from 1959 to 1961. He died in October 2016 in the United States, where he had obtained political asylum in 1992.

11. Although it should be noted that voting for higher-level council offices like these was not universal until 1959, and most of the voters in this 1956 election were drawn from lower councils. Lemarchand (1970: 81–82) suggests that restrictions on who could vote and the range of possible candidates favored Tutsi, but it is also questionable whether most Rwandans were orienting toward ethnicity in their voting decisions prior to 1959 (Linden 1977).

12. *Ubuhake* is the form of clientship on which the well-known, rigid colonial formulation of the Tutsi patron (*shebuja*) who owns cattle and the Hutu client (*umugaragu*) is based. See Maquet (1961) for a classic formulation of this account. While *ubuhake* has featured centrally in the classic ethnography on Rwanda, other types of clientship have coexisted with it, for example *ubukonde* land clientship.

13. It is important to note that these stereotypes do not imply that those who inherited Tutsi ethnicity through patrilineal descent never occupied the client role in a patron–client relationship, but what I focus on here are the ethnic markings of patron and client roles.

Chapter 2

ETHNICITY'S SPECTER IN POST-ETHNIC TIMES

∽

One afternoon in late February 2009, I was driving with the Abbé Célestin, a Hutu priest of the Butare parish with an easy smile and a sociable manner. Célestin, like many Butare residents, liked to show foreigners around the rural surroundings of the town, so he invited me to join him on visits he had to make to three smaller parishes scattered between Butare and Nyanza. As we sped north away from Butare along the narrow, but well-paved highway, Célestin noted my grip on the armrest and said with a chuckle, "*Je roule vite, eh?*" [I drive fast, eh?]. But when we turned onto a dirt road not far past Save, our progress was slowed not only by the rough terrain, but also by pedestrians who flagged down Célestin's bright blue Toyota to greet him and ask for support or prayers. Célestin was growing anxious about being able to make all of his scheduled stops. "But I have no choice, I have to stop and talk to them," he explained as he pulled over to chide a young girl for letting the toddler in her charge wander too close to the road. "If you don't, you are not appreciated. You have to be careful. If you're educated—a priest, a professor, or even our former [Hutu] President Habyarimana—if you have been shaped [*formé*] by elites, people may say you're more Tutsi than Hutu." Here, Célestin invoked ethnic categories to communicate what kind of person he thought a clergyman ought to be—someone who has time for "ordinary Rwandans" and who is not unduly caught up in the world of elites. Yet paradoxically, his phrasing also acts to distance him from those who still "think ethnically." He is careful to say that "people" may accuse you of Tutsiness. The implication is that he, Célestin, does not think that way; he is merely reporting what less enlightened Rwandans might say about him if he fails to uphold their expectations.

At least since the colonial period in Rwanda, the question of what kind of person one is and ought to be has been inseparable from ethnicity and ethnic boundary production. Chapter 1 established the unstable loci of qualities and capacities that grew throughout the colonial and postcolonial periods to define "Hutuness" and "Tutsiness," the key conceptual categories that drive the analysis in this chapter. Hutuness, as I argued, connotes capacities for hard physical work, a concern for equality, but also dependency, an inability to think for oneself, and low-status work, especially rural cultivation. Tutsiness, by contrast, is constituted by the qualities of intelligence, independent thought and action, and high-status occupations including leadership positions, but also a tendency toward dissimulation, greed, and a willingness to exploit others. The question today—and the one that animates this chapter—is what happens to ethnic categories at the level of everyday practice in a political moment in which they are no longer supposed to exist? In light of the RPF moratorium on ethnic identifiers, what are people "doing" with ethnic categories when they speak them, contest them, refer to them obliquely, or claim that they do not matter anymore?

The purpose of this chapter is to theorize and ethnographically ground Tutsi and Hutu ethnic categories in the contemporary social world of Butare and the difficult ways they bear on the question of what kind of person one is or ought to be. I argue that ethnicity in Rwanda's "post-ethnic" moment is characterized by uncertainty, innuendo, ambiguity, and the danger of interpretive disjuncture between the speaker and the audience of evaluative commentaries on people's actions, character, and choices. Building out from work that identifies the dangers of open talk about ethnicity in post-genocide Rwanda and the strategies by which Rwandans nonetheless try to discern each other's ethnic heritage (Hintjens 2008; Mclean Hilker 2009), I draw out another strand of uncertainty around the place of "ethnic talk" in everyday life. Interpretive doubt also arises about the question of whether people are "thinking ethnically" at all when they make evaluative commentaries about other people's moral qualities. Regardless of a speaker's intention, the problem is that people can always choose to read ethnic interpretations into remarks that invoke stereotypical ethnic qualities but that avoid (whether calculatedly or not) explicitly ethnic terminology. In order to claim a modern, inclusive, liberal stance on ethnicity, most Butare residents adhere quite readily to the RPF moratorium on ethnic labels. As such, much more typical than openly ethnic references are commentaries on other people's work ethic, level of generosity, or degree of dependency on others—judgments that evoke the qualities constitutive of ethnic stereotypes. The listener is thus left wondering: was this an "ethnic" commentary? And whether it was or not, what does this say about the moral status of the speaker? Crucially, this type of uncertainty does not strictly afflict ethnographers or other relative outsiders to Rwandan society. Butaréens, too, express that they cannot be sure whether people are making "ethnic" commentaries on each other's actions because ethnic labels refer not just to heritage but also to a person's qualities and capacities. As Simbi observed in the context of a conversation on the state moratorium on ethnic labels, "Tutsi, Hutu—these terms have never been clear—not even to us! We've always used them in different ways. I could call you 'my Tutsi' even if you're Hutu because maybe you're someone who sponsors [pays school fees for] me. Or I could say that you lack generosity as a way of saying you're just like a Tutsi" (Butare, May 2014). The difficulty is that patron–client relationships and accusations of lacking sociality *need not* be characterized in ethnic terms, but avoiding those labels never rules out the possibility of an ethnic reading, since the speaker cannot dictate how her remarks will be received. Hence, for both researchers and for Rwandans, the uses of ethnicity in making sense of the moral status of others are never unproblematic. It is this uncertainty and the ways that people put it to work or suffer its consequences that are the focus of this chapter.

To be clear, the uncertainty I describe here should not be read as a sign of inadequate understanding on the part of foreign researchers. Instead, it is precisely what tells us about the *experience* of striving to be a "good Rwandan" or "peaceful self" in the post-genocide moment. In the Rwandan context, attention to the problem of ethnographic uncertainty is fundamental to building an analysis that adequately captures the feel of social relations and interactions that raise the specter of "the ethnic." By ethnographic uncertainty, I mean that analysis and interpretation must make space for the ambiguous character of social interactions in the sense that Piot (1993) describes. Indeed, this is less a form of "secret communication" or deliberately concealed esoteric knowledge than the "relational contexts" in which understandings of hierarchy, equality, the good, and the contemptible are worked out in daily life (Piot 1993: 354). Since we cannot assume that social actors have perfect knowledge, certainty, or unequivocal interpretations of the interactions and situations in which they find themselves, ethnographers learn what it is to dwell in post-genocide Rwanda in part by being subject to the same interpretive uncertainties that Rwandans face when it comes to ethnicity in post-ethnic times. What matters is not simply the degree to which one embodies the admirable or contemptible qualities evocative of Tutsiness or Hutuness. I argue in this chapter that just as crucial is whether people seem to still think in terms of ethnicity at all or whether they have embraced the RPF's powerful contemporary fiction that ethnicity does not exist. Even as the openness of possibilities for interpretation raises the danger that one can be accused of "thinking ethnically," ambiguity is simultaneously what lets people live up to the post-genocide imperative to eschew ethnicity. A focus on the uses of ambiguity helps us to understand not only social boundary production in Rwanda or in post-conflict societies, but also the practical indeterminacies that more generally characterize how people use idioms of ethnicized and racialized difference (e.g. Brubaker 2004; Harrison 2002).

The Great Ethnicity Debate: Rwanda and Beyond

The nature of ethnicity in Rwanda and the question of just what kind of distinctions Tutsi, Hutu, and Twa denote has been *the* central debate in the Rwanda scholarship since at least the late colonial period (e.g. Maquet 1961). In a context in which people categorized as Hutu, Tutsi, or Twa have no particular linguistic, settlement, or kinship boundaries distinguishing them, questions arise as to just what is "ethnic" about these categories, what their origins are, their relation to other social categories like clan, lineage, class, and status, and how ethnic boundaries operate in daily life (e.g. de Lame 2005; Gravel 1968; Hintjens 2008; Lemarchand 1970; Mamdani 2001; Maquet 1961; C. Newbury 1988; D. Newbury 1980). These debates are testament to the lively and complex, but also devastating social life that ethnic categories in Rwanda have had, both past and present.

Although ethnic politics took on an extraordinary tenor in the 1994 genocide, debates on Rwandan ethnicity parallel those in the wider Africanist literature and beyond. First, in Rwanda and elsewhere, scholars have focused on the conditions under which ethnic difference comes to matter politically, particularly the coincidence of ethnic boundary production with decolonization (A. Cohen 1974; Lemarchand 1970; Newbury 1988; Williams 1989; Wilmsen and McAllister 1996). Second, two main configurations of ethnic boundaries populate the ethnographic record on Rwanda and constitute an opposition that mirrors larger debates on the nature of ethnic difference (Barth 1969; Brubaker 2004; R. Cohen 1978; Eriksen 1993; Nagata 1974; Okamura 1981; Williams 1991). On the one hand, there is an absolute, "either/or" perspective, and on the other a fluid, situational approach. In the case of Rwanda, the rigid, caste-like understanding of ethnicity based on patrilineal descent found its classic expression in Maquet's (1961) "premise of inequality" between Hutu and Tutsi. Against this reductive, descent-based view of ethnicity grew a set of counter-perspectives that saw Tutsi and Hutu as social-relational, flexible categories that overlap with differences like region, class, clan, and that find expression in ethnic stereotypes (e.g. de Lame 2005; Gravel 1968; Lemarchand 1970; C. Newbury 1988; D. Newbury 1980). However, immediately after the genocide, the "either/or" view of ethnicity was again central because of the impulse to account for the role of the ethnic binary in the violence. Scholars traced the historical production of the "Tutsi–Hutu" opposition and emphasized the relatively recent crystallization of political factions around an either/or view of ethnicity (e.g. Chrétien 2003; des Forges 1995; Mamdani 2001; Prunier 1995) to counter the "ancient tribal hatreds" narrative promoted by the international media during the genocide. However, Fujii (2009: 104) argues that ethnicity was more than a rigid binary even in 1994, as the killing of Hutu as well as Tutsi meant it was not always clear who the main targets were.

As the initial imperative to explain the genocide receded, scholars, especially ethnographers, began to recover the social-relational view of Rwandese ethnicity. Many emphasize how ethnic boundaries overlap with north–south regional divides, status and class distinctions, and citizenship categories in order to destabilize RPF claims to having excised ethnicity from the social order by outlawing Tutsi and Hutu labels (Buckley-Zistel 2006; Burnet 2012; Fujii 2009; Jefremovas 1997; McLean Hilker 2009; Thomson 2013). Still, scholars do not deny the ongoing significance of "inherited" ethnicity, as they also highlight the constraints posed by one's ethnic heritage in the post-genocide moment. Inherited ethnicity governs who can openly mourn their dead at genocide commemorations and how one stands in relation to categories like victim, survivor, and perpetrator (Burnet 2012; Doughty 2016; Vidal 2004), which profoundly shapes how people participate and belong in their social worlds. Thus, even at historical junctures where either rigid or mutable perspectives on ethnicity dominate the literature or Rwandan politics, the other is never ruled out completely.

Yet in spite of decades of dispute on the nature of Rwandan ethnicity and the origins of these categories, there seems to be little disagreement among contemporary scholars that the RPF's moratorium on ethnic labels has failed to eliminate the categories for which they stand from the social world of post-genocide Rwanda. Eltringham (2004), Burnet (2009), Hintjens (2008), Thomson (2013), and Vidal (2004) have detailed how the labels of genocide victim or survivor versus perpetrator map onto the Tutsi–Hutu distinction and produce new, politicized categories that legitimate Tutsi suffering and downplay or deny that of Hutu. Fujii (2009) and McLean Hilker (2009) have found that Rwandans continue to use ethnic referents to evaluate people's relative wealth or prestige. What became apparent through the everyday social situations that I observed and recorded during my fieldwork is that the question is not whether a rigid or situational view of ethnicity has greater explanatory power in the Rwandan context. I suggest that both configurations exist and matter in Rwanda today, which is one of the central factors that gives rise to the ambiguity of precisely *if or how* ethnicity matters in any given social interaction or evaluative commentary. Hence, both ethnic "heritage" and ethnically marked capacities and situational behavioral traits converge to produce layered complexities as to what kind of (non-)ethnic subject a person is. My interest is precisely in the ethnographic question of how rigid and flexible configurations of "the ethnic" *intersect* in the everyday lives of Rwandans. I draw out the practical tensions raised by this always ambiguous and open-to-interpretation convergence of absolute and situational ethnicity in the "post-conflict" moment as people grapple with the question: "What kind of person should I be?" Certainly, rigid, "heritage-based" ethnicity limits the identities people can felicitously perform. But ethnically marked moral qualities, personal capacities, and behavioral traits can also cast doubt on "inherited" Hutu or Tutsi ethnicity and place profound constraints on how people know themselves and others.

Managing the Specter of Ethnicity: Fixity, Flexibility, and Their Limits

The following analysis may appear to carelessly jettison the foregoing discussion of the interpretive *uncertainty* of when ethnicity matters in everyday life in Butare, because it takes up the difficult confluence of rigid and flexible ethnic boundaries in everyday social life. It might be read to suggest that ethnicity does, indeed, matter in the following situations and that the social actors in question are interpreting these moments ethnically. If I seem to err on the side of such interpretations in these ambiguous contexts, it is only to underscore the potential for this reading, since both scholars and Butare residents report that ethnicity continues to matter. My aim is to draw out the layers of uncertainty about how and when ethnicity matters by demonstrating how this interpretive work is complicated by the dual configurations of ethnicity—rigid and flexible—that have animated everyday life, postcolonial politics, and scholarly debate in Rwanda. Indeed, I use "Hutu" and "Tutsi" in this analysis not to imply that, if asked, any of the people involved would have said they were actively performing "Tutsi" or "Hutu" qualities, but rather to show how, in practical terms, the specter of ethnicity ambiguously arises when Butaréens evaluate each other's conduct in terms of class, occupational, moral, regional, or other distinctions that constitute ethnic stereotypes. As Mitchell put it in his seminal work on urban ethnicity:

> The social meanings of ethnicity, therefore, depend directly on the wider social context of which it is only a part, since the meanings have social significance in that they enable behaviour to be predicted. This view of ethnicity as a set of situationally determined meanings leaves open, of course, the possibility that there could be several contradictory definitions of ethnicity possible for a set

of actors in a social situation so that the meaning which comes to prevail will need to be negotiated by the actors. (Mitchell 1974: 23)

The following three vignettes demonstrate how social agents navigate the local (ethnically marked) politics of inequality and the genocide. I show how Butare residents manage the dangers of ethnicity's specter through quotidian acts of moral agency, that is, deliberate acts based on "strong evaluations" of the worth of one's desires and possible actions (Taylor 1985). Such evaluations are made against standards of moral regulation, that is, "proper forms of expression," both linguistic and non-linguistic, that constitute "moral repertoires" out of which social identities are produced (Corrigan 1981: 319). Indeed, choices about what kinds of acts constitute "the good" indicate a great deal about how ethnicity continues to raise difficult questions about what kind of person one is and ought to be in the post-conflict moment.

Those Who Work Hard at Umuganda

Umuganda ("contribution" in Kinyarwanda) is community work that takes place nationwide in Rwanda on the last Saturday of each month. It was first introduced under President Habyarimana's populist rural development campaign of the 1970s, but it was quickly co-opted by the elite for personal gain. Wealthier people stopped participating and corruption in high government ranks meant that work groups were ordered to till the personal fields of state officials (Longman 2010a: 123). After the 1994 genocide, *umuganda* was revived as a strategy of unity and reconciliation: working together to rebuild the country. It is, in principle, compulsory for all adult citizens and each person has a card that must be signed by the neighborhood head (*chef du quartier*) to mark her or his attendance. However, many, if not most, affluent town residents choose to pay a fine instead of participating, so, depending on the neighborhood, numbers can be quite thin. *Umuganda* usually consists of cultivating fields, maintaining public property, planting trees, picking up litter, or building houses for genocide survivors. Fortunately, on the occasions when I attended, the activity was tree planting, a form of work for which even I had the necessary skills.

I attended *umuganda* with Charles, the NUR professor first introduced in Chapter 1. According to patrilineal descent rules, Charles is Hutu, a fact that he never revealed to me directly. I gleaned it from a February 2009 conversation in which Charles complained that people think he and a friend (someone who had previously divulged his Hutu ethnicity to me) do favors for each other because of shared ethnicity. Charles regularly attended *umuganda*, but he sometimes reported somewhat sheepishly that when the assigned work was to build houses, he would end up just standing around because of his lack of experience in construction. Charles grew up on a rural hill in the neighboring province of Gikongoro, but he is a long-time resident of Butare. He first arrived there as a secondary school student to attend the prestigious Groupe Scolaire established during the colonial period. He later attended the NUR as an undergraduate student, a time from which he remembers many of the professors who eventually became propagandists for the genocide or, sadly, its victims. During the civil war (1990–1994), Charles married his wife, whom he met while studying at the university. Like most Hutu men, he says little about where he was and what he was doing during the civil war and genocide. During the many years I have known Charles, he has spoken only in passing of where he was during the war, and when he did so, he only vaguely talked about how that was a time when he had "real problems." Shortly after I first met him in 2004, he told me that his (Hutu) father was killed in the genocide, but he has not spoken of it to me since. To my knowledge, Charles was never imprisoned or indicted as a genocide suspect, so he was spared the ordeal of standing trial at *gacaca*. Unlike many NUR professors who reside in the capital, Kigali, and commute to the campus, Charles and his family reside in Butare. On this basis, Charles often staked a claim to being a "simple" person who is not seduced by the lure of the capital. However, his frequent trips to Kigali for meetings and conferences were the subject of scrutiny and speculation among the neighbors: who invited him to the capital so often, and what did he do there that let him buy a house, a car, and fund both his own and other children's education?

We participated in *umuganda* in Charles's mixed-income neighborhood of Ngoma. On the morning of *umuganda*, the *chef du quartier*, a young, energetic acquaintance of Charles's with a light-hearted demeanor, was waiting on the street to organize participants. The street, the main artery through Ngoma, was rather quiet. Since businesses are required to close on the mornings of *umuganda*, not many people were on the road into town. Surveying our calm surroundings, the *chef* expressed concern that few people would come to help. He wondered how we would be able to plant all of the saplings that were to be dropped off with so few hands. He then proceeded to make a joke about my small frame, which suggested that he was not particularly confident that I would be much help in this regard.

We conversed casually for about thirty minutes while waiting for the trees to be delivered, during which time a handful more people arrived. Some were wealthier residents dressed like Charles in the Adidas or Reebok tracksuits often worn on weekends by the affluent, but they paired them with the heavy rubber boots favored by rural agriculturalists. Others were low-income neighbors dressed in eclectic combinations of second-hand clothing and who could be counted on to bring the wheelbarrows, shovels, and other tools required for *umuganda*.

Once the trees were delivered, we set out in a group of only eight to begin. At the start, all participants were men, all of whom appeared between the ages of forty and sixty-five. One woman, wearing jeans and a polo-style shirt, joined us about thirty minutes later. She greeted me with a joking "Bonjour, monsieur!" to signal the oddity of a young white woman attending *umuganda*. Only one man, a low-income neighbor, had brought his wheelbarrow along to cart trees around. Since we could not all follow him around if we wanted to distribute trees evenly and efficiently throughout the neighborhood, Charles volunteered to go back to his house to retrieve the wheelbarrow that normally is only used by his domestic worker for hauling firewood and by his gardener. He appeared pleased to be contributing agricultural tools not usually supplied by those who do not make their living using them. With his wheelbarrow, we were able to split into two groups and make our way around the neighborhood. As we moved along our way, good-natured banter characterized exchanges between participants. They teased each other about their planting techniques and their level of know-how when it came to agricultural tasks. Other residents would occasionally arrive to join the work, but most passers-by, upon seeing the work group, quickened their pace. The workers shouted to those who passed and asked them where they were going and why they had not come to share in *umuganda*. To some extent, their shouts were in jest, but they also demonstrate real resentment and criticism of those who buy their way out of shared work—agricultural work that has the markings of the rural peasant majority of the country. Charles has a good reputation in the neighborhood in large part because of his willingness to join in shared work with his lower-income neighbors instead of paying the fine. The *chef du quartier* appreciates that someone of his status works hard at *umuganda* and is quick to do Charles small favors, like witnessing his passport application, a request that could easily be put off for weeks by a *chef* who is unhappy with the applicant. While the moral agency of participating in shared physical work is a crucial way for wealthy town residents to maintain good reputations and relationships with neighbors, I could not help but notice that the work group, nonetheless, split off along lines of those who work in modern, urban sectors and the urban poor who make their living in ways not unlike the work of *umuganda*.

A Public Declaration of Subordination

Alexandre, a government functionary at the district office for Huye,[1] was scarcely seen in public without a carefully tailored suit and impeccably shined dress shoes, even on weekends. He is of Hutu heritage, a fact I inferred because he was first introduced to me as the brother of a Butare shopkeeper who had disclosed her Hutu ethnicity to me. I crossed paths with Alexandre late one Friday morning while I was at the district office to see the local immigration officer to collect my research permit. The Rwandan government touts the professionalism of its civil servants, who are expected to be at their desks at 7am and to be reliably present during business hours. In the RPF's campaign for a modern state bureaucracy, they have appropriated the corporate language of customer service to remake the image of their offices, which the population and foreign visitors alike have long criticized as incompetent and disorganized. I knew something was afoot in the image renewal of state agencies when I applied online for my entry visa to Rwanda in the spring of 2014, and the email I received with the visa attached had in its signature line, "Your satisfaction is our duty, Rwanda Directorate General of Immigration and Emigration."

In practice, however, it can still be as difficult as it always was in Rwanda to find civil servants in their offices. On that morning, Alexandre was on his way out of the district office building in the middle of regular hours to run some personal errands. He called out to me from the other end of the dimly lit hallway to ask me where I was going, and he insisted on giving me a ride since the sun was blazing on that cloudless June day. He advised me that I would have to make some stops with him because his errands were pressing, but that he would drop me off at my destination afterwards.

I climbed into Alexandre's shiny, black Toyota RAV4. As much as I tried to avoid being chauffeured around Butare, I did appreciate the air conditioning on this day. We drove to the town center and parked on the side of a dusty road near the market. As usual, the street was bustling with pedestrians, motorcycle and bicycle taxis looking for clients, and prepaid card vendors for the mobile phone networks. Even with the car windows up, I heard one of the local street kids shout to me, "Give me money!"—a demand now articulated in English, not the (slightly fractured) French plea, "*Donnez-moi l'argent!*" to which I was routinely subject up until around 2009.[2]

No sooner had we exited the vehicle than a young man in stained clothing—perhaps a day laborer—called out not to me, but to Alexandre, "Boss, boss!" Alexandre turned as the young man sidled up to him. "Boss, I beg of you please, I am a father and a husband. I work hard to support my family, but I have nothing left, so my clothes are dirty as you can see. Boss, could you buy me a T-shirt? I know you are good man, a good Christian. I trust that you will help me." Without hesitation, Alexandre agreed to buy the man a T-shirt from a nearby vendor at the market. The man, upon receiving his gift, pressed his palms together and bowed toward Alexandre—a typical gesture of deference and respect. As we parted company with the young man, I remarked to Alexandre that he must get requests like this one routinely, and I asked how he manages them all. He explained to me that he has sympathy for young men like this who ask for only simple things. "How could I deny him a T-shirt?" he asked rhetorically. But then Alexandre went on to explain that this young man—and many others like him—is strategic. Unlike some prospective clients who come to a private home to ask for money and who can more easily and quietly be refused, this man had made a bold, loud, public request for assistance.

> He knew that my refusal would not be looked well upon by those around us. People in this town know who I am. This is why people will approach you in public. They know you are under pressure to agree. Otherwise, people will say you don't care about those struggling to get by. They'll say you are content to drink your beer on the veranda of the [Hotel] Ibis while others cannot feed their families. And like I said, it was just a T-shirt—a few hundred Francs. To deny him that would have looked like the worst kind of greed.

These two social situations speak to the everyday convergence of "inherited" and situational ethnicity. Both Charles's and Alexandre's selfhood is situationally marked by the stereotypes of Tutsiness in spite of their Hutu heritage. Charles's PhD from a Belgian university, coupled with his work as a NUR professor, mark him as a member of a "traditional" elite set apart by wealth and education. Likewise, Alexandre's university degree and his occupation as a civil servant mean that the sources of his and Charles's privilege share the pattern established by the colonial education system in Rwanda that produced "Tutsi" privilege by virtue of ties to the world of the modern.

What is compelling about the situation of *umuganda* was that Charles's Hutu heritage was not enough to definitively offset the social dangers of "Tutsi" wealth and education. In that situation, relations of work brought out Charles's "Hutu" capacities for physical labor. In order to have a reputation as someone who, despite wealth and privilege, "knows how to work hard,"[3] Charles recognizes the significance of shared physical work in forging good relationships. Indeed, the criticisms leveled at those who passed the workers without joining in attest to *umuganda*'s importance. Given the history of *umuganda* being co-opted to serve elites, and given that the *chef du quartier* worries about completing the work because many residents refuse to participate, Charles can perform the positive qualities bound up with his Hutu descent category and set himself apart from "Tutsi" stereotypes of a lazy, exploitative elite. To share in physical work with low-income town residents is an act of moral agency whose value rests on the vision of social equality between good "peasant citizens" first glorified by PARMEHUTU and its supporters.

However, Charles's participation in *umuganda* may not have a singular interpretation because his Hutu heritage is not sufficiently powerful to conclusively define what "kind" of person he is. He, with the other affluent neighborhood residents at *umuganda*, worked separately from their low-income neighbors. The humble act of taking part in shared agricultural work was complicated by the act of setting themselves apart from the urban poor (although it is worth noting that the urban poor may have chosen to separate themselves from the affluent). The ambiguities of these acts are symbolically well captured in affluent residents' pairing of brand name athletic clothing with the knee-high rubber boots typically worn by cultivators, as well as in their teasing about each other's lack of agricultural skills. Here, it is the social relational dimensions of ethnicity that place limits on how Charles can perform the admirable traits marked by his inherited Hutuness. Indeed, as a Hutu by descent and someone who grew up cultivating with his family on a rural hill, Charles might be well positioned to fit in with his low-income neighbors and perform solidarity with them through shared work. However, his class and status ultimately limit his capacity, and perhaps also his desire, to be "of" the low-income majority. As Célestin remarked in the opening vignette, one is easily perceived as "more Tutsi than Hutu" if one is close to power.

In the case of Alexandre here, in social-relational, situational terms, his position in the patronage relationship with the man who asked for the T-shirt "overrode" his Hutu descent category and lent him the stereotypical capacities of Tutsiness. In patron–client exchange in Rwanda, the patron role is tied to Tutsi stereotypes, and the client role to Hutu ones—an opposition that hardened in no small part due to colonial-era ethnography in Rwanda (e.g. Maquet 1961). The ethnic heritage of the young man who approached Alexandre was unknown to me, but what is important was his deployment of the "normal capacities" of Hutuness to "get things done." Indeed, his public "declaration of dependence" (Ferguson 2013) meant that he placed himself in the position of stereotypical Hutuness by deferring to Alexandre, calling him "boss" repeatedly, and invoking Alexandre's good reputation for helping others. Whether Alexandre's performance of the patron role is received as intended, however, is another matter. On the one hand, his "client" may spread his reputation for generosity and bolster Alexandre's "Hutu" concern for redistribution to offset the negative moral evaluations to which people like Alexandre, who wear tailored suits and drive shiny late-model vehicles, are subject. But on the other hand, Alexandre's public embrace of his patron role potentially furthers his vulnerability to the social dangers of "Tutsi" wealth and privilege. He is open to the accusation that, like a "Tutsi," he wants to trap clients in servitude by agreeing to their requests for aid, a possibility that is captured in comments I routinely heard from Butare residents of all income levels about how the wealthy will only give if they think they can get something in return. Hence, Alexandre's Hutu heritage is not enough to level the hierarchy of patron–client exchange, and it must be performed in ways that can either succeed or fail.

Be that as it may, it would be a mistake to read ethnic descent categories as always flexible or open to question in Rwanda today. As much as social agents know how to put the ambiguity and flexibility of ethnically marked categories to work, the politics of the violent past simultaneously produce rigid boundaries that can make inherited ethnicity difficult to escape. A final account of the difficulties that Charles faces during the annual genocide commemorations each April illustrates this point.

Ethnic Heritage and the Politics of Remembering

It was 3 April 2008, and the annual genocide commemorations were set to begin in a matter of days on the 6th. I had stopped by Charles's office for advice on an administrative matter related to my research permit, when talk turned to the imminent start of the official commemoration period, which he warned me would close down government offices and delay the processing of my file. He leaned back in his chair, sighed, and mused about how he wished he could leave town that week, because it is such a hard time to be in Butare. "You'll notice a change," he said, as he knew that this was the first time I had been in Rwanda during the annual commemorations. "The streets are quieter—as you know, the shops and bars and businesses must close all afternoon for the ceremonies." He paused and continued cryptically, "In principle, everyone must attend to remember the victims, but there are those who opt out for various reasons." I asked what kinds and got a similarly elusive response. All Charles would add was that sometimes a person has responsibilities that prevent attendance, but sometimes they avoid the ceremonies for "personal reasons."

Simbi's remarks to me during a commemoration ceremony several days later at the Butare stadium shed light on Charles's vague phrase, "for various reasons." He surveyed our surroundings and whispered to me:

> As you know, everyone is supposed to attend these ceremonies, but there are far more people in Butare than are here at this stadium. For the survivors, some refuse to come because they simply can't bear to relive their grief. You've seen at these ceremonies how one person in the audience falls [collapses onto the ground in throes of grief] and then all around them others begin to fall too. But then there are those who are called Hutu. I have friends who say that they can't bear coming to these ceremonies because of how the survivors look at them. They stare them down and treat them like killers. Sometimes they even publicly accuse them of being *génocidaires* who have come to revel in survivors' misery. How can they be expected to come and remember when people look at them like they're criminals? (Butare, April 2008)

Like Célestin, Simbi speaks the ethnic label, "Hutu," but he distances himself from it with the passive construction, "those who are called" Hutu. He implies that it is not he who calls them this way, but others. Simbi told me that he has sympathy for both survivors and perpetrators, the latter because in 1994, "they only did what their fathers and grandfathers had been rewarded for doing in the past. When these *pauvres* [poor people] take the stand at *gacaca* and are asked to explain themselves, I believe them when they say they don't know why they did what they did" (Butare, July 2008). In espousing sympathy with both Tutsi and Hutu, Simbi asserts a liberal outlook on ethnicity, even as he invokes now-outlawed labels.

In spite of his misgivings, Charles attended the genocide commemorations, as he does every year. He chose to go to the ones at the university campus, which he characterized as "more informative" than the ones in the neighborhood. This choice was a deliberate act of moral agency shaped at least in part by the constraints of his Hutu heritage. Even though no one has made a concrete accusation of genocide crimes against him, Charles knows that he must contend with the suspicion that has been cast on all Hutu men in the post-genocide moment, since RPF politics paint all those occupying the status of Hutu male as potential *génocidaires* (Burnet 2009). Indeed, Charles's mindfulness of these dangers demonstrates that his descent category can never be completely overcome by the ethnic markings of his class position. Even though Charles lost a close family member to the violence of 1994, he cannot publicly mourn that loss (cf. Burnet 2009; Vidal 2004). He attends the annual genocide commemorations, but must do so as a mourner for Tutsi victims, not for his Hutu father, or at least not openly so. He knows the importance of situating himself on the side of RPF unity and reconciliation initiatives, and so he participates in conferences and *sensibilisation* (consciousness-raising) meetings aimed at understanding and preventing future violence. And even as his contributions to these initiatives and his own scholarship help to legitimate today's official narratives of Rwandan history and ethnicity, his reticence about his activities during the period of the civil war through the genocide belies anxieties surrounding the questions that Rwandans so often wonder about each other: Where were you in 1994, and what were you doing? How are you situated in terms of "citizenship categories" (Doughty 2016) of victim, perpetrator, returnee, "moderate Hutu," or survivor? As others have shown (e.g. McLean Hilker 2009: 90), these questions are ways that Rwandans know how to "get at" ethnicity in its rigid, descent-based manifestations, just as they know how to make "ethnic" commentaries on situational conduct through reference to stereotypes based on wealth, status, or behavioral traits.

Ethnicity without Labels?

The place of ethnicity in post-genocide Rwandan social life is complicated not only by the rigid and flexible dimensions of Hutuness and Tutsiness, but also by the state moratorium on ethnic labels. Still, the unclear boundaries between these overlapping social distinctions in Rwanda are not an entirely new, post-genocide problem produced by the outlawing of ethnic labels. Of all the people with whom I discussed my research interests, Irène, a NUR graduate and aspiring journalist in her thirties, provided me the most explicit formulation of this issue. Irène explained that Rwandans have always known how to make use of the overlaps between ethnic and other social boundaries. She cited an idea that I have heard from many Butare residents over the years: that cleverness in Rwanda is judged by a person's capacity to speak indirectly about a topic, but still have her or his message heard and understood (cf. Bellman 1984). However, even though oblique references to shared conceptual frameworks of "Hutuness" and "Tutsiness" are by no means purely a product of the "post-ethnic" moment in Rwanda, the moratorium on ethnic labels and the new legal sanctions associated with its violation today compound the problem of uncertainty. More important, these politico-legal shifts in official policy on ethnicity raise new stakes and dangers around the question of whether Rwandans still invoke ethnic frameworks to make sense of others' actions and evaluate the relative worth of their forms of agency. Hence, the problem remains: how can we know when the social actor is making use of ethnic frameworks in evaluating and interpreting the social actions of others? The answer is that one *cannot* know, and it is this uncertainty that is the defining characteristic of ethnicity in Rwanda today. Because Tutsi and Hutu categories are not clearly distinguishable from and are mutually marked by stereotypes of class, occupation, region, and education, the possibility for an ethnic interpretation of evaluative remarks remains uncomfortably open.

In what follows, I provide a series of ethnographic vignettes to draw forth the uncertain and ambiguous ways in which the specter of "the ethnic" arises even in the absence of ethnic labels. The first one, which took place during an excursion to Gisenyi, demonstrates one of the least ambiguous connections between ethnicity and other forms of difference that I heard during my fieldwork. Based on the connections established in that first incident and the broader interpretive frameworks provided by popular Tutsi and Hutu stereotypes, the three vignettes that follow show how even "non-ethnic" commentaries on people's conduct nonetheless raise the possibility that people are "thinking ethnically."

Northern "Peasants"

In March of 2009, I was traveling in the northern province of Gisenyi with Pauline, the Tutsi genocide survivor introduced in Chapter 1. Gisenyi is known to be Hutu-dominated,[4] and southerners, including Butare residents, often contrast their more "integrated" populations with the stereotypically anti-Tutsi stance of the north (see Guichaoua 2005; Lemarchand 1970). While observing roadside pedestrians, Pauline remarked, "You know, there have never been many Tutsi here in the north—they've never been welcome. People here, they aren't educated. They're rural cultivators, true peasants." Her seamless integration of ethnicity, ruralness, education, and occupation shows just how closely these forms of difference are intertwined in collective representations (see also Burnet 2012: 34)—a connection that I suspect she felt freer to make in Gisenyi, where, as she put it, "no one knows me."

In Butare, these linkages were usually subtler. Talk that ambiguously raised ethnicity through reference to other social divisions is common there, where, as Chapter 1 explained, sharp disparities of class, occupation, education, and ethnicity were coproduced throughout the colonial and postcolonial periods. Indeed, Butare residents are vigilant about avoiding ethnic labels not only because of the worry that one's interlocutor might be a government spy, but also because educated residents often self-present as "modern" subjects who do not get embroiled in ethnic schisms. Most people took care to avoid ethnic talk around me, too, for both of these reasons, I suspect. Nonetheless, simply because there is potential for ethnic readings does not mean that actors intend to communicate an "ethnic" message. It is the indeterminacy and the *excess* of meaning produced in these situations that are ultimately of interest, a finding that sheds light both on why de-ethnicization is much more complex than RPF efforts to outlaw ethnic labels might suggest and on the practical interpretive problems to which this gives rise.

A Dispute between Business Partners

Rose is a Tutsi genocide survivor and small business owner who has lived in Butare for most of her life. In 2008, she was the owner of a general store not far from the market, one that also had a hair salon attached to it. Rose had rented out the hair salon to various different people to manage it for her over the years, because she did not have the energy to manage both branches of the business. She has struggled to find honest managers for the salon, and a number of times over the years she has had to break off agreements with people who refused to pay their rent on time. In the spring of 2008, Rose was struggling with just such a situation. Chantal, a Tutsi genocide survivor in her early thirties, had taken over management of the salon in December

2007. Since Chantal had paid her rent promptly for several months, Rose had decided to offer Chantal management of the general store in addition to the salon. The reason was that the oldest of Rose's three surviving daughters had recently married and had a child. They lived in the eastern Rwandan town of Rwamagana, and Rose was spending weeks and sometimes months at a time helping her daughter with the new baby. She no longer wished to be tied to Butare to look after her businesses, and Chantal had appeared trustworthy.

Rose's agreement with Chantal stated that Chantal would pay 500,000 RWF[5] each month to rent both the store and the salon, and any earnings beyond that would go to Chantal. By the spring of 2008, however, Chantal was three months behind on her rent, and her refusal to pay was trying Rose's patience. One afternoon when I was visiting Rose at her store, she described how Chantal had been avoiding her. She had seen Chantal sneaking into the salon very early in the morning to take the earnings to the bank without running into Rose. This pattern began after Rose had confronted Chantal and threatened to break off their agreement if she did not pay her debts. In her exasperated state, Rose complained to me about Chantal's character flaws.

> I've known this girl [*cette fille*] for many years—I've known her since she was a student in Butare in the late '90s. You know what her problem is? She loves money too much, this girl. At first I asked her for 600,000 RWF each month, and she accused me of expecting her to work for me like a slave. I told her that 600,000 was fair, since it's all my capital—the building, the equipment—everything. She even tried to get her husband to buy all new equipment for the salon so that she wouldn't have to use mine, but he refused. So we agreed on 500,000, but in practice she pays what and when she feels like paying me. She knows I go away from time to time to see my children and grandchild, so she takes advantage of my absences to avoid paying her rent. I know she has the money, but she tells me she doesn't. She keeps money that doesn't belong to her. I know people like her, and she loves money. She loves it too much. (Butare, 2008)

Rose's and Chantal's mutual accusations of greed and dishonesty ambiguously evoke a host of negative "Tutsi" stereotypes. Nonetheless, it was out of the question for me to ask Rose if she was accusing Chantal of "acting like a Tutsi" when she said that Chantal loves money too much and lies about being unable to pay. For one thing, as a Tutsi by heritage herself, Rose could have interpreted that question as an affront to her own character, too. But more important, I would have shown myself as an ignorant ethnographer who does not understand the local "rules" of what can and cannot be said openly. Rose is considered quite influential in Butare, because she was married to a well-respected local government official—a Tutsi man killed shortly after the genocide arrived in Butare in mid April 1994. She expressed concern that she is under surveillance by the local authorities today, because they sometimes showed up at her home and business from time to time under pretenses that can only be characterized as strange. According to Rose, the RPF is suspicious of Tutsi survivors, especially educated urban dwellers who are not official party members, because there are dissenting voices among them who accuse the RPF of causing the genocide with the October 1990 invasion of Rwanda. For someone like Rose who worries that even minor missteps could label her a political subversive, the only reasonable answer to the question of whether she was accusing Chantal of "Tutsi greed" is that she no longer thinks that way. And yet the possibility of an ethnic commentary on Chantal's conduct remains an interpretive possibility in light of the clear parallels between Rose's criticisms and longstanding popular Tutsi stereotypes.

A Dishonest Student

I met Jean-Claude, a young, urban man who identifies as a genocide survivor, through a mutual friend in March of 2008. At the time of my fieldwork, he was a National University student and employed at a local peace building NGO. However, Jean-Claude, who is Tutsi by descent, was not particularly committed to his academic pursuits. He openly admitted to me that he paid low-income students to do his coursework and that his main concern was to make money, build a house, and become a "self-made man." As he explained:

> The best thing I can do is work on building my house and make as much money as I can. I make RWF 200,000 a month at one of my jobs, and RWF 300,000[6] a month at my other one. I already have my house almost built—it's a little [outside of town], but it's more than some profs have, you know! A lot of them rent houses from the university, but here I am, I already have my own house ... I have my whole life to study and learn; right now, I want to make my wealth. I'm doing poor students a favor by providing them with work! (Butare, May 2008)

Jean-Claude's academic dishonesty elicited judgments from other students about who works hard and who benefits. Another student, Marie, who is Hutu by descent, comes from a rural area outside Butare. She regularly asserted that she took her studies seriously and invoked the notion of exploitation, trickery, and the corrupting influences of urban life to explain Jean-Claude's behavior and that of other high-income students: "It's only the students who have jobs or who come from rich families in cities who are dishonest in their academic work. These *gens de la ville* [sic], they're the ones who have no conscience and who do not have a problem with cheating," she explained. She contrasted habits like Jean-Claude's with her own honest hard work—qualities she attributed to her rural upbringing. "In the [rural] hills, we learn how to work hard," she explained. "You have no choice if you want to survive." Marie never asserted that Jean-Claude was "acting like a Tutsi" when she critiqued his practices of exploiting low-income students for his own gain. Nonetheless, based on the content of ethnic stereotypes, terms like *gens de la ville* or "students who come from rich families" could be replaced with the term "Tutsi" and still communicate essentially the same type of evaluation. There is no question that this conversation could be read through the strict opposition between the moral qualities of urban versus rural people or related class distinctions. Indeed, some of the strongest themes in people's everyday talk concerned hard work, dignified versus undignified work, and "success," but to reduce them to commentaries on work and class relations overlooks the porous, indeterminate boundaries between them and ethnic distinctions.

A Subordinated Worker

One afternoon in March 2009, I was conversing with Emmanuel, a bartender at a local motel restaurant in Butare. He is a post-1994 Tutsi returnee to Rwanda and at the time of my fieldwork had completed two years of university. Because of the spatial organization of the motel, many arriving guests encountered Emmanuel's bar before they reached the reception desk. As we spoke, an incident took place similar to ones I saw transpire on other occasions. A man in a suit carrying a briefcase and one other bag strode down the steps toward the bar. Rather than proceeding directly to the reception desk, he stopped, curtly told Emmanuel that he wanted him to take his bags, and slid them toward Emmanuel, who silently took them behind the bar. After the man had disappeared into the restaurant, Emmanuel lowered his voice and told me what he thought of this interaction.

> I hate it when motel guests ask me to look after their bags. First of all, it's not what I'm paid to do. But they see me here, and they think they can just toss their things. The reception is right around the corner, but they hand it to me instead … Some things haven't changed since traditional Rwanda. It's like when chiefs took poor peasants with them to carry their belongings when they traveled. This is very subservient work in Rwandan tradition.

Here, Emmanuel intimates that he interpreted this encounter through reference to an ethnically stereotyped relation. As Eltringham (2004: 163–76) has shown, Rwandans (especially those with secondary or post-secondary education) are well versed in competing narratives about the role of colonialism in the country's past. They know how Catholic missionaries worked to ensure that virtually all chiefs were Tutsi, and they are familiar with the stereotypical opposition of Tutsi rulers to Hutu peasants. Emmanuel's reference to chiefs and peasants evoked these popular stereotypes and communicated how incensed he was by the guest's treatment of him, since he counts himself among the educated. Nonetheless, one could read this incident strictly as an unequal encounter between an affluent professional and someone in a low-status job. Emmanuel did not say that the motel guest was "treating him like a Hutu." However, in his invocation of the subordinate peasant porter for a high-status chief, Emmanuel raises the problem of the relation between class and ethnic distinctions. What is particularly interesting is how this case shows that descent is not the only way to take on an ethnically marked subject position. As an "ethnic Tutsi," Emmanuel implied he was put in a position of "Hutuness." Seen from the view of ethnicity as a social relation, there is no contradiction between having Tutsi heritage and situationally being in a position marked by "Hutu" traits. The possibility that Emmanuel was interpreting his situation "ethnically" can likewise be grasped through Barth's (1969: 21) point that ethnic boundaries can and do persist despite— and because of—the "'osmosis' of personnel through them."

As I already suggested, a direct inquiry to Butare residents as to whether they were actively categorizing each other as Hutu or Tutsi in any of the situations described here would not receive an answer that a researcher could easily take at face value given today's strict state prohibitions on openly ethnic talk. And yet the interpretive problem remains. We can still wonder, was Charles "thinking ethnically" when he chose to participate in *umuganda*? Was Emmanuel saying that the motel guest put him in a position of Hutuness? Was Rose accusing Chantal of acting like a "greedy Tutsi"? Indeed, what does it mean to "think ethnically"? Must one think or say the term *Hutu* or *Tutsi*, or is an oblique reference to ethnically marked traits enough, since people can always take what they want from it (McAllister 2013)? Since ethnic difference is inseparable from quotidian concerns like inequality, ill-gotten gains, and (im)moral conduct in everyday life, the suppression of ethnic labels produces an *excess* of possible interpretations—ethnic and otherwise— for how people account for what "kinds" of persons they are dealing with. The indeterminacy raises the possibility that people still think "ethnically" in a moment when it is politically dangerous to do so and when state leaders direct "modern," "post-ethnic" subjects to put "parochial" ethnic schisms in the past.

In the case of people like Charles, Rose, and Alexandre, this problem is compounded by their status and position in the social world of Butare. While their relationships reveal especially starkly the complex operations of ethnic boundaries, their social positions are not without constraints. The incidents and situations I have described occurred when I had known these Butaréens between five and ten years. All of them trusted me not to inform on them to the state for using ethnic labels, but they still took care to present themselves to me as people who are "above" thinking in terms of "parochial" schisms like ethnicity. More generally, Butare residents take pride in the town's reputation for peaceful interethnic relations (Jefremovas 1997) and they cite the local resistance to the genocide for weeks after it had begun in Kigali as evidence that ethnicity "doesn't matter" in Butare the way it does elsewhere. By conforming to RPF directives to delete ethnic labels from their vocabularies, Butare residents appear very much to be "good Rwandans" or "peaceful selves" who are leading the call to leave ethnicity in the past. Indeed, educated residents' desire to espouse liberal attitudes toward ethnicity, and the fact that their livelihoods depend on the legitimation of the RPF account of ethnicity, may go some way to explaining why other researchers (e.g. Fujii 2009; McLean Hilker 2009) found more frequent, open references to ethnicity, whereas high-status Butare residents carefully—compulsively, even—avoided them. But simultaneously, the open-endedness allows people to manage those dangers by framing interpretations of others' conduct in terms of class, occupation, or the moral qualities of urban versus rural people—whether they intend an "ethnic" commentary or not. Openness of interpretation is a source of both power and danger in post-ethnic Rwanda, since the intentions of the speaker and the interpretations of the listener remain always indeterminate.

Conclusion

In light of these interpretive uncertainties, does studying ethnicity in Rwanda today inevitably mean arriving at an interpretive impasse? As Carlota McAllister (2013: 110), drawing on Frank Kermode (1979) proposes, the impossibility of interpretive certainty is not necessarily a failure because of what we can learn from the problem of uncertainty itself. The world and its interpretations, Kermode (1979: 145) reminds us, are "hopelessly plural." Even though I cannot be certain when Butare residents are thinking ethnically, the question is nonetheless worth pursuing because it places the researcher in the same practical ambiguities that Butare residents face, namely the open-endedness of when ethnicity matters, how it matters and with what effects. Indeed, the centrality of ethnicity in Rwanda's violent past renders the questions of how one can be placed "ethnically" and what "kind" of person that makes someone especially pressing, not only at the level of the state formation agenda but also in everyday practice.

Even as rigid configurations of ethnicity take on special significance at certain historical moments—as in the crystallization of political parties around ethnicity at independence, in the genocidal constructions of the 1990s, or in the RPF's rigid Tutsi/victim versus Hutu/perpetrator dichotomy—there has never been a single criterion that Rwandans can use to conclusively and in all situations resolve how they and others belong ethnically (Newbury 1988: 51–52). Ethnicity during the Rwandan genocide had an unmistakable binary quality, but in everyday life it simultaneously matters in ways that exceed the question of heritage. Indeed, the forms of moral agency and self-presentation that Butaréens deploy in everyday life—be it opting into *umuganda*, offering charity to others, or being reticent about what one was doing in 1994—are marked by ethnic stereotypes and bound up with the intersection of both rigid and social-relational dimensions of ethnicity. These dual configurations of "the ethnic," coupled with the post-genocide moratorium on ethnic labels, render the question of how ethnicity matters today compelling, fraught, and also elusive, not only for the ethnographer but also for Rwandans.

Today, the bearing of ethnicity on personhood takes on increasingly layered contours. Not only does what "kind" of person you are still depend to some degree on the ethnically marked qualities and capacities of "normal" personhood you are perceived to embody. Now, the question of whether you continue to use ethnic stereotypes as frameworks by which to evaluate and interpret others' behavior also bears heavily on what "kind" of person you are, when modern, development-minded and forward-looking Rwandans should be leaving ethnic schisms in the past. But there is yet another layer of contradictions here, too. Even the RPF-led rejection of ethnic boundaries for an inclusive, pan-Rwandan identity cannot escape the ambiguities and innuendos of ethnic reference points in Rwandan politics. Indeed, ever since the late 1950s when UNAR called on Rwandans to unite as brothers under the *mwami* (see Chapter 1), exaltations for ethnic unity and shared Rwandanness have been suspect and, crucially, marked as a Tutsi strategy of concealing the traditional ethnic hierarchy.[7] That a Tutsi president leads the charge to eradicate ethnic divisions does little to dispel this suspicion. Hence, to claim the modern, liberal perspective on ethnicity—that it is illusory and does not matter—can paradoxically raise the markers of Tutsiness with its connotations of eliteness and a penchant for subterfuge. In spite—or because—of the ways Butare residents participate in the project of making the "New (post-ethnic) Rwanda," the genocide and its politics stubbornly intrude into the present and into their everyday worlds. The difficult place of ethnic categories and the difficult work of navigating their dangers and strategic possibilities are some of the ways that the violent past permeates the "post-conflict" moment and fundamental moral questions about self, other, belonging, and exclusion. The next chapter takes up another locus of ways in which personhood, the violent past, and questions of belonging come up against each other as Butare residents grapple with what it means to live a moral life in the wake of the devastation of 1994.

Notes

1. Even though I largely retain the pre-2006 place names because Rwandans still use them more often in everyday talk, here I refer to the new administrative unit of Huye and its district office. By the time of my fieldwork in 2008, 2009, and 2014, everyone in town referred to the district office as the Huye office. Huye is one of eight districts that comprise Southern Province, and it encompasses what used to be known as Butare town.
2. Rwanda's bid to join the British Commonwealth was approved in 2009. It was not long before demands for money by the urban poor changed to reflect the fact that English was the new language of power and affluence.
3. This phrase came up with remarkable frequency in routine conversation with Butare residents as they evaluated each other's moral worth and capacities for hard work.
4. Most areas of Gisenyi province had only 1–7 percent Tutsi residents before the genocide, when those of Tutsi heritage comprised 14 percent of the national population (Guichaoua 2005).
5. Roughly US$725
6. Roughly US$290 and US$435, respectively.
7. It is not only Tutsi leaders who invoke the rhetoric of Rwandan unity in the service of bolstering their political legitimacy. Desrosiers and Thomson (2011) convincingly argue that there are continuities between the "benevolent leadership" of former Hutu President Juvénal Habyarimana and Paul Kagame. Even as both regimes used unity as a mask for ethnic favoritism, the difference between Habyarimana and Kagame is that the former relied on a vision of "complementary ethnic identities" while the latter aims to replace them entirely with a pan-Rwandan identity (Desrosiers and Thomson 2011: 434), a strategy with antecedents in the late colonial rhetoric of the pro-Tutsi UNAR.

Chapter 3

LIVING WITH ABSENCE

∞

It was early morning in central Butare, and Pauline had invited me to share coffee with her before she began her workday. We sat in the shade on plastic chairs in the grounds of the daycare center she runs, while the dew on the grass rapidly evaporated in the morning equatorial sun. Tiny birds of blue, yellow, and red flitted from branch to branch of avocado and passionfruit trees, and the sounds of schoolchildren making their way down the road permeated the quiet surroundings. A thick file of paperwork sat ominously on her side of the small wooden table between us. It was tax season in Rwanda in 2009, and Pauline was worried about not being able to make her payments before the 31 March deadline. We had been discussing these and other quotidian challenges she faces running her business when her thoughts took what seemed to me an unexpected turn:

> You know, a survivor I know came to see me the other day. She lost all of her family in 1994 except for an uncle and a sister-in-law. I have the impression that she isn't well. It seems that some of her family's remains were recently found not far from here. What's a person to do when they hear that kind of news?

For Pauline, who faced significant obstacles—both logistical and emotional—to rebuilding her livelihood without her husband, children, and other kin networks after 1994, routine pressures like tax payments are never all that far removed from the history of violence. Nonetheless, her interjection about another survivor's plight into our discussion is not merely anecdotal, but speaks to a broader relationship between remembering and personhood that I argue is central to understanding what it means to have lived through the violence of the Rwandan genocide. Narratives like Pauline's that attest to losses in the 1994 genocide arose routinely in the course of everyday conversation with educated Butaréens, especially Tutsi survivors. These informal practices of remembering, which my field notes indicate arose several times a week and sometimes more than once a day, were typically directed at establishing how many and what kinds of relations people had lost or the circumstances of their deaths. Accounts were more like short interludes in conversations than formal memorial practices symbolically demarcated from the everyday as in official commemorations. Sometimes seeing a person or place or object seemed to precipitate these testimonials, and sometimes it was not clear to me what brought them on. Even though these interjections went by quickly, their duration is not indicative of their significance when it comes to grasping the routine effects of violence on personhood and everyday social relationships. Strikingly, survivors spoke less often about their own losses than of the numbers and categories of kin lost by other town residents, many of whom were no more than acquaintances. In this practice, I argue, lies a crucial dimension of how violence affects the self and social relationships, one that takes seriously the relationship between the living and the dead. Indeed, to speak and think of the dead is not only an important form of exchange between the living and the dead, but also a form of claims-making by the speaker to (erstwhile) belonging in Butare.

This chapter tells how informal memory practices lay bare how people live out the routine effects of decimated lines of kinship, friendship, and other relations in a post-conflict moment. In it, I take everyday practices of remembering as a rich site from which to understand and theorize how the absence of key relations—especially kin relations—bears upon personhood and how survivors struggle to know themselves and others in the contemporary moment. I shift the emphasis away from national-level memory politics to a form of moral work that genocide survivors undertake when they informally—yet habitually—attest to their own and others' losses in the genocide. I call this "work" because of the *effort* undertaken to reckon with the violent past—work that is *moral* because it constitutes a "continuous practical judgment in the living of a moral life," a life composed of both "speaking the future and speaking the past" (Lambek 2006: 213). Indeed, remembering is a moral practice because memory is itself a function of social relationships (Lambek 1996). It is an obligation, both social and ethical, that concerns what is owed to others, including the dead. Through informal remembering, survivors give expression to concerns about personhood and their place in the world that remain peripheral in prominent frameworks on memory and violence. The argument is predicated, first, on the challenges that genocide survivors—especially educated ones—face in claiming to be fully "of" Butare, and second, on the view that one's social relationships, especially kinship and exchange of shared substances like food or drink, are constitutive of one's personhood (Geertz 1973; Mauss [1925] 1967, [1938] 1985; Strathern 1988). It is in the context of a devastating history of violence in which persons have lost so many relations that these dimensions of remembering come into particularly sharp relief. Indeed, the dead are by no means absent from the world of the living, but their presence is a terribly partial one that survivors struggle to maintain.

It was in conversations about relationships of work, friendship, kinship, neighborliness, and clientship that these memory practices were most likely to emerge. Such conversations took place in private homes, at the National University, at people's workplaces, or on walks around the town and its surroundings. The urban survivors whose memory practices I bring forth in this chapter had lived in town between five and forty years, but all of them had a rural upbringing and all faced the daunting task of rebuilding their livelihoods after the devastation of the genocide—two points that they emphasized when wishing to express commonality with the rural majority. Once again, I am mindful that educated urban dwellers' experiences do not stand for those of all Rwandans or even all Butare residents. However, the post-genocide sense of social dislocation that my research participants express is by no means restricted to people of their social position; for example, Claudine Vidal (2001: 6) has noted similar findings among survivors in other towns and in rural areas. Thus, while educated residents might be especially at pains to articulate their knowledge of what happened and to whom in 1994, all genocide survivors must contend with the problem of how to manage the absence of relations. I focus on this subset of Butaréens because the moral demands of remembering and the post-1994 difficulties of claiming belonging are especially visible among a mobile elite with strong affective ties to the local.

Informal narratives of loss were recounted to me most often in one-on-one conversations that arose during participant observation, not formal interviews. Indeed, all of the narratives I present below came from informal talk in the course of daily activities and goings-on. They were therefore "naturally occurring" in the sense that I never aimed to elicit them with direct questions about the past. However, a researcher's presence also affects the social situation and what is said or not in ways that cannot be easily ascertained, and people's knowledge of my interest in memory practices may have elevated the frequency of these narratives. At the same time, informal talk between Butaréens about those lost in the genocide was not always directed toward reporting these losses to me, which suggests that these accounts do constitute everyday practices in the sense of patterned, shared, concrete human activity (Reckwitz 2002: 249–50; Taylor 1993: 52). But what forms of knowledge, politics, and sociocultural expectations might pattern these practices, and in turn pattern my account of how they punctuate everyday life?

The narrative practices I recount here focused overwhelmingly on the losses of Tutsi victims remembered by Tutsi survivors. Those familiar with Rwandan politics today might wonder at my focus on their memory practices when it is well recognized that scores of Hutu lost family in the genocide and its aftermath, too. Since I worked with both Hutu and Tutsi town residents over the course of my fieldwork, this chapter seems to uncritically reproduce the Rwandan government's denial of Hutu victimhood in the genocide and alleged RPF crimes against Hutu throughout the civil war of the 1990s and after they took power in July 1994. However, recollections of Hutu loss of life remained less accessible to me since they were only rarely raised in private settings with trusted interlocutors. Rwandans who speak openly of Hutu deaths open themselves to accusations of "revisionism" and spreading the "double-genocide" thesis, a dangerous crime because it undermines the narrative of Tutsi victimhood that is central to the RPF's political legitimacy. The exception to the public denial of Hutu suffering and loss of life is the demarcation of the "Hutu moderates" category with respect to genocide victims. As Eltringham (2004: 75–76) notes, however, this category is only used retrospectively in reference to Hutu killed in the 1990s for their opposition to the genocide. The troubling implication is that all "moderate" Hutu are dead and that those still alive colluded in the campaign of violence. Scholars have noted a veritable "conspiracy of silence" by the Rwandan government when it comes to Hutu victimization (e.g. Richters 2010: 177; Vidal 2001: 45). One of the starkest manifestations of these politics was in the *gacaca* trials, where only Hutu crimes against Tutsi victims were heard and acknowledged. As a prominent feature of post-genocide social life, *gacaca* testimonial practices may have given partial shape to the content of informal memory practices, since the latter tended to reproduce both *gacaca*'s emphasis on Tutsi victimhood and its emphasis on collecting factual information on who wronged whom, the identities of victims, and the circumstances of their deaths (National Service of Gacaca Jurisdictions 2004). Yet the informal remembering that I describe here also expresses forms of distress for which much less space was made in *gacaca* testimony, including feelings of guilt, regret, or ongoing obligations to the dead on the part of survivors. In any case, while struggles for official acknowledgment of subaltern or marginalized memory are common in other postcolonial settings (e.g. Werbner 1998), the current political moment and its restrictive standards of victimhood explain why we do not find substantial studies on the subject in Rwanda. Nonetheless, this fraught situation raises a compelling question: if survivors' informal recollections are not attempts to set the record straight against a national narrative that denies their victimhood, why are they at pains to articulate them?

Beyond Memory, Nation, and Psychosocial Healing

Questions about remembering, and by extension forgetting, the violent past in the Rwandan context are by no means absent in the post-genocide scholarship, but two sets of frameworks tend to dominate it. The first considers the politics of memory and nation building and how narratives of the past are implicated in forging national identifications, reconciliation, or forms of exclusion. In Rwanda, the political uses of memory raise the question of what a "just allotment" (Ricoeur 2004: xv) of memory and forgetting might be in terms of the nation's capacity to forge unifying forms of belonging. On the one hand, scholars ask whether national memory politics are reproducing the ethnicized fault lines of the 1990s. Many researchers express concern that even as the government frames public remembering of genocide victims in terms of promoting unity, it risks reproducing the opposition between reified groups: Tutsi-victim versus Hutu-perpetrator. These concerns are linked to the state restriction of victimhood to Tutsi at official commemorations of the genocide and the suppression of open dialogue about the past (Burnet 2009; Hintjens 2008; Vidal 2004). On the other hand, some scholars suggest that remembering violence on a public level might provide the means to overcome past conflicts by forging national unity and reconciliation and thereby prevent future violence or denial of genocide (Staub 2003). Many scholars have focused directly on this tension between remembering violence as obstacle versus pathway to peace and take up these questions vis-à-vis commemorative events and judicial processes (Buckley-Zistel 2006; Longman and Rutagengwa 2006; Rettig 2008).

A second set of approaches focuses on the relationship between memory and the psychosocial injuries of political violence. Some Rwanda scholars have characterized remembered violence—or the inability (or refusal) to narrate it—as a form of suffering to be addressed through therapeutic interventions for individual or social healing (Staub 2003; Steward 2008). These approaches engage with the issue of post-traumatic stress disorder (PTSD), its degree of cross-cultural universality and longstanding debates around the nature of traumatic memory, its relationship to "normal" memory, recovery from psychosocial wounds, and intergenerational transmission of trauma (Argenti and Schramm 2010; Herman 1992; Young 1995). Here, the normative question of how much to remember or forget arises again, although the concern is as much with the psychological wellbeing of the individual as it is with collective cohesion (and it is worth remembering that the analogy between the individual and collective healing from the effects of violence is not uncontroversial [Young 1993]). In terms of Rwanda, central questions revolve around what healing interventions ought to look like, especially whether truth telling by victims and perpetrators and remembering violence is, indeed, cathartic (Brounéus 2010).

When I first returned to Rwanda in 2008 to conduct my doctoral research, I intended to study the relationship between violence, memory, and post-genocide reconciliation—perspectives that I saw as grounded in the two sets of approaches I just described. Had I adhered to the types of questions these frameworks make it possible to ask and answer, I expect I could have read survivors' attestations to loss through them. Indeed, I could have theorized them as ongoing preoccupations with the past and evidence that ethnic schisms persist in the face of government reconciliation and de-ethnicization policies. I might have suggested that a compulsion to recount one's own or others' losses indicates ongoing psychosocial suffering from experiences of violence. Perhaps people speak more often of others' losses because it is a less painful way to communicate what happened in 1994 than is talking about one's own absent relations. There were certainly times during my fieldwork when people showed concern for the question of what individual or collective "healing" entails or what the national political stakes of remembering violence might be. Nonetheless, I found that the significance of informal memory practices in Butare exceeds these approaches. In those excesses, I found that another compelling question preoccupies many Rwandan genocide survivors: how do people who suddenly, and moreover violently, lost many or even most of their relations in the 1994 genocide locate themselves in relation to others? There are many possible approaches to this question, but here I look to memory, the temporal axis of personhood (Antze and Lambek 1996: xxv). To draw on Antze's (1996) felicitous phrase, albeit in a very different ethnographic context, by *telling stories*—even very short ones interjected into other lines of conversation—survivors are *making selves* in the absence of relations that constitute the person. Indeed, parallel to how Carsten (2000) has shown that relatedness is forged through shared substance, sentiment, or space, in Butare shared experience and *knowledge* of one another's loss and dislocation also constitute grounds on which people engender belonging.

Personhood in the Absence of Relations

In Butare, a central site of the production of the local elite past and present, educated town residents place a great deal of importance on the moral dimensions of being embedded in local networks, on being "of" the town and belonging with others. This importance is grounded not only in the history of violence, but also in the particular challenges faced by the elite in claiming belonging in Butare, ones that reach back to the colonial production of a local, educated elite who straddle (at least) two worlds. One afternoon in May 2008, I was crossing town on foot with Simbi. It had not rained in a week, and clouds of deep rust-colored dust were blowing across the road to the market. As we passed some storefronts outside the market entrance, a young man seated on the ground outside a pharmacy made a remark to Simbi. "I've seen you. You spend a lot of time with *bazungu* [white people, foreigners]," he said. "If you aren't careful, you will no longer be able to understand ordinary Rwandans' problems." Simbi was visibly troubled by this accusation, since he prides himself on his ability to talk to all kinds of people, especially rural and low-income people. Simbi did not know the young man who admonished him, which speaks to the degree to which people's conduct, especially the conduct of those deemed privileged in some way, is monitored and open to commentary by other town residents. To be called or treated as a stranger carries a particular sting for affluent Butaréens. It connotes an accusation of being more interested in forging ties to the resources, forms of knowledge, and power of Westerners. To ally oneself too much with Westerners can lead to disparaging accusations of having become a *muzungu* (sing. of *bazungu*) or no longer being able to understand the problems of "ordinary Rwandans." Besides this episode with Simbi outside the market, on three other occasions that I am aware of, such accusations were leveled at friends of mine for having been seen with me. Because of their wealth and modern Western dress, many Butaréens complain of being charged the "*muzungu* price" at the market. On a similar note, after visiting a Canadian friend in Ottawa in 2008, Pauline returned home to discover that a neighbor had been spreading rumors that she had left for good and no longer cared about Rwanda and its people. These rumors had necessitated weeks of damage control during which Pauline had to correct residents' impression that she was no longer residing in the town. Indeed, for no one is the moral importance of remaining "of" Butare more significant than for the affluent town residents I knew—those who travel internationally for conferences and consultancies, study or pleasure, and who speak the colonial language of French (or increasingly, English) effortlessly. The claim to belonging takes on particular significance in light of a postcolonial political economy that makes intellectuals, small business owners, and other affluent Butare residents symbolically and materially distant from "ordinary Rwandans." Indeed, the educated, wealthy urban dweller is morally suspect from the perspective of the low-income urban and rural majority, who are known to blame social inequality on "educated people," whom they accuse of hijacking the benefits of development aid for their own gain (Sommers 2012: 44). While I often heard low-income town residents complain that it is as though local professionals and entrepreneurs "live in another world," claims by materially privileged residents to knowing about others' losses and having suffered together in 1994 are a form of moral agency that might mitigate such accusations. Educated Butaréens no doubt faced similar challenges in claiming belonging due to class differences prior to 1994, but what is crucial is that they perceive a sharp contrast between how they fit into their social worlds before and after the genocide. Some may idealize the degree to which they were thought to belong before, but it is perhaps all the more significant if they do: to remember pre-genocide modes of belonging as relatively unproblematic lays bare how the absence of robust kinship networks compounds educated urban dwellers' sensitivity to social divisions between themselves and the low-income majority.

Concerns over being treated or perceived as a stranger are evident in survivors' anxieties about where they fit in today. Many lament how few people they still know in Butare. As Hélèna, a survivor in her forties who works for a local HIV/AIDS NGO, revealed one day when Simbi and I were paying her a visit at her home,

> I was born on this hill, but since 1994 I've lived all over. Brussels, the US, Japan, Kenya, and now I am back. But it hardly feels like my home … everyone I know is gone. They were all killed, so I don't know anyone anymore. The only people I know now are the prisoners who work on the roads here who greet me when I pass. Can you imagine? (Butare, February 2009)

On another occasion, I had been on a long walk all over town with Pauline, through the main streets and the back roads. I crossed paths with her again the next day, and she looked sullen. She explained that our walk the previous day had reminded her of the absences of those she used to know:

> Everyone I know is gone, and the new neighbors look at me like I don't even belong when I've lived here all my life! Can you believe that we walked around the entire town yesterday and I only ran into three people I know? Three! Everyone I knew is gone. I don't even want to know the new neighbors. I thought I was the one who was watching them, but I couldn't believe it when I realized that they're watching me like I'm a foreigner too! (Butare, February 2009)

It is in this space of loss and absence that the significance of survivors' informal practices of remembering is located. Below, I recount a series of these narratives. I chose these particular ones not because they stand out as remarkable, but for their representativeness of the accounts one is likely to hear in informal conversation. Regardless of their precipitating factors, all assert a claim to knowing what happened in Butare and to whom.

A Suffering Friend

One afternoon in March 2009, Daniel, a National University graduate, and I were with Hélèna at her home. We had been discussing the improvements in local police responses to incidents of domestic violence when, for reasons I do not know, a younger sibling brought out an envelope of photos and handed it to her. "That's me there," she said, pointing to a picture of herself and several other young female family members taken some years ago before the genocide. "Almost everyone in this photo is gone now. We were so close back then." Hélèna reflected on the impunity of the perpetrators of the genocide, and then turned to speaking about the losses of a female friend of hers:

> You know, I have a friend who only just found out at *gacaca* that it was her own husband who was responsible for killing her whole family—her mother and father, her siblings, all her relations. Can you imagine? Her own husband. He never even told her. He just went out one day, killed them all and never said a word. And the craziest part? She stayed with him after that! I said to her, you have to leave him after what he did. But she said she couldn't because he's the only one [husband] she's ever known.

The Loss of a Sister

On a long hike in the rural areas around Butare, Simbi had been quizzing me about my knowledge of local agricultural crops—knowledge deemed crucial for anyone who claims to "know" Rwanda. All of a sudden, we were passed by an acquaintance of his from their student days at the university who was careening down the hill on his motorcycle, hands and feet in the air while waving to Simbi. As he disappeared around the corner, Simbi, laughing at his antics, explained,

> *Il est fou, ce type* [This guy's crazy]! You know, he survived the genocide, but he lost his mind after what happened. It's true, they killed his whole family— parents, uncles, aunts, everyone. But what really did him in was when they killed his twin sister. He's never been the same since then, although he has calmed down a bit since they found her body. Before that, he used to talk of nothing but revenge, but now he's mostly harmless. But before, I used to see him in the *cabarets* [neighborhood bars] and he would always be looking for a fight. I had to stop him myself a few times. (Butare Province, July 2008)

Enumerating Acquaintances' Losses

On another occasion in June 2008, Simbi and I were crossing town together on foot. We ran into a prominent local official and small business owner who had been attempting to help Simbi secure a stable job as a favor to Simbi's brother-in-law. After we had parted company, Simbi explained, "He lost his wife and three children in the genocide. He suffers every day without them." Shortly thereafter we crossed paths with a middle-aged woman whom Simbi knew from the now defunct University Club gym. As is typical, we paused, exchanged greetings, and they shared news for a few moments before we moved on. As we began to walk again, Simbi told me, "She is a [genocide] survivor and she lost all seven of her children—can you imagine?"

Living with Guilt

Butare residents said that June 2014 was strange, because it rained more than it had in April, the month that usually brings the heaviest rain in Rwanda. One day when an unexpected downpour began mid afternoon and sent everyone running for shelter, I found myself talking to Christophe, a restaurant server, who for reasons I do not know began recounting to me a story of a Hutu professor who had recently died. "In 1994, he hid his Tutsi wife for weeks; he turned away the *interahamwe* several times when they came looking for her. His children were Hutu because he was Hutu, but he worried that if they came to kill her, they might kill the children, too. Then one day, he said to her, '*ma cherie*, you know I love you. But do you want to go on hiding like this? It's no life for anyone; you must be brave.' She understood what he was asking her to do, so she went out and showed herself to the killers. And of course, that was it. People say he was never right again, and up to his death, he wondered if he'd done the right thing."

Knowing the Private Lives of Others

One afternoon in May 2008, I was at the university chatting with a recent graduate, Nicolas. We had been conversing about his job prospects and the possibility of his pursuing graduate study when, for reasons I was unable to discern, he began to recount the tragic losses during the genocide of a mutual acquaintance of ours, Florence, who works at the National University. Nicolas, a genocide survivor himself, explained the complications that Florence has had to face in her family life since 1994.

> The first problem is that it was some of her in-laws who killed her husband and four of her five children. Can you imagine? But more than that, she told me once that she feels it is her fault that only she and her youngest child survived. Before the genocide, her husband had told her that he thought four children were enough, but she wanted more. Her husband was angry when he found out she was pregnant, and he told her that meant that the first four children

were for him, but the last one was for her. Now, because he and the four oldest were killed, she thinks that the others died because he had claimed the oldest children as his and left the youngest to her.

The Loss of a Husband

Often I would accompany Pauline on errands, and she would narrate to me what had happened to other survivors as we passed by their homes, places of business, or a burial site. As we passed by a quiet neighborhood bar one afternoon in March 2009, she told me what had happened to the Tutsi survivor who now owns and operates it. "You know this place? It's a woman who owns it now, a survivor. Back in '94, her husband had the foresight to take her and their four boys to Burundi after the genocide started in Kigali. But he came back after he left them there. He thought it wasn't dangerous here in Butare because the killing hadn't started here yet. He thought, 'oh, if I come back, maybe I could recover a few of our belongings.' But he was killed at their home and she never saw him again" (Butare, March 2009).

Two perspectives on the relationship between personhood and remembered violence bear attention in order to situate these narratives. First, some may argue that attestations to other town residents' losses are not "memories" at all in the sense that they may not concern what the speaker saw first-hand. However, if we take remembering as an active process that transmits knowledge of the past between persons (Connerton 1989), then such practices are not outside the realm of "memory." In none of the previous narratives do people claim vicarious memory of events they never witnessed; they are instead remembering the fact of others' losses and that there were once persons with them who are now gone. Informal remembering thus functions as a form of collective memory in the sense of a shared body of knowledge (Wertsch and Roediger 2008)—in this case, about who lost whom in the genocide. This is not to say that this body of knowledge is uncontested, static, or unchanging, but since Butare's genocide survivors are remarkably knowledgeable about how many and what kinds of relations others lost, I heard little debate over these facts.

Second, if remembering and personhood are mutually constitutive, then any strict dichotomy between individual and collective memory obscures the fundamentally social nature of the person. In order to focus on the social constitution of personhood through these practices of remembering, we must, as Olick (1999: 346) suggests, overcome our common tendency to treat individuals and collectivities as distinct kinds of entities. Among the survivors with whom I worked, memory is a practice through which the shared body of knowledge of who lost whom in 1994 is deployed to make moral claims about social relationships and their absence. Indeed, a shared body of knowledge on losses incurred in 1994 is built through intersubjective remembering that is inseparable from the processes by which they struggle to reconstitute personhood in the absence of significant others.

What was striking about these accounts was that everyone knows everyone else's details of how many family members, what types of relations they were, or even the painstaking details of how and where those people died. In a small town like Butare, perhaps this should be expected, and yet it was remarkable given how often it emerged that affluent residents did *not* know each other or that they know very little about each other beyond their stories of loss in 1994. Moreover, to keep straight the details of so many people's hardships requires a level of care that is unusual between people who are not particularly close. It would be easy to dismiss these narratives as little more than the routine gossip that characterizes social relationships in small towns. I see these more as memorial practices than gossip since the latter tends to thrive when the facts are uncertain (Merry 1997: 51), but even if we do read gossip into how Butare's survivors speak of others' losses, it is nonetheless noteworthy as a central way of demonstrating one's belonging and "insider knowledge" of the lives of fellow town residents. By asserting knowledge of others' losses, survivors evoke the absence of the relationships that constitute their own personhood and that of other survivors. Therefore, to speak about the genocide and what happened to people is not just evidence that national reconciliation policies are failing or that they are unable to heal from the trauma of violence. Informal memorial practices, when situated in their social contexts and in webs of social relationships, speak to the problem of selfhood in the absence of others, and while they may tell us something about the state of ethnic schisms and psychosocial "healing," they cannot be reduced to them.

What is central is that these narratives and reflections are doing moral work; they are among the few ways left by which these town residents can stake a claim to having had the relationships constitutive of personhood and rootedness in Butare. When people can no longer actively live their relationships with family and other relations, they invoke those absences, as well as what happened to other survivors as a way of saying, "I have knowledge of this town and its residents, and I am still 'of' this place." These claims to belonging are not merely a researcher's report of her interlocutors' conversations or descriptive accounts of who lost whom. Instead they are speech acts in Austin's (1962) sense: by deploying them, survivors are "doing things" with words, and they are deeply aware of the potential for infelicities should their claims to belonging not be received as intended. Indeed, survivors track out these relationships beyond their own families because to know about the losses of even distant acquaintances is what does some of the most important work of grounding survivors as members of their social worlds. This is in no way to say that survivors disingenuously instrumentalize their own and others' losses to make strategic claims about belonging. Claims to the absence (and therefore, erstwhile presence) of the relationships that constitute personhood are directed as much inward to assuaging doubts about one's selfhood as toward making claims about one's moral status and connection to Rwanda. Indeed, seen from the perspective of relational personhood in which the self is always being built out of relations with others, to lose those relations is to lose a part of one's own person. Paradoxically, then, the violence is what severed survivors' relationships, their connections to "here," *and* what permits them to continue to show how they fit in with others in their social worlds through memory practices. *Tracking out* the networks in which they used to be embedded, coupled with exchange relations maintained with the dead, imperfectly replace practices of *living out* the relationships that used to constitute their personhood. Indeed, these attestations to loss are never just about the past, but are always also about how that past paradoxically connects persons to and disconnects them from their social worlds. Since it goes without saying in Butare that everyone has terrible problems since 1994, to have suffered with others is a way that mobile town residents often accused of becoming strangers or *bazungu* stake claims to ongoing locatedness and attachments to local people and places.

The Moral Economy of Exchange with the Dead

At a coffee break during a meeting of a Butare peace-building organization in July 2014, Olivier, the organization director, told me a story of how thinking of the dead acts as a "gift" of care on the part of the living, one that the dead reciprocate with benevolent interventions in their affairs.

> I have a neighbor who lost her husband during the 1994 genocide. I can tell you this because it's no secret—she married another, but she never stopped thinking about the one she lost. She didn't love the second as much, and he was violent with her. One night during the [genocide] commemorations a few years back, she was lying in bed, and her first husband appeared to her. He was wearing the suit that he wore on their wedding day. He spoke to her, and he said, "I want you to know that I love you and I will never stop. I know that you have been suffering, but my love will protect you." She knew it wasn't a dream because she wasn't really asleep, so she knew that he had come to her. And after that, she felt more at ease, more stable, and her second husband even became less violent toward her. You know, there is no small number of stories like this that circulate of people whose lost loved ones have come to them this way and who protect them.

As the foregoing discussion implies, in Rwanda, the deceased are not inert or absent from the world of the living, and relations with them are important to survivors. The notion that the dead are still involved in the affairs of the living is not a new, post-1994 phenomenon in Rwanda. People emphasized to me that in Rwandan cosmology, ancestor spirits can make malevolent interventions in the lives of the living, but thinking of them regularly, as did Olivier's neighbor, or making other symbolic gestures of exchange maintains good relations with them (see also Taylor 1992). For many survivors, the duty to think of the dead has become all the more pressing with respect to those who died so violently in 1994 and whose memorialization is bound up with broader political questions of doing justice, forging peace, or condemning international inaction to stop the genocide (Vidal 2001). In this section, I detail how Butaréens try to maintain some semblance of relations with the dead in everyday life.

On a 2008 stroll through a wooded area on the outskirts of town, Simbi emphasized that historically in Rwanda, it was not the body of a dead person that was treated with care, but the memory or the name of the person. As an RPF soldier during the civil war, he is not a civilian "survivor" as many of my other interlocutors were, but as a post-1994 Tutsi returnee to Rwanda, he faces similar problems of forging belonging that survivors do. To assert his rootedness and authority on matters historical, Simbi routinely drew on his elderly father's recollections of the colonial period and customary sociocultural practices in southern Rwanda:

> In our tradition, the body was not important. In fact, Rwandans can't stand being near corpses—we always disposed of them quickly. So people would wrap the body in a mat, they would make their way into the forest, and they would abandon the body. Then they would run—as fast as they could—because they were afraid of the body but also because they were afraid of the animals who would come and eat the remains! (Butare, May 2008)

Scholarly accounts of precolonial burial practices (e.g. Vidal 2001, 2004) mirror Simbi's description in many ways, but they also reveal a greater diversity. Rwandan funerary practices have historically varied considerably by region and even from family to family (van't Spijker 1990: 39). Bodies were not always abandoned in uncultivated areas, and interment of deceased relatives within the enclosure of the rural homestead (*rugo*) was also common (ibid.: 91, 98). Nonetheless, Pauline confirmed Simbi's assertion that burial sites were historically insignificant for Rwandan memory practices, but she underscored the importance of the practice of *guterekera*. *Guterekera* is a tradition of honoring the deceased. It is predicated on the notion that the dead continue to concern themselves with the affairs of the living and that the living can invoke the ancestors' assistance by making offerings to them. In *guterekera*, beer, meat, or whatever the deceased used to enjoy is shared between the living and the dead by sprinkling some on the ground (Taylor 1992: 142; van't Spijker 1990: 18). As Pauline explained during an interview in her living room in February of 2009:

> If the dead person liked to drink, then everyone would drink. If he was known for giving to the poor, then everyone would do that. But it wasn't just to honor the memory of the dead person. It's also because people were afraid. Afraid that the dead would come back and say that people aren't doing anything for them! They may come back and do harm to people; they can be nasty spirits, so each time someone dies, the living retain their relations with these people.

While many urban dwellers today tend to disparage "traditional" beliefs about the dangers posed by the dead, what emerged is that educated Butaréens by no means live in a completely disenchanted world. For them, the dead can still be helpful forces if treated with due care and respect. Mauss famously wrote that reciprocal exchange is a "moral transaction, bringing about and maintaining human, personal relationships between individuals and groups" (Evans-Pritchard 1967: ix), and in this case, death does not sever exchange obligations completely. Where variation arises is in how these exchanges should be practiced and the degree to which burial sites and bodies in addition to the memory of genocide victims should be treated with care.

During my fieldwork, I heard a number of survivors—although by no means the majority of those I knew—express a desire to restore dignity to victims whose bodies were haphazardly tossed into mass graves or simply left to decompose. For them, formal public commemorations, elaborate monuments, and re-interment of bodies are things that the living owe to the dead (Vidal 2001: 16–17; 2004: 279). During the annual genocide commemorations is when memorials see the most foot traffic, when crowds of Butare residents participate in walks to memorials around the town, and when survivors and their supporters hold all-night vigils at memorial sites. For some, however, being near to the dead is an important part of keeping their memory close no matter the time of year. Thomas, the university student and executive member of a student survivors' organization who first appeared in the Introduction, had proud ancestral ties to the precolonial royal court at Nyanza. He talked about going to memorials when he needed to reflect on an important decision. As he explained, "I survived, so I want to bring value to my life. So I go and pray to the spirits of the dead to help me do good things with my life." It was primarily younger Butaréens like Thomas who professed a duty to physically visit burial sites beyond the week of mourning, perhaps because they grew up in a context in which their government was placing an emphasis on building memorials that was unprecedented in Rwanda's history. Indeed, many Rwandans express concern that the state has "centralized" memory of the violence through its official sites and uses memorials as a means to an end in order to "market" the genocide internationally (Meierhenrich 2011: 285). Hence, not only are the making of memorial sites and the duty to visit them to remember contested issues, but so are the uses to which those sites are put, be they for public or private uses.

In April 2008, Simbi and I participated in a number of events during the week of mourning that draw out debates over what is owed to the dead. Among these was a formally organized commemorative march to the Ngoma genocide memorial from the town hall in central Butare. At nine in the morning, the hall was brimming with several hundred residents awaiting the start of the walk. Although no one stood up to make a formal announcement, somehow word spread through the crowd that it was time to depart. Upon exiting the hall, Simbi encountered a young man he knew from his days as a scout leader and who joined us for the duration of the walk.

The mood of the walk was solemn as we made our way to Ngoma. Some people appeared to have come alone, while most walked in groups of four or five and engaged in muted conversation along the way. No one brought children, and the youngest participants seemed to be youth in their mid teens who had come alone. Simbi's old acquaintance was quietly relating a story about a family friend of his who survived the genocide, but who did not know his own father when he came face to face with him years later since he had been separated from him in 1994 when he was still an infant. Simbi murmured something about how these stories show the depth of the effects of the violence, and we fell into silence. Upon arrival at the memorial, the crowd formed a large circle around the crosses and white tiled burial markers. Simbi and I were positioned quite far back in the crowd, so it became difficult to see and hear what the three officiants—Catholic, Protestant, and Muslim religious leaders—were doing. While the march had been quiet and solemn, an incongruous scene began to emerge. Most in attendance stood in silence and listened to the proceedings; a few sat weeping quietly on the fringes of the crowd. But among us was no small number of attendees who had neglected to turn off their mobile phones, which were ringing with remarkable frequency, and people were taking phone calls as the ceremonies proceeded. Their behavior was not lost on Simbi, who pointed out to me the dirty looks that others were giving the telephone talkers. "You see?" he said. "People come here because they just want to be seen. It's suspicious if you don't show up—people think you might have supported the genocide. So they come, but they're only going through the motions." He paused to consider his own words, then continued. "But in a way it makes sense and you can have sympathy for it—this imported practice from the West of cemeteries has little meaning for us."

According to Simbi, then, jarring contrasts in conduct at formal commemorations can be explained by competing ideas about what is owed to the dead and the question of whether "imported" burial practices can and should be imbued with moral significance. Whether or not he was correct to read instrumental performances into why some (especially, as he implied, Hutu) attend the commemorations, he also points to why many Tutsi survivors who lost scores of family members are not especially eager to participate in these events. Unlike Thomas and a handful of others I knew in town, the majority of those I worked with underscored why it is not compulsory to attend official commemorations or visit sites. For this reason, if one were to only study formal memorial occasions like the commemorative march I just described, it would result in a very narrow view of memory practices and how they link to questions of belonging. As Rose once put it, "You think of those you lost every day. I don't need a ceremony to remember." Similarly, Pauline expressed horror at the idea of visiting memorials. She told me that she regretted once having accompanied a Belgian friend to the Murambi memorial, because the sight of room upon room of preserved victim remains disturbed her sleep for weeks.

Whether one places importance on visiting burial sites or not, exchanges with the dead still involve thinking of them in exchange for assistance or protection. Pauline described to me on more than one occasion how her husband and children whom she lost in the genocide still help her whenever she overcomes a major challenge. As she remarked one day after she had just dealt with a rather delicate problem concerning a business partner who was behind on his rent and utility bill payments, "I know it's they who are helping me. It's my husband and children—not God or Jesus! If I didn't still feel them here with me, if I didn't believe they were always close, I wouldn't even be able to walk." A number of survivors expressed guilt if they go too long without thinking of certain victims. "I think of the closest family I lost all the time," Rose said in reference to her husband and children. "But then sometimes I realize that several weeks have passed since I thought of an aunt or cousin or brother, and I feel guilty [coupable]."

What is central is that, while thinking and speaking about genocide victims is a way of maintaining good relations with them, it is moreover a way for survivors to remain connected in some way to the relations that constitute their personhood. As Pauline once said, "You feel like pieces of them [kin; friends] are still here somewhere, even though you cannot know exactly. If I left Rwanda for good, I would feel guilty." The dead are active agents in the present, not only because, controversially, some of their bodies have been left exposed at memorial sites as reminders of the scale of devastation in 1994, but also because of the moral duty to maintain relations and the claims to (erstwhile) belonging in one's social world that they make possible.

These limited exchange practices with the dead raise perceptions of injustice among Rwandan genocide survivors that remain peripheral in approaches focused primarily on national memory politics or healing from trauma. Survivors express anger not only for what perpetrators of violence took from them, but also, crucially, for what accused or convicted perpetrators still have. Survivors who are at pains to maintain limited forms of exchange with the dead resent that many perpetrators still have relations and support networks. Since prisoners must rely on their families rather than the state for provisions, one or two days each week, a stream of mostly women can be seen making their way to the Butare prison and carrying food, small amounts of money, or other items requested by inmates. While prisoners are not permitted to visit with their family members on these occasions, what they have are people to whom they can return home when they are released. Moreover, because prisoners in Rwanda are required to build infrastructure like roads and drainage ditches, they are permitted out in public in limited ways, albeit bearing the stigma of the bright pink prison uniform. In Butare, prisoners also run an auto repair garage and build furniture to sell to the public. From these points of contact with the general population, they maintain relationships of exchange and commerce with their family members and other townspeople.

Meanwhile, genocide survivors like Pauline express a sense of dislocation in the absence of relations and resentment of those accused of genocide crimes who do not suffer in the same way survivors do. As she explained, she does not "know who she is anymore" in the absence of her pre-1994 relations, but those who are released from prison have families to whom they return. For her, this injustice is something she is faced with on a daily basis since victims and perpetrators released from prison now share the same public space.

> Now I walk around Butare, I go to Uganda on the bus. Am I really living? Yes, I have my projects, I know how to use money, but when I get into bed at night, *I don't know who I am anymore* [emphasis added]. I'm tired so I'll sleep, I sleep for a second, then I feel myself wake with a start—ok, I can't stay awake anymore so I sleep. ... I've been forced to conclude that we have no country. We have victims who suffer injustice and we have killers who come and live with us. And the killers? They walk around, free and happy, they drink with their friends in the *cabarets*, they build houses, they have sex with their wives, they take the bus to Kigali with us. Can you imagine?

While in practice many ex-prisoners did lose family members or do not easily resume their relationships upon returning home, for those who lost the majority of their kin relations in 1994, there is nonetheless resentment toward perpetrators who have people with whom to rebuild relations at all. Concerns like these should not be read simply as evidence that Tutsi survivors harbor resentment toward the blanket category of "Hutu = perpetrator." Rather, they speak to a different scale of injustice, namely the everyday anguish of living with absence and no longer knowing oneself. The significance of having relationships and the hardship and disconnect that comes from their absence is perhaps best captured in something that Pauline reported *génocidaires* having sometimes said to those Tutsi whom they spared during the genocide: rather than dying right then, the survivor would instead die a slow "death of sadness" in the absence of everyone to whom she or he was related.

Conclusion

Informal talk about the 1994 genocide and its victims is a practice that speaks to the ruptures in relationships constitutive of survivors' personhood and the ways in which the violent past enters into everyday practices of making selves and forging relationships. That educated survivors are at pains to assure themselves and others that their claims to "hereness" are legitimate demonstrates that there is no contradiction between having ties to power on the one hand and being devastated by loss and dislocation on the other. What their informal memory practices reveal is that people now navigate complex predicaments of what it means to dwell in a present that is marred by the absence of friends, family, and neighbors with whom they once socialized and with whom they were engaged in relations of mutual dependency—a problem that is by no means restricted to educated survivors in Butare. Indeed, it is the challenges that these Butaréens face in claiming locatedness that puts the effects of the sudden and widespread loss of kin on relational persons into particularly sharp focus.

A feature I have underscored about these ways of forging personhood through remembering is that they go by quickly in the course of everyday talk. At the outset of this chapter, I defended their short duration against accusations that they might simply be of little significance, but at this point I want to suggest that the brevity of these practices has a broader significance of its own. In other words, even as people are at pains to undertake the moral work of remembering, to dwell too long on the past comes with dangers of its own, ones bound up with the moral imperative to become agents of change to bring about a "better" Rwanda. In the next chapter, I elicit a set of competing demands when it comes to how the violent past enters the present, and the moral choice to think positively and become "modern" selves.

Chapter 4

CREATIVITY, POSITIVE THINKING, AND THEIR PERILS

∞

Simbi is known in Butare for his broad smile, easygoing demeanor, and his booming laugh that fills a *cabaret* (neighborhood bar) when he shows up to drink a beer. Over the years I have known him, I have noticed that he takes special pleasure in regaling others (perhaps foreign anthropologists especially) with stories of his youth. His stories share a pattern. Whether they recount the time he defiantly swam across a river at age eleven when everyone said it was too dangerous, the time when as a scout leader he nearly landed his entire troop in a Congolese prison because he refused to defer to the border guard, or the time when at age sixteen he ran away to join the RPF and fight the civil war, his tales always position him as a dissident figure—one who is fiercely independent, who will take a moral stand even at personal risk, and who refuses to conform as a matter of principle.

But just how autonomous was Simbi? The status claims that Simbi asserted through these narratives—claims to being immune to the Rwandan "logic of contagion" (Fujii 2009) and to value autonomy above all else—were undermined by his chronic unemployment and economic dependency on others. As someone with a university degree and a family well connected to local elite networks, it was a mystery to other town residents why Simbi's employment stints were inevitably short-lived. During my 2008 fieldwork, he was unemployed having just been let go from a local peace-building NGO. By 2009, he had secured a job with a Belgian-sponsored NGO working on malaria prevention, a job that even provided him with a spacious house and live-in cook. His time there was brief, however, and a few months later he was unemployed again. He cited problems with his employer, whom he accused of disliking his independent streak, as the reason for his dismissal. At this point, he found himself both homeless and unemployed, so he went to live with his father in a rural sector on the outskirts of Kigali. By the time I returned to Rwanda in the spring of 2014, Simbi was back in Butare and living with an elderly aunt, who had agreed to house and feed him in exchange for help at home. Any time I have been at a gathering of Butare residents at which the conversation turned to Simbi, I heard them wonder why his employment problems seemed so intractable. It was not only behind his back that people would question his priorities. As he told me once, "My sisters always say to me, why can't you just accept wearing a tie at work, why can't you just settle down and marry like other men your age? And I drive them crazy by telling them I'm not like other men my age! [laughs heartily] They don't know what to say to me then!" (Butare, May 2014).

In spite of Simbi's efforts to self-present as an autonomous person, I heard town residents speculate that he secretly preferred not to work but to depend on others. Odette theorized that, because Simbi had lost his mother at a young age, he wanted to be cared for by women, whether his aunt or me, through his more than occasional dependency on me for meals and small sums of cash for incidentals. She suggested that Simbi's problem was "discipline," citing his tendency to spend his money on cigarettes and alcohol rather than cultivating prudent saving habits. Charles, who knew Simbi through a colleague, remarked on several occasions that Simbi was not "serious" or "well organized." He wondered aloud why Simbi did not seek to marry. Rose once suggested that perhaps he was still dealing with a deep *traumatisme* from the war, and this is what kept him from becoming financially independent. In any case, as much as Simbi was well liked around town, he was also the subject of gossip, criticism, and sometimes pity.

While in the eyes of other town residents his unstable financial situation undermined his claims to being a modern, independent subject, Simbi, for his part, relied on these very attributes to explain his perpetual difficulties in securing steady work. Blaming his malaria NGO employer for being unable to handle his independence at work was just one of many of Simbi's explanations to himself and others of why he is one of the few in his NUR graduating class who have not found steady employment in a modern, urban sector.[1] His strategy calls to mind what Elliot Liebow (1967) termed "manly flaws" in black American "streetcorner" men's explanations for their personal inadequacies, unemployment, trouble with the law, or failed marriages. Parallel to Liebow's analysis of how those men assert that they are "too manly" to be faithful spouses, law-abiding citizens, or good employees, so Simbi's explanation for his chronic unemployment relies on what I call his "modern flaws." Modern flaws for Simbi are a strategy by which he can retain personal dignity even as his claims to modern selfhood are dangerously undermined by his chronic dependency on others. Indeed, in the unapologetically hierarchical society of Rwanda, Simbi claims that he is "too modern" and "too independent," such that his "modern flaws" prevent him from meeting Rwandan employers' expectations of their subordinates: deference, subservience, and obedience. As Simbi put it late one afternoon when we sat in a quiet corner of a neighborhood *cabaret* sharing large green bottles of the local beer, Mützig:

> Working for someone else, that is like slavery. I'm working for this woman [at the malaria prevention NGO] right now, but I can't do it forever. That's not a life. She expects me to take orders from her, to hop when she says to hop. So I'll do this for a while, but eventually, when I earn enough to start something, I'm going to work for myself. I've already started raising goats and rabbits, so I'll make my living that way. I'll sell the rabbits to the local restaurants, and I'll make cheese from the goat milk. *My goal is to be a self-made man.* (Butare, February 2009, my emphasis)

Simbi said the phrase "self-made man" in English when the rest of this conversation took place in French, which suggests that this is an idea borrowed directly from the Anglo-American tradition of enterprising individualism. The figure of the "self-made man" has appeal for middle-class and aspiring middle-class urban Rwandans. Indeed, it aligns with the crucial distinction that Butare residents of all levels of wealth and education draw between "working for oneself" and "working for others"—an opposition that animates this chapter and that is shot through with politically charged questions about modern personhood and nationhood in Rwanda.

It is difficult to obtain reliable statistics on how many Rwandans succeed in starting up business ventures of the "modern sector" type that Butare residents desire (e.g. tourism, hotel/restaurant, internet cafes, boutiques), because "self-employment" statistics can include much less prestigious forms of work, such as domestic work and subsistence farming. This is why the African Development Bank (2014: Table 6) could report that in 2005–2006, 47.8 percent of all Rwandans were self-employed. Furthermore, "unemployment," "informal employment," and "self-employment" overlap in official reports—a reality on which a writer for *The New Times*[2] drew for a piece entitled "Unemployed = Self-Employed," which advised unemployed Rwandans to re-baptize themselves as "self-employed," since "entrepreneurship is a hot topic" and "[a]nyone who starts a business is given hero status—instantly classed as brave and innovative for taking risks in these 'difficult economic times'" (Keza Gara 2012: para. 2). In the absence of reliable figures on entrepreneurship in Rwanda (successful and otherwise), anecdotal reports are what remain. Butare residents talk about people who try to "start something up," only to have bank loans run out or to falter under crushing tax burdens[3] for small business owners in Rwanda. As Chapter 1 described, stalled, abandoned construction projects around Butare stand as testaments to these failed business plans. When ambition and practical constraint collide in entrepreneurial ventures that fail or fail to launch in the first place, questions arise for Butaréens as to what precisely makes the difference between those who succeed and those who fail.

I argue in this chapter that work relations, moral languages of work, and work-related aspirations in Butare are contradictory, politically charged loci of the post-genocide imperative to envision the self as a modern project of improvement. Crucially, in the post-conflict moment in Rwanda, self-improvement is caught in the contradictions of "peaceful selfhood." While both state leaders and ordinary Butare residents link the quest for personal prosperity and self-worth to possibilities for peace, the moral languages of work antithetically evoke and reproduce the politics of the genocide.

Practices and patterns of labor and work are not simply modes by which economic needs and wants are satisfied. They are also constitutive and productive of individual and collective subjectivities and forms of sociality (Hardt 1999: 89). This chapter traces the linkage between working for oneself and self-worth, along with a growing turn toward entrepreneurship, creativity, positive thinking, and calculated risk taking as admirable personal qualities. It elucidates the contested rise of the "enterprise" ethos that configures the self as a project on which to work, one that can and should be developed not only in one's private life, but also crucially through one's job (Fioratta 2015; Freeman 2014; Illouz 2008; Rose 1992: 149). In adopting these ideas in their self-making projects, Butaréens assert a claim to inclusion in rather than exclusion from the modern global order and its contemporary political and economic forms that, since the era of Reagan and Thatcher and the emergence of the "enterprise culture" (Heelas and Morris 1992), especially champion self-reliance, self-sufficiency, and personal responsibility for one's lot in life. Crucially, positive thinking is inseparable from the enterprise culture because the latter turns social issues (like unemployment) into questions of personal character to be solved at the level of individual psychology. It is a culture in which a positive, upbeat outlook—no matter how bleak one's prospects, or in this case, no matter how much one suffers with the legacy of the genocide—is a prerequisite for personal success.

While these ideas about entrepreneurship, financial independence, and self-making seem incongruous with the history of violence, Butaréens also draw them together in important ways. The striking post-genocide emphasis on entrepreneurship and enterprise is partially linked to the greater foothold that Protestant and Pentecostal churches and their prosperity doctrine have secured in Rwanda in the wake of the genocide, when many people abandoned the Catholic Church because of its role in the massacres (Longman 2010a). Yet the moral importance of enterprise has traction beyond adherents to these relative newcomer religions in Rwanda, as my overwhelmingly Catholic research participants similarly extolled the virtues of questing after personal prosperity. There is a positively Smithian perspective that circulates among town residents, one that unites individualism, hard work, and civil peace with local ideas about what kinds of persons were capable of making the genocide happen. Indeed, Adam Smith (1982) famously argued that individuals each pursuing and maximizing their own economic interests produce civil and stable social relations, and some Butaréens position such social relations as good insurance against future violence. In a typical assertion of this ilk, Charles mused one evening over dinner:

> Perhaps capitalism means that we don't need each other anymore. And I'm not sure that's a bad thing. But it also means that perhaps we fear each other, because you never know when someone is going to come after you, trick you, steal from you. The problems we've had here in Rwanda, the war, the genocide, they were related to problems of poverty and resentments that some people had more than others. *If everyone would just work to get by on their own, if they'd use their creativity to start something so that they'd have some means, then maybe we wouldn't have these problems in Rwanda.* (Butare, February 2009, my emphasis)

Here, Charles implies that the genocide was precipitated by (Hutu) resentment of (Tutsi) wealth and prosperity. Even as he recognized that resentment over others' success is an ongoing problem that produces fear and mistrust of lower-income Rwandans, he invoked the virtues of creativity, entrepreneurship, and getting by on one's own, and expressed faith in their ability to produce greater peace and prosperity in Rwanda. Charles's view is typical of the way Butare residents draw an association between the entrepreneurial self and the self who is capable of peace. Modernity, in this perspective, is characterized by opportunities for all "enterprising selves" to pursue not only their own livelihoods, but also their own self-development (Heelas and Morris 1992: 4)—in this case, to become "peaceful selves." The problem, as I will argue in this chapter, is that the ability to pursue one's own prosperity without resenting others' success is not among the range of capacities that Butare residents attribute to "normal personhood." Indeed, successful entrepreneurs have capacities considered *extraordinary* in Butaréens' moral frameworks—ones that place them ahead, at the vanguard of bringing an ethic of enterprising individualism to Rwanda. However, it is precisely because these capacities are considered beyond the ordinary that there are perils to success in Butare. People wonder, are entrepreneurial gains ill-gotten? Town residents warn of the dangers of success, which they express in the idiom of "jealousy," a problem that they report can lead to theft, sabotage, or even murder.

In spite of Butaréens' adoption of ideas like the "self-made man" and the linkage between individual prosperity and peace, it would be a mistake to interpret these invocations as mere replications of a stereotypically rugged American individualism and its classical liberal and neoliberal iterations. There is a peculiarly Rwandan significance to the value placed on working for oneself as a mark of modern personhood that emerges from the nexus of Rwanda's socially charged history of dependent work relationships and patron–client bonds coupled with the increasingly globalized phenomena of "enterprising selfhood" and "positive thinking" as transformative forces (e.g. Heelas and Morris 1992; Peale [1956] 2012). Hence, while others (e.g. Sommers 2012; Thomson 2013) have shown that low-income rural and urban Rwandans privately critique their government's wholesale embrace of development practices that bypass ordinary people's interests for elite ones, this chapter elicits the ambivalent orientation of (aspiring) middle-class Butare residents to RPF calls for "good Rwandans" to "work hard," develop the "right mentality," and contribute to building the "New Rwanda"—a "self-sufficient" member of the global economic order (Kagame 2015; see also Ansoms 2011; Purdeková 2012). On the one hand, Butare residents recognize that, in practice, not everyone can be an entrepreneur in spite of their best efforts to answer those state calls for "hard work," creativity, and enterprise. They see that the decline of durable patron–client relations has precipitated a crisis in economic security and an assault on personal dignity for those who must depend on others to get by. The combination of judgment and pity directed at Simbi is but one case in point. On the other hand, there are elements of the RPF's paternalistic brand of neoliberal reform and entrepreneurial spirit that Butaréens find meaningful as they aim to live up to the demands placed on the self in the wake of violence. I turn now to town residents' ambivalences toward enterprise culture and entrepreneurial selfhood (Freeman 2014) and how those ambivalences are produced through the politics of dependent work relationships and patron–client bonds, the history of violence, and the power of positive thinking and personal development.

Working for Oneself versus Working for Others

The ethnographic record demonstrates that diverse types of patronage and personal dependency were historically among the most important modes of social organization in Rwanda (Newbury 1988; Rwabukumba and

Mudandagizi 1974; Vidal 1969). These relationships—past and present—are tightly entangled with ethnic boundary production, dignity, and prestige, or lack of them (see Chapters 1 and 2). Out of that history grows the contemporary distinction Butare residents draw between working for oneself and working for others. It is a prominent feature of everyday talk, but it is also a central criterion by which Rwandans configure status. Sommers notes that "the poor" (*abakene*), "the vulnerable" (*abatindi*), and "the most vulnerable" (*abatindi nyakujya*) are distinguished in part by the fact that they "work for others." By contrast, "the rich" (*abakire*) employ others and "can solve any problem as they know many people" (Ingelaere 2007: 12, quoted in Sommers 2012: 33). When Simbi characterized working for others as slavery, he pointed to a crucial set of shared meanings that are attached to employee–employer relations in contemporary Butare. Town residents are known to map any type of hierarchical, dependent relationship onto patron–client bonds—even when working for others in modern sector wage or salaried employment like Simbi's NGO job. Indeed, people of diverse levels of income and status are quick to invoke patron–client bonds to characterize work relations that they perceive as exploitative. One such example was that of Emmanuel, the motel bartender from Chapter 2, who compared the guest's treatment of him to the way chiefs used to treat their (Hutu) porters. On another occasion, a restaurant server at a popular establishment in central Butare privately complained to me that his boss acts like a *chef* who controls the *petits paysans* (little peasants). "I've gone to school!" he exclaimed as he contested his "peasant" status. "I speak French, I know how to handle money. But here in Rwanda, when you work for someone else, they treat you like you're no more than a common peasant. You have to say, *oui chef!*" (Butare, April 2008).

Even though there are clear qualitative distinctions between employer–employee relations and patron–client bonds, in Rwanda they share the feature of being openly hierarchical and putting subordinates in positions of servitude. Sometimes, the factors that unite low-status wage work and clientship are not only the potential to be treated like a personal servant, but also the employer's influence over living arrangements and other "non-work" aspects of employees' lives.

I met Françoise in 2008 when she was twenty-nine years old and working as a cleaner at a motel popular with budget travelers in central Butare. She came from a rural sector of Cyangugu Province in western Rwanda not far from the Congolese border. Unlike many young Rwandans who grew up in the rural hills, Françoise spoke fluent French. She said that she was lucky to have learned it since it helped her secure urban work. She attributed her luck to having been the oldest child in her family, which allowed her to remain in school longer than the others, because as more of her siblings reached school age, the more difficult it was to pay their tuition fees. When she and her five sisters were orphaned during the 1994 genocide, Françoise left home to seek work to support her siblings. Many workers in low-skilled jobs are migrants to Butare who lack the means to house themselves in the town. Hence, Françoise and the other motel employees all slept in shared rooms—one for male and one for female employees—rented by the motel owner. The employer–employee relationship was thus cross-cut by the patronage-style relationship in which housing was provided to employees unable to provide it for themselves. I interviewed Françoise one afternoon in July 2008 about her experiences as a migrant worker in Butare.

LE: What is the most difficult part of your life right now?

Françoise: [Sighs] Life is not easy. It's true, I have some family at least, but I never see them. I start work here [at the motel] at 8am, and I have to work all day until 10pm without having anything to eat. The work is very tiring. I have to haul heavy buckets of water, clean rooms, wash clothes and sheets by hand, and clean up after the guests. I never have time to relax; I can never go to pray and my body feels exhausted all the time. Sometimes I even have to clean my boss's house and for no additional pay. But I am responsible to my boss, and so I have no choice. I ask myself how much longer I can withstand this. The pay is not enough to make me want to stay—only 6,500 RWF each month [roughly US$9 at the time of fieldwork].

Françoise's entire life was structured around the demands of her ill-paying job. Indeed, her employer determined not just what her work responsibilities entailed but also when she could eat, when she could leave the motel premises to pray (or to do anything else), and where and when she slept. She was vulnerable to exploitative demands to clean her boss's house for no additional compensation. Françoise's experience of her relationship with her employer was that it exceeded the confines of paid work duties. This sheds light on why town residents so often liken their paid jobs to the servitude relations that characterized precolonial and colonial-era patron–client bonds.

Of all the types of subordinate work in Butare, the most disparaged and undignified is the role of household domestic workers. By and large, domestic workers are rural Rwandan youth[4] whose families require their wages to make ends meet. As far back as 1978, 15 percent of Butare's workforce comprised such household workers, a figure approximately 7–8 percent greater than other small towns in Rwanda at that time because of the high population of North Americans and Europeans in Butare who employed domestic workers (Sirven 1984: 475). Today, it is difficult to find statistics on numbers of domestic workers, because they are subsumed under other categories in national and regional statistics. Nonetheless, domestic service is one of the most common sectors in which young Rwandans find work. By

2010, 30 percent of all 15–34-year-old workers in Rwanda were employed in non-farm wage employment, a category that comprises mostly domestic work, but also construction (African Development Bank 2014: 32).

The duties of live-in domestic workers in affluent Butare households underscore in extraordinary ways the status differentials between employers and employees. The domestic worker is the first in the household to get up in the morning and the last to go to sleep at night. In the morning, she or he prepares the tea, coffee, bread, and fruit normally served for breakfast in urban households. After cleaning up the family's morning meal, the floors must be mopped, since they get dusty in the dry season and muddy in the wet season. Laundry is done by hand (washing machines are non-existent in Butare) and must be completed in the morning in order to let the clothes dry in the hot afternoon sun. Next is the preparation of the midday meal, which must be ready at just the right hour to accommodate schoolchildren's short lunch breaks. In the afternoons, a domestic worker may wash dishes, chop wood, wash windows, boil drinking water, or sweep away dead leaves and debris outdoors before preparing the evening meal. They eat their meals in separate quarters, never in the house with the family. While they share in the food that they prepare for the family, they are only permitted to consume "lower status" foods, which means they are never given meat and eat only grains, starchy vegetables like manioc, potatoes, and green plantains, and beans for protein. Before retiring for the night, domestic workers inspect employers' shoes and polish them as needed. Urban Rwandans insist on clean, polished shoes, especially in the dry season when dusty unpaved roads make shoe cleaning a daily task. It is no surprise that turnover of domestic workers is high in most households. In the families in whose houses I spent the most time, I never saw a domestic worker who lasted more than six months. Sometimes their departure was due to problems with the employer, occasionally young women would "fall pregnant" and return to their rural homesteads, sometimes they were fired for stealing, and sometimes they would simply disappear without any explanation. The organization of household labor and the constraints it puts on the lives of domestic workers is an especially stark example of how working for someone else looks and feels akin to slavery, according to Butare residents. The wage does little to mitigate this impression: in 2008, families paid about 4,000 RWF (US$6) each month in wages to domestic workers. By 2014, people reported paying 10,000 RWF (US$13).

I rarely heard workers like Françoise in low-status, poorly paid jobs express a desire to work for themselves some day. Perhaps it was simply too unlikely a scenario for most of them, or perhaps it was because they were all too familiar with a different kind of "working for oneself" that has a different set of connotations, namely subsistence farming. But when it came to well-educated Butaréens who came from families with some means, the desire to work for oneself was typically expressed through sentiments like Simbi's comparison of his white-collar NGO job to slavery. Simbi was by no means the only person in Butare to draw such an analogy. I asked Thomas, a fourth-year agronomy student at the NUR and Tutsi genocide survivor, what he planned to do when he graduates during a conversation at the office of the survivors' association he helped to coordinate. He responded:

> What I want is to work for myself, not for someone else like a beast. I'm hoping to have a farm—I am an agronomist after all. I could raise pigs and goats and sell their products. I have a friend who might lend me some land in Cyangugu. I'm working on a proposal to secure some funding from the state as well. (Butare, July 2008)

Thomas compared working for others to the condition of a "beast," or an animal put to work in the service of agricultural production. Indeed, both Simbi and Thomas expressed a wish to "start something up" (*démarrer quelque chose*) related to animal husbandry, which might seem a surprisingly humble form of work for men aiming at "modern" autonomy and self-employment. Nonetheless, it is important to note that the kind of animal husbandry to which they aspire is hardly at the modest scale of a handful of goats or chickens common on rural homesteads. Rather, both men envisioned a commercial livestock venture in which they would work for themselves and would also hire others to work for them. When I returned to Rwanda in 2014, Thomas had not realized his ambition of working for himself, but he had secured a post in the Ministry of Agriculture and had married. Legal marriage has become a real sign of status in contemporary Rwanda. It has been on the decline in favor of less formal unions, since to marry, a suitable husband must be able to build, purchase, or rent a house in which to establish his family—something that is painfully out of reach for most young Rwandans (Sommers 2012: 202–4). Thomas is thus in a privileged minority, because his job permits him to rent a house and support a spouse in Kigali, which means that (provided he and his wife have a child), he has transitioned into successful adulthood by Rwandan standards. Nonetheless, when I met up with him in Kigali after my five-year absence from the field, he expressed some regrets that he is still working for someone else. He complained that his superior sends him out on field expeditions for weeks at a time, and while he quickly added that it is a good job that he is grateful to have, he wondered aloud what life would be like if he was "free." He continued, "Perhaps once I've saved some money, then I'll finally start something of my own." More than simply a wistful contemplation about where the grass might be greener, Thomas was making a claim about the ideal kind of person he would like to become and the centrality of self-sufficiency to that vision.

It is not that Simbi's short-lived NGO job or Thomas's government job are not respectable positions, or that they indicate a failure to participate in "modern" forms of work. In Rwanda, "modern" livelihoods and work relations are not restricted to entrepreneurial ventures. Employment in a wide range of governmental, managerial, and "white-collar" jobs can earn town residents social recognition. Still, there is something special about working for oneself that holds allure even for those who make comfortable livings in other ways and who may or may not ever make a serious attempt at entrepreneurship. Voicing an aspiration to work for oneself is more than anything a *claim about oneself* and what kind of person one is, not a series of concrete plans a person has for her or his career and livelihood. To claim an aspiration to self-employment is to assert one's capacities for personal development and the concern that traditional, hierarchically organized employment will only stifle one's personal potential. Indeed, as elements of the "enterprise culture" find expression in urban Rwanda, so too the idea is gaining traction that work need not be a source of constraint on one's autonomy, but rather is an avenue for its fullest and purest expression (Rose 1992: 153)—provided, of course, that one develops one's creative capacities and "starts something" of one's own rather than working for others "like a beast." By reproducing—at least selectively and situationally—the rhetoric of the "enterprise culture" with its emphasis on personal development, creativity, and innovation, Butare residents are using a language of power to align themselves with forms of personhood that are valued in the global economic order. Thus, regardless of whether a person succeeds in "starting something" or even begins to make the attempt, vocalizing the aspiration acts as a way of asserting one's personhood as distinct from that of the majority who are "content to work for others" or who "desire direction" so that they do not have to "think for themselves," in the phrases Butaréens deployed to disparage their low-income co-citizens. In this sense, expressing the desire to work for oneself might be more important than achieving it in practice, since the expression of the wish does the crucial work of setting the person apart as someone with the "will to improve" (Li 2007), unlike those who are content with subordinate positions or who lack the thirst for autonomy. It is the claim to be *striving* for something more—even if those strivings are never enacted or never bring the wished-for outcomes—that is a crucial mode by which people work to assert successful, modern personhood (Fioratta 2015).

Even among those who take concrete steps to achieve autonomy in their livelihoods, there is a profound unevenness that characterizes how people succeed or fail to meet the criteria of a person who truly works for herself or himself. Even for those who seem to have all of the trappings of "working for oneself," there are plenty of ways that their status can be called into question. Léon was an entrepreneur in the restaurant industry in his late thirties with a checkered work history. Of all the aspiring "self-made men" I met in Butare, he was the most doggedly ambitious and the least risk-averse—a quality that has been both detrimental and fundamental to his success over the years. I first met him in early 2008 when he was renting a small café/ restaurant from Pauline, the local daycare owner discussed in Chapters 1 and 3 who had inherited this restaurant property from a relative who died in the genocide. Léon's wife, Claire, was also involved with the restaurant and kept the accounting ledgers, but Léon saw himself as the visionary behind their business. In my very first conversation with him in the grounds of the restaurant where I had gone to meet up with Pauline, he narrated his work history and his hopes for the future.

> Ever since I was a young boy, I have wanted to work for myself. I went to high school to study math and physics, but I ended up learning to become an electrician. I told myself that I would work for someone else for five years only, and then I'd do something on my own. What I've always wanted to do was own a restaurant. When I was young, my aunt owned one, and I would go help her there in the afternoons when I finished school. My father died when I was only thirteen. After he was gone, my mother said that since I am the oldest, I had to become the head of the household. So I worked in my aunt's restaurant to help support my family; I had six younger siblings to look after. I even sold peanuts on the street for a while just to make a living. Now I've been operating this restaurant for ten months. It is going well, but it was hard at first. My friends tease me about having a math degree, being a technician, and owning a restaurant, but it's good because I have always wanted to work for myself. I like to be independent. I get by on my own and I never ask anyone for anything. People come here and they say, how did this *petit Rwandais* do all of this? *Moi, j'évolue toujours.* (Butare, February 2008)

With the verb *évoluer* (to develop, progress, change, or evolve), Léon invokes the basic tenet of enterprise culture and the therapeutic-entrepreneurial ethos in which the self is a project to be worked on and optimized—a project realized in large part through self-development in one's work life (cf. Freeman 2014). It is not just Léon's business or livelihood that grows or "evolves" through his tenacity; it is he *himself* who "evolves" and "develops." His choice of *évoluer* to characterize the project of his business and his own self thoroughly expresses the meeting of mobile precepts of the enterprise culture (Heelas and Morris 1992) with its emphasis on personal improvement and European colonial-era distinctions between elites and ordinary people. The noun form, *évolué(e)*, is a term that emerged under Francophone colonial regimes to refer to members of the colonized population who, through exposure to European formal education, styles of dress, values, etiquette, and religious practices, became "evolved" or "Westernized" persons. Hence, the increasingly globalized "enterprise culture" was not the first set of ideas that emphasized self-improvement as the path to prestige, even as it may have placed new emphasis on self-sufficiency and autonomy that were by definition denied to colonial-era *évolué(e)s* by virtue of their structural dependency on the colonial governance apparatus.

However, Léon's status claims were undermined when it emerged several months later that he had been dishonest and was mismanaging his funds. According to Pauline, his landlady, he had wasted (*bouffer*, to gobble up[5]) his money and was six months behind on his rent and utility bills, and his employees had not been paid in two months. One day in May 2008, I was in the midst of an interview with Simbi in a quiet corner of the garden of Léon's restaurant, when we heard a scuffle inside. We jumped up and went to investigate and found one of Léon's disgruntled employees holding him by the throat. He was threatening Léon and ominously told him that it was a good thing that he had been hoarding all his employees' pay, because he would need it for his hospital bills. In another incident that cast doubt on Léon's economic autonomy, he asked Simbi for 80,000 RFW to help cover the cost of a new refrigerator that he had purchased on credit. I was surprised that he requested this loan in front of me and two other people, since he always prided himself on his apparent self-sufficiency. Simbi suggested that he did it because he felt he had no choice. Léon was surprised when Simbi pled lack of funds. Since Simbi was well connected to *bazungu*, and since Rwandans say that *bazungu* are synonymous with money, people simply assumed he had disposable income. Pauline complained that Léon had foolishly spent his funds on building up side projects like tourism and hosting large entertainment events for which he purchased expensive sound equipment. "He wants to become too big too fast—that is his problem," as she put it one day when she, by her own admission, was finally fed up with him.

> He thinks he's like the *grandes personnes* [important people], but he doesn't know how to run his business. He needs to focus on the essentials instead of getting distracted by these other projects. You know, he had another restaurant on the other side of town that failed for the same reason. Now I worry he'll never pay me what he owes me. You see how people are here? They want to have everything right away; they're not patient and they don't want to work for it. I thought I could trust Léon, but now I see he's a crook [*escroc*]. (Butare, July 2008)

Léon's relationship with Pauline fell apart in the winter of 2009. He claimed that she was placing too many limits on his business expansion plans after he had invested in a number of improvements, including the construction of a clay oven in the kitchen, paving of garden pathways, and the purchase of new garden furniture and parasols. She accused him of not respecting their agreement, both because of his unpaid rent and bills and his violation of her stipulation that he must not turn the restaurant into a destination for late-night drinking and carousing. Following his departure from her property, Léon made two more unsuccessful attempts to open restaurants. Léon's wife, Claire, had privately expressed her worries to me that they would never have any savings, because as soon as money came in, Léon spent it on one of his many "projects." He delighted in boasting about the number of projects he had on the go (including aspirations for a tourism agency, a sound production studio, and an association to help the "vulnerable"), which speaks to his embrace of the "enterprise" ethic in which people should never "rest on their laurels," should be "ambitious and competitive," "show enterprise," and "energetically '[go] for it'" (Heelas and Morris 1992: 3, 8). Indeed, Léon invoked a different breed of "modern flaws" to account for his checkered work history. While Simbi cited his modern flaw of boundless independence to account for his shortcomings, Léon would cite his excess of entrepreneurial ambition to try to turn his failures into modern virtues. "People say I'm too ambitious sometimes," he explained after Pauline had asked him to leave her premises. "But how do you grow otherwise? How do you evolve? Maybe not all of my projects work out, but it's better to be too ambitious than not to have any ambition at all" (Butare, July 2009). Nonetheless, in spite of his bombastic claims to work for himself, Léon's uneven track record, dubious spending decisions, unpaid bills, and eventual requests to friends for loans undermined his status claim to self-sufficiency. Thus, even though Léon had successfully made a home for his family in Ngoma, supported all three of his and Claire's children's education, and had temporarily demonstrated successful entrepreneurial ventures, people in Butare used a range of criteria to evaluate his self-claims, which resulted in an uneven and ambiguous reputation among other middle-class town residents.

By the time I returned to Rwanda in 2014, Léon and Claire's entrepreneurial ventures had grown less precarious and fly-by-night. Together, they were running a new restaurant in central Butare that was one of several operations under the auspices of an enterprise that Léon had dubbed "LéoMax Initiative Promotion." While Claire attributed their newfound stability largely to the fact that their youngest child was by then in school, which allowed her to participate in (and supervise) Léon's business transactions to a much greater degree, Léon, in a move much more expressive of post-genocide transformations in valued forms of selfhood, credited their newfound stability and success to his creativity, ingenuity, and positive thinking. I turn now to the emergence of these values among middle-class Butare residents and the ways in which they take up these growing, globalized directives for how to achieve a "good life."

The Positive Thinking Imperative

In light of the recent, devastating history of violence in Rwanda, there is something incongruous about the ways that enterprise culture, "positive thinking," and their benefits are gaining traction among urban dwellers. In a social world in which suffering has been so profound and widespread, we might expect to find outright hostility to the idea that one can think or smile one's way to a better life. In this context, the imperative to think positively might be received purely as an imposition—the last indignity foisted upon a population still reeling from the devastation of 1994. It calls to mind Feldman's (2004)[6] critique of "emplotted narratives" of hope after hardship that "schedule" recovery from trauma with artificial endpoints and that act as marketable "feel-good stories" for international audiences and development donors. On the other hand, understood through the question of what kinds of selves are valued in post-genocide Rwanda, it is perhaps no surprise that positive thinking has found purchase there. Indeed, conversations with Butare residents reveal the imperative to "be positive" (*soyez positif* or *soyez optimiste*) as a force to combat the effects of "negativity," a term whose content is flexible depending on the context in which it is invoked. I heard "negativity" used to explain anything from the causes of endemic poverty (cycles of poverty and negative thinking prevent innovation), to jealousy of others' success ("negative" people do not focus on how to build their own success and are mired in negative thoughts about what others have that they do not), to the 1994 genocide itself (anti-Tutsi sentiment fueled by the "negativity" of hopeless and disaffected men helps to explain why ordinary people took part in the massacres). If negativity is linked to these three central social and political problems that have plagued Rwandan society, past and present, it is no wonder that the power of positive thinking has a real appeal as a solution to these ills.

In part, the imperative to avoid negativity is also a moral choice to help others—one's negativity, like all influences in Rwanda, is thought to be contagious (Fujii 2009), and it can drag down one's fellows. I noticed that if Butare residents make too much of problems thought to be too common to remark on (for example the death of a relative, employment problems, or illnesses), others subtly sanction this "negative" talk with the response, *c'est comme ça la vie* (that's how life is) or its closest equivalent in Kinyarwanda, *wihangane* (try to bear/withstand it). These responses are directed at downplaying the complaint of the speaker, because the events of the civil war and genocide mean that everyone must assume that their interlocutors also have their own problems and ongoing forms of suffering to confront, so the moral choice is not to burden anyone else with "negative" talk. But rather than simply suppressing one's suffering to spare other people, positive thinking and cultivating an upbeat outlook are ways by which the emergent middle class can solidify its position at the vanguard of the emergence of the "New Rwanda." Indeed, by cultivating a positive attitude about Rwanda's future and their roles in it, Butare residents assert their belonging in the wildly popular global movement to prosperity through self-help and positive thinking. In February 2009, I watched President Kagame give a speech on Rwanda Television in which he encouraged the population to smile more, especially when they see foreign tourists, as a way of changing the public image of the country. A 2015 networking meeting in London, England hosted by the Business Council for Africa to encourage foreign investment in Rwanda was entitled "Rwanda: Land of a Thousand Hills and a Million Smiles." It is this kind of upbeat outlook on Rwanda and its future that shapes and expresses emergent post-genocide "structures of feeling" (Williams 1977)—inchoate yet patterned cultural schemas (Illouz 2008: 156) that in Butare meld positive thinking, enterprising ambition, creativity, modern self-making, and possibilities for a peaceful nation.

While the meaning of "positive thinking" as an ideal or a practice is by no means singular, I mean mental strategies directed toward envisioning exclusively good outcomes in one's life and to overcoming or preventing unpleasant thoughts (Youll and Meekosha 2011: 28), and a general upbeat attitude to the possibilities that the future holds. In practical terms in Butare, this meant maintaining an optimistic outlook in spite of any and all hardships, adversity, or forms of suffering. I was struck during my 2008, 2009, and especially my 2014 fieldwork when I found myself face to face with signs of the dubious, yet profoundly pervasive Euro-American idea that "positive thinking" is a transformative force for success at work and in one's personal life (Ehrenreich 2009). For example, when wandering through the streets of Rwandan towns, I encountered elementary schools with bright hand-painted signs announcing their decidedly "upbeat" names: "Bright Happy Nation Academy" or "Bright Generation School."

One of the most robust sources of ideas about positive thinking in Rwanda comes from none other than President Kagame himself. I quote from his speeches, all of which are collected and archived on his website, paulkagame.com, not to suggest that Rwandans uncritically absorb and reproduce his rhetoric. Rather, I suggest that like all languages of power, Kagame's development rhetoric is a resource on which social actors can draw; it is part of what Illouz (2008: 164) calls "publicly available repertoires to frame languages of selfhood and individualism." Kagame's speeches and his Twitter feed, on which he enjoys over a million followers at the time of writing, are studies in the convergence of the North American obsession with positive thinking and enterprise culture with the imperative to build a "New Rwanda" and a "New Rwandan."[7]

> When the government mobilizes resources and shares them with its citizens— among them students—and when they graduate, if they have learnt well ... if they have good ideas and a positive mindset, they do not wish to be on government's assistance. Instead they help the government to lift others who are still lagging behind ... Technology and technical skills are universally known to be the key to development. Scientists among you have to give us solutions we should depend on. They should come up with solutions of innovation leading to entrepreneurship that can allow an individual to develop themselves [sic] and develop others, which also allows the country to prosper. We should not be queuing holding a basket waiting for people to drop aid into it. That's not how we will achieve self-reliance; we cannot live carrying a basket for other people to drop aid into. (Kagame 2015)

> You should be proud of yourselves for being who you are. Never ever want to be somebody else; be yourself and only improve yourself so that you can be better. Many of you have gone traveled wide [sic]; America, Europe or Asia, and you have seen and learnt various things, there is a lot to learn out there. But you don't learn to turn into somebody else. You learn to be a better person. Even Rwanda as a nation we want to learn and be inspired by others but most importantly we want to be a better Rwanda, not another nation. (Kagame 2012a)

The following posts come from President Kagame's Twitter feed in 2015:

Paul Kagame @PaulKagame

Feb 1
Happy Heroes Day. We celebrate #IntwarizuRwanda,[8] the resilience of the #Rwandan Spirit & hard work of Rwandans in our country's transformation

Mar 25
#Rwanda's transformation is about everyone having a stake & believing change is up to us

Apr 7
We remember&honour [sic] the millions of lives lost, with utter determination to confront our challenges as we build a dignified nation! #Kwibuka21

The ideas and imperatives expressed here are in no way unique to the Rwandan president. On the contrary, they are expressions of the idea that psychologist Erik Erikson popularized in the 1950s, namely the upbeat, optimistic notion that "every crisis provided the opportunity for the self to grow and develop mastery over the world" (Illouz 2008: 158). Indeed, that crisis has brought opportunity is a fundamental feature of Kagame's public addresses as he exalts the population to seize the opportunities afforded by the national project of making the "New Rwanda." The question is, how do these ideas and emergent structures of feeling find expression in "micropractices" of telling stories, evaluating one's own and others' conduct, and making sense of the choices and actions others take (Illouz 2008: 156)? In what ways do Butare residents make use of, challenge, or undermine them?

Positive Thinking, Creativity, and Entrepreneurship

With respect to work, livelihoods, and entrepreneurial ventures, Butare residents link the therapeutic imperative to "be positive" to another equally valued quality of modern, prosperous, autonomous selves, namely "creativity." A conversation in the spring of 2009 with Léon, Simbi, and David—a fourth-year agronomy student and acquaintance of Léon's— yielded just this kind of association. Seated around a table sharing drinks in the garden of Léon's restaurant, we were discussing the prospects for youth employment in Rwanda. Ever the anthropologist, I was trying to gently suggest that Rwandan youth faced structural barriers to stable, lucrative employment—a perspective to which I expected the perennially unemployed Simbi to be sympathetic. While these men gave a cursory acknowledgment to the challenges facing young people—urban and rural—in their search for stability and adulthood, they quickly insisted that a focus on those barriers does no good because it only keeps a person focused on the negative things in life. In a polemic that (Rwanda-specific references notwithstanding) might have been lifted directly from the pages of Norman Vincent Peale's ([1956] 2012) landmark contribution to the self-help genre, *The Power of Positive Thinking*, David explained:

> Our problem in Rwanda is that people are not sufficiently creative. The idea that original research happens at the university—*c'est une comédie*. Rwandans don't do research. Research means innovation, and Rwandans only stick to their old ways—old ways of cultivating, ways of raising animals. Nothing changes. Ideas are not produced here—they come from outside. And have you ever heard of a Rwandan writing a novel? What would they write about? Instead they read books from elsewhere. Even with the genocide, they let outsiders monopolize the writing about it, and because they are not creative, they think they have nothing to contribute. Creativity—it's about figuring out what *you* can contribute—your special skills—which no one else has. But Rwandans are too stuck in negativity. Negative thinking—it prevents creative thought. In order to be creative, to figure out how you can start something of

your own, you first have to find your positive energy. If you can create that positive energy in yourself, then you will get an idea, you'll figure out your special skills, and you'll find a way to use them to progress [*évoluer*]. (Butare, May 2009)

Here, David provides a textbook example of how urban dwellers disparage the majority as "ignorant," "stubbornly set in their ways," and "not able to cope or adapt to a new situation" (Sommers 2012: 78). However, unlike most officials who limit their criticisms to rural Rwandans, David accused even his fellow *universitaires* (academics) of lacking innovative, creative capacities. As he spoke, Simbi and Léon nodded approvingly and emitted the characteristically Rwandan non-verbal vocalization of agreement, "Ehhhhh." Just as Peale ([1956] 2012: 15) wrote that negative people lack self-confidence and that positive thinking stimulates "creative attitudes," so David, Léon, and Simbi expressed faith in the linkage between "positive energy" and self-development for creative entrepreneurial ventures. Given that positive thinking as a movement was born of American pop psychology (Ehrenreich 2009; Illouz 2008), and given that most Americans (or at least the ones to whom Rwandans are exposed) are infinitely wealthier than the average Rwandan, it is perhaps no surprise that for some Rwandans, positive and creative energy seem to be the mystical factors that spell the difference between economic success and failure.

In June 2014, Léon insisted on taking me on a tour to visit the various "projects" that constituted LéoMax Initiative Promotion. The main LéoMax office is a single room of no more than six by seven feet in which he has crammed a desk for himself and two tiny tables on which precariously perch two obsolete computer terminals used by his two young female assistants. He explained that he is trying to save on overhead costs to maximize the inputs available for his projects. The LéoMax enterprise consists of the restaurant that he runs with Claire, a small bakery that was at the time of my fieldwork still under construction in a rural district about forty-five minutes from Butare, and a training center located in nearby Save for youth aspiring to become domestic workers. Léon showed me the project study he had written as a recruitment tool for potential investors (I suspect that he showed me this document for that same reason). More a manifesto on how to promote entrepreneurship and personal development among the poor than a detailed study of domestic workers' problems, the document first enumerates the challenges they face, including inability to cook an edible meal or wash clothes properly, risk of abuse (physical, verbal, and sexual) from their employers, lack of labor laws for informal workers, injuries due to poor kitchen safety training, and social isolation. It then becomes apparent that Léon's training center and his solution to overcoming the "misery" of domestic workers lies in the combination of teaching practical housekeeping skills with instilling entrepreneurial qualities into his disciples. "I found my creative force," he explained with a proud smile when I asked why he had chosen to train domestic workers.

> Now I feel a responsibility to help the most vulnerable, the ones who don't have the capacities to make a life for themselves without help from someone else. What we have to remember is that you cannot give what you don't have. And domestic workers face so many problems because their employers ask of them things they aren't capable of doing. They don't know how to do laundry properly or how to care for the children—accidents happen sometimes because of their poor knowledge. That's what we do here—we give them competencies so that they can make contented lives, even in this modest kind of work. (Gisagara, June 2014)

When I visited the training center with Léon in June 2014, it was fully operational, and a class of roughly thirty youth was in session—one that Léon awkwardly interrupted in order to introduce me to the students. When we arrived, Léon showed me around the facilities, which included a large and tidily kept outdoor kitchen and laundry facility where youth were taught to cook and do washing, and a sparsely furnished model house where they practiced sweeping, bed making, and other tasks. He explained that it was through this facility that he aimed to fulfill the objectives outlined in his study/manifesto to better the lives of domestic workers. While it is difficult sometimes to trace precisely where ideas come from, Léon's study indicates a direct linkage between Rwandan entrepreneurial ambitions, self-making, and the influential ideas of psychologist Abraham Maslow, who seamlessly linked the full development of the self with the capacity for creativity (Illouz 2008: 160–61; Maslow 1993). Léon articulated it in the following way in his study/manifesto:[9]

> We aim to help those who work in domestic service find their place in society according to the following objectives:
> – Promote the autonomy of domestic workers and give them basic training according to their needs and to promote their self-esteem
> – Provide professional training (for a domestic life)
> – Form cooperatives for domestic workers to promote a vision of hard work in the whole country of Rwanda
> … Specific measures must be taken with a view to improve work, productivity, and conditions of [domestic] work in the informal economy, to facilitate its integration into the formal economy, and to encourage entrepreneurship … To take action against poverty, we must climb, step by step, the pyramid of Maslow![10] We need to take into account the personal situation [of each

domestic worker], the state of her environment, and her own motivations for building her own development project [i.e. the worker is her own development project]. By this activity, she will acquire social ties, a productive role recognized by her village and useful to all inhabitants of this village. She will attain social recognition, dignity next to her peers. In this way, she will have climbed three steps of [Maslow's] pyramid—one action for three steps [*sic*]! ... Motivation is the keyword for escaping poverty; the interior desire to climb the steps of Maslow's pyramid. If we also bring to this effort creativity, the cocktail will galvanize [*dynamiser*] the poor person to choose the best path to get out of poverty: his project will be born! (My translation from the original French)

Léon's approach to assisting vulnerable youth is shot through with the tendency of urban elites to view rural youth as those who must be "guided, shaped, led, influenced, directed, and persuaded" (Sommers 2012: 81). Indeed, he positions himself as just the kind of benevolent, yet paternalistic expert required to direct youth to better lives. Strikingly, Léon seeks to inject an entrepreneurial ethic into those engaged in the most menial form of "working for others." In drawing on psychologist Abraham Maslow's (1943) "hierarchy of needs," Léon expresses the idea so fundamental to modern entrepreneurial culture that "self-actualization" is a fundamental human necessity (Illouz 2008: 160–61). Léon's aim, in teaching entrepreneurial skills to low-status workers, is to produce capacities for self-development in the service of not only economic, but also therapeutic interventions in the lives of the rural poor. Following Maslow, Léon takes stock of the potential of rural youth, and he seeks to assist them in "actualizing" that potential. He assesses the potential of rural youth as inherently limited compared to those of educated urban dwellers, and his aim is not to help them transcend their low-status positions, but rather to fill them to the best of their abilities in order to achieve self-respect. Implicit in his endeavor is a functionalist view of inequality, in which the modern division of labor requires both high- and low-skill members of the workforce (Davis and Moore 1945). The trouble is, if in the end the domestic worker fails to find dignity in her work, she only has herself to blame, because she did not complete the process of "self-actualization." Léon seeks to produce entrepreneurial domestic workers capable of asserting their special training, experience, and pride in their work. Just as largesse and generosity are thought to be social benefits of enterprise culture (Heelas and Morris 1992: 9), so Léon's paternalism paradoxically smuggles a dependent, clientelistic relationship back into the project of instilling autonomy in vulnerable populations, as he aims to demonstrate the power of his positive thinking to transform not only his own life but also the lives of others.

The Struggle to "Remain Positive"

Even as positive thinking grows into a veritable moral duty in post-genocide social life, Butare residents simultaneously acknowledge that an upbeat orientation to hardship is by no means effortless. Indeed, one must work hard to cultivate the ability to remain positive in the face of difficulty and to harness that power to unleash one's creative force. And as vigilant as one tries to be about remaining positive, there are slips and lapses that betray the strain of these post-genocide demands on the self. Even as I spent many an hour over the years listening to Simbi wax philosophical about the spiritual benefits of Tai Chi and meditation to build inner strength and "positive energy," in his darker moments he confessed to feeling terribly discouraged, powerless, and ineffective. In July 2014, Simbi was in a period of particular despair. I suspect this is because I had been employing him as a research assistant, and my imminent departure spelled a return to unemployment. As we shared a meal at the end of a long workday, he expressed his worries and the challenges of staying positive.

> I'm growing afraid of my instability lately. You know that I say I'm not afraid of anything, but this is really bothering me. It's gotten so bad that I've started to feel imprisoned by it. I freeze up when I think about finding a job—even jobs I'm trained to do. I lock myself in the bathroom and I ask myself why I'm even doing this at all. I get very depressed when I think about my instability. I am even willing to work for free for a while if it would turn into something. I have an associate with several small businesses who keeps telling me I should work with him. I keep trying to arrange meetings to discuss it with him, but he keeps putting me off. And the worst part is, he keeps asking for my input on how to improve his business—it's like he wants my expertise without having to pay for it. If he can't afford to pay me right now, that's ok. I'd still work with him if we could come to an agreement that would benefit me in the future. I've had so much rejection that I hate the thought of asking someone else for a job. I need encouragement, support. You know, I have *ideas*. If I could just work for someone for a couple of years until I have money to start something… (Butare, July 2014)

Simbi's sense of desperation in this moment poignantly contrasts with his usual performance of "modern flaws" and an unbreakable positive outlook. Indeed, he expresses a willingness to temporarily submit to exploitative, uncompensated work if it would let him eventually build the means to "start something up."

Similarly, I listened as Odette narrated the painstaking process of rebuilding her life for her surviving children after having lost most of her family in the genocide—a story that she always punctuated with the importance of finding a way to stay positive so that you do not remain "stuck" in negativity. Sitting one day in the grounds of the restaurant she runs, she pointed to all of the work that she had to do after 1994 to rebuild her business. "This whole building was barely intact after the genocide," she explained, gesturing to the largest structure on the property. "The *interahamwe* was using it then—for sleeping, for storage—I don't know what. But it was all but destroyed when I returned. I had to buy all new bricks because they'd been stolen to build houses for the killers." She continued:

> Even though I've rebuilt my business, the genocide, it still lives here. Up near the front gate, there was a roadblock set up [during the genocide]. They were stopping Tutsi there and they were killing victims. They were throwing the bodies down the slope to right where we are sitting now. I worry that someone is going to show up here someday and tell me there is a mass grave on this property. I worry about finding bones. [Sighs, pauses]. You know, Laura, sometimes I wonder why I bothered to rebuild after we lost everything. By chance, I was able to make my life again. I worked to start over, and I think I've done a lot to rebuild this country with all of the taxes I pay. And I do so even as it wasn't me who destroyed the country—it was the country that destroyed me! But sometimes I think, what is to stop them from coming to *me génocider* [commit genocide against me] again. But I suppose I did it because if you remain in your negative state, then the killers have won. I've heard them say it myself—they want to see us in misery and poverty. (Butare, March 2009)

In Odette's narrative, the struggle to remain positive emerges with devastating clarity, as she speaks about how the genocidal past threatens to insert itself into the present at any time—perhaps in the form of yet unexcavated mass graves, perhaps in the form of renewed violence at some indefinite point in the future. As Illouz (2008: 183) notes, privileged people may deploy these types of narratives to make claims about how being of the elite does not necessarily make life easy. In the Rwandan context in which educated urban dwellers seek grounding and belonging among their compatriots (see Chapter 3), it is perhaps no surprise that Odette asserts that her life is still a struggle. But her words also betray a sense of her own powerlessness. She says that "by chance" she was able to rebuild her life, which, perhaps in contrast to the pillars of "positive thinking," suggests a sense of fatalism and the idea that one's life outcomes are out of one's hands. As she explained, "People say I'm strong, they praise me for what I've been able to do. Maybe I have my strength, but I feel like I could lose it at any moment. Then what would I become? But I cannot think that way. Maybe I'm strong because I have no choice. What is the alternative?" (Butare, July 2008).

Like so many other Butare residents, Odette and Simbi check for signs that they are failing to live up to the demands of remaining positive—ones shaped not only by the post-genocide quest to become a new kind of self, but also in Odette's case a disciplined effort to ensure that killers do not "win" by miring her in the past. They engage in practices of what Ehrenreich calls self-monitoring in the quest to remain positive. As she writes, "emotions remain suspect and one's inner life must be subjected to relentless monitoring" (Ehrenreich 2009: 89). When slippages cast doubt upon the self, positive thinking—in part configured as a means to dignified work and realizing one's potential—becomes a form of work all its own (Ehrenreich 2009: 90).

Even as the imperative to be positive can be oppressive when one finds little about which to be positive, it also functions as one of the only forms of agency to which those who find themselves dependent, constrained, or haunted by the legacy of the genocide can lay claim. Simbi may not have control over his material conditions, but he does have control over how he feels about his predicament. He would emphatically assert that although he is *enfermé* (imprisoned) by unemployment and poor prospects, nothing can ever confine his spirit. In this way, positive thinking is a crucial form of agency available to Butare residents like Simbi who have fallen short of realizing modern, autonomous selfhood in their work lives and livelihoods. Similarly, Odette lost almost everything and everyone important to her in the genocide, and she still endures a great deal of hardship for it. But she nonetheless asserts that she will not remain mired in the negative thoughts that consumed her in the years immediately after 1994.

What all of this suggests is that the capacity to remain positive in the face of discouragement and adversity is *itself* a mark of the modern, peaceful self in Rwanda. Entrepreneurs, whether they succeed because of good connections, an existing sum of capital, or some mystical power to prosper through positive thinking, are remarkable precisely because they *exceed* Butare residents' expectations of "normal" capacities. They are exceptional in a world in which most urbanites can never achieve the goal of working for themselves. In this sense, *normal personhood* is precisely what prevents the majority from becoming self-sufficient entrepreneurs. A lack of entrepreneurial spirit is read as "typical" Rwandan adversity to risk, "backwardness and resistance to development" (Sommers 2012: 200). As Anthony Cohen (1992: 187) writes, in enterprise culture, individuality is only recognized in exceptional circumstances. On the one hand, a person can stand out for extraordinary achievement, as people like Léon strive to do with projects like his school for domestic workers. Parallel to Sennett and Cobb's (1972) classic argument on the hidden injuries of class, dignity and modern personhood in Butare depend on the capacity to stand out, to not be ordinary. One might protest that this linkage between personal dignity and the capacity to stand out is peculiar to a bounded, autonomous, Euro-American configuration of the person. However, it is precisely the rise of an urban, educated middle class in

Butare who embrace "enterprising selfhood" that has produced new standards for what it means to be valued—ones that rely on cultivating individuality. The sad irony is that with the rising value on forms of agency emergent from enterprise culture—helped along in no small part by President Kagame's incessant talk of hard work, autonomy, and personal responsibility (Ansoms 2011; Kagame 2015; Straus and Waldorf 2011)—from this perspective, those who fail to become autonomous or remain positive (which are, of course, inseparable) must then locate those failures within the self, not in the broader context of structural barriers to prosperity. The "tools of freedom" (in this case, positive thinking) "become the sources of indignity" (a failure to do so) (Sennett and Cobb 1972: 30).

On the other hand, according to Cohen (1992: 187), people might stand out because they deviate from "normal" expectations. Simbi—with his refusal to conform to the dictates of hierarchical workplaces and his eschewal of marriage—was perceived by townspeople and his own family members alike as stubbornly nonconformist. In response, Simbi tried to turn his obstinacy into a virtue by suggesting that his "modern flaws" prevented him from finding stable work or settling down. But without autonomy and self-sufficiency to back up his claims, the tragedy of Simbi's strategy for dignity is that he stands out for all the wrong reasons. And yet, even in the absence of economic self-sufficiency, his tenacious commitment to remaining positive in the face of discouraging lay-offs and chronic unemployment is the one way that he can still claim his autonomy. The person who can remain positive, even if s/he cannot achieve the markings of entrepreneurial success, can still claim a defiantly positive attitude even when faced with a future with no clear prospects. Hence, if Simbi asserts the claim to remain positive even as he sits by and watches others prosper, then he is asserting that, against the expectations of "normal personhood," there is something remarkable about him still. Unlike "normal" Rwandans, he will not become mired in jealousy—a problem that town residents say threatens the wellbeing of successful entrepreneurs in Butare.

The Perils of Success

To become remarkable, to work for oneself—these are not simply happy success stories in Butare. In June 2008, the town was abuzz with an incident in which a local businessman had gone missing. He owned a transportation company and a hotel in the town, and I was told that he had a favorable reputation because he had a light-hearted demeanor, and he treated everyone with respect, regardless of their socioeconomic position or occupation. The story went that he had gone to a meeting with associates in Gitarama, roughly halfway between Butare and Kigali. After that, he was not seen for two and a half weeks, at which point his body and that of his business partner were found in the Nyabarongo River. Speculation abounded, since this killing was evocative of the tossing of Tutsi bodies in the river during the genocide.[11] The victim was indeed Tutsi by heritage, so people wondered if it was not a grievance lingering from the genocide. Nonetheless, of the eight different people who debated with me what had happened, six were convinced that it was revenge for his entrepreneurial successes. "Why else would they have killed his business partner, too?" one person asked rhetorically.

Somewhat less severe in its consequences since no one was killed, Léon recounted to me an incident at his restaurant in 2008 that he interpreted as an attempt to cast a shadow over his business and generate rumors that it is a dangerous place where bad things happen. Three men were drinking together one evening in one of the small, enclosed hut-like structures in the restaurant garden. These huts are a typical feature of Rwandan *cabarets* that afford each party a measure of shelter from the elements and privacy from prying eyes. Two of the men had come together, Léon explained, and they invited the third man to join them in their hut since he was alone—a common practice among men in *cabarets*. They ordered numerous rounds of Primus, a local beer, and nothing seemed amiss for several hours. But then, at around 11pm when the servers were cleaning up for the night, they found the third man alone and unconscious on the floor of the hut. When he came to, he told the servers that the two men had drugged him and stolen his bicycle. When Léon heard about the incident the next day, he interpreted it as sabotage. He said that the two men were jealous of his success and wanted to make people afraid to come and drink there in the evenings. He even wondered if the third man who was discovered in the hut was in on the plot rather than a hapless victim caught in the wrong place at the wrong time. When Pauline heard what had happened, she too expressed concern as the property owner: "This is just like Rwandans, you know. They're treacherous. They see that you are doing well, that you are making a successful business, and they come after you. And you never know when they'll come. They pretend like everything is fine, like they are your friends. And then—pow! It's like in 1994. We never knew what they were planning, and then one day, that was it" (Butare, May 2008).

While in neither of these cases (or any other similar ones I heard of) was it ever certain that jealousy over the victims' success was what precipitated these incidents, what is significant is that this was the reasoning by which Butare residents explained them. It speaks to a genuine fear by entrepreneurs that their success will catch up with them in ways that they liken to the motivation behind the 1994 massacres—to level ethnic (or ethnically marked) social inequalities and right wrongs against the marginalized majority. However, when Butaréens *criticize* those who are suspected of going after the successful, they once again draw a line between themselves and the majority who have merely "normal" personal capacities—ones that lead them down what Butare residents say is the all-too-common path of jealousy and reprisal when faced with others' success. By criticizing alleged vigilantes, they set themselves apart as those who "belong" in Euro-American enterprise culture—the kinds of selves who are productive, focused, and capable of creative, positive thought and, crucially, peace.

In spite of the embrace of enterprise values that this chapter has drawn forth, it would be remiss of me to leave the reader with the impression that Butare residents have no critical distance from these ideas. Indeed, even as many of the stories they tell about themselves and their aspirations contain more than a touch of contempt for the rural poor, they are also keenly aware that the experiences of most Rwandans are painfully distant from the world of Butare's educated residents. Sometimes, the conditions in which rural Rwandans live excuse their inability to "stay positive" in the face of hardship. As Bernadette put it one morning in February 2008 as she prepared to travel to her rural natal hill for an uncle's funeral, "*la campagne, c'est la misère!* [the countryside is misery] You don't spend any more time there than you have to. You see *les pauvres* [the poor], and you know that there is nothing in the world that could change their lives." And as Charles explained on an excursion to visit his mother in rural Gikongoro:

> Do you see how people live in the hills? They have nothing here. Sometimes I really wonder about the idea that everyone can develop and succeed. There are barriers sometimes. It might be poverty, it might be politics. You know, I was quite nearly blocked from studying at university, because it was the old [Habyarimana] government. I was from the south, and back then, the government favored northerners for all of the seats at the university.[12] It didn't matter how well you scored. And now the government talks about guaranteed schooling for children, but most of those schools have no books. How can they grow under those conditions? We have a difficult history here in Rwanda, and there is a tendency for the rich to keep the poor in poverty. They want people below them, they want to know they're above the majority. They want to keep the poor running around like ants in their service. (June 2014)

As much as Butare residents express the values of enterprise culture in the stories they tell about themselves and others, in other moments they are also critical of those same values and imperatives because of their experience of what it means to live in a postcolonial society and the difficult legacies of structural inequality that this produces. What Charles expressed here might also be read as a response to a moral imperative to stay humble and show sympathy for the poor (see Chapters 2 and 3), but in either case, the criticism of enterprise values and the idea that everyone can and should pursue "self-actualization" still stands. Charles knows that he was only able to complete his post-secondary and graduate education because of the regime change after the 1994 genocide. Most important, he knows that his life could easily have turned out otherwise.

Conclusion

Work relations and work aspirations are socially and politically charged sites from which to understand contemporary practices of self-making in post-genocide Rwanda. While urban Rwandans do not simply adopt neoliberal values wholesale, the ways in which they use them tell a great deal about what kind of selves they aspire to be, especially when the question arises of how they can know that the violence will not happen again. In an altogether Smithian style, a social world of independently enterprising subjects is thought to be a formula for peace, because industriousness produces prosperity and quells jealousy. But beyond that (arguably dubious) formulation for forging a peaceful future in Rwanda, there is something profoundly appealing about the project of self-making through work and enterprise.

Rwanda's overwhelmingly Catholic population notwithstanding, the virtue that Butare residents attach to economic striving shares striking parallels with the Protestant work ethic (Weber [1905] 2002). The difference, however, is that Butaréens are not seeking confirmation of salvation in the next life as Weber's Protestants did. Rather, they seek confirmation of their very capacities for modern, peaceful selfhood. Indeed, envisioning the self as a project on which to work through economic endeavors and positive thinking inverts the logic of the longstanding Rwandan view of the person as always in the process of becoming. Whereas the relational self is always being built out of relations with others, the entrepreneurial self searches for *interior* sources of self-making and self-improvement. And where could the idea that the self is "still in the making" (Illouz 2008: 182) be more appealing than in a social world like post-genocide Rwanda? When people have endured such overwhelming losses, when they struggle to know themselves in the absence of others, when the obstacles to remaking one's life appear insurmountable, and when people wonder, will I ever be seen as anything other than a victim, a *génocidaire*, a Tutsi, or a Hutu, the idea that the self is fundamentally malleable, not yet complete, that one can be someone or something else, is profoundly alluring. Treating the self as a project powered by "positive energy," even when that project is stalled, is a way to set oneself apart as a modern, peaceful self—someone with capacities that exceed "normal personhood" and on whom hopes for the "New Rwanda" largely hang. They are the kinds of persons who embrace "the will to improve" (Li 2007), and who are all the more remarkable for doing so when the weight of the past and the demands of the present are as burdensome as they are in post-genocide Rwanda.

And yet, even as entrepreneurial strivings and self-making seem a radical break from patron–client bonds and exploitative employer–employee relations, the types of evaluations that people make of successful entrepreneurs and the low-income majority map eerily onto that ambiguously bounded locus of class/occupation/ethnic/rural-urban moral categories investigated in Chapter 2. That rural youth are characterized as in need of direction, leading, and guidance (Sommers 2012: 81) sounds hauntingly similar to the old colonial stereotype that Hutu desire a "strong and leading hand" (Lemarchand 1970: 43). That Odette and Charles can draw parallels between jealousy over economic success and the motivations behind the 1994 genocide (even as they would also be quick to draw clear qualitative and quantitative differences between them) nonetheless speaks to a worldview in which there is still something about ethnicity and the history of violence, about stereotypical Tutsi privilege and Hutu marginality, that shapes how Butare residents make sense of inequality and its social consequences. The next chapter elucidates how peace-building experts in Butare try to instill yet another set of transformations to the post-genocide Rwandan self, ones directed toward trying to ensure that violence will not happen again.

Notes

1. Simbi completed his university degree in 2005, when 42 percent of Rwandans aged 14–35 were unemployed (Ministry of Youth, Culture, and Sports 2005: 16), so it is perhaps no surprise that he has had difficulty finding a job. Anecdotally, however, Butare residents claim that he graduated at a time when there were few enough university graduates that anyone with a diploma could secure urban work. Whether this is true or not, it explains their blaming of Simbi for his condition rather than lack of job opportunities.
2. *The New Times* is the main English-language newspaper in Rwanda. It is known for its pro-RPF stance, and for this reason it is a useful source from which to glean state rhetoric on remaking Rwanda.
3. Officially, business income is taxed at 30 percent (Rwanda Revenue Authority, n.d.). This tax burden is enough to sink many a start-up venture, but small business owners also spoke of extra "lump sum" payments that the Rwanda Revenue Authority will collect without warning as part of a national imperative to decrease Rwanda's dependency on foreign aid.
4. Youth is a social rather than an absolute category (Clark-Kazak 2009), and in Rwanda, unmarried people up to their thirties can fall into this category if they have not achieved the cultural markers of adulthood, namely having married and had at least one child (Ministry of Youth, Culture, and Sports 2005).

5. To say that someone has "eaten" something is commonly recognized in Africanist ethnography as an idiom for something having been wasted. For one example, see Riesman 1977: 49, 91.

6. See also Booth 2001: 786; Langer 1991; Ricoeur 2004; Stover and Weinstein 2004; Theidon and Laplante 2007; Young 1993, 1998 for similar critiques.

7. As architect of the transition to English from French as the "elite" language of Rwanda, Kagame gave these speeches and made these Twitter posts in English.

8. Intwari z'u Rwanda means Heroes Day in Kinyarwanda.

9. I avoid providing a citation for this document, even as an unpublished manuscript, because "LéoMax" is a pseudonym, and the full title of the work reveals the real name of Léon's enterprise.

10. Maslow's (1943) hierarchy of needs is graphically represented in a pyramid of five levels. The most "basic" needs are at the bottom, and Maslow envisioned them as prerequisites for meeting "higher" needs. In this way, movement up the pyramid represents stages of personal growth. At the very bottom, the most basic needs are "physiological," including nourishment, shelter, air, and other requirements for human survival. On the second level are "safety" needs, meaning physical safety and personal security, mental and physical health, and basic financial security. Third on the hierarchy of needs are "love and belonging," which should come from kin, friends, colleagues, and members of social groups such as religious groups, civic, or professional organizations. Fourth on Maslow's pyramid is "esteem," meaning self-esteem and self-respect as well as respect for others. Finally, at the very top of the pyramid is "self-actualization," which refers to capacities for creativity, growth, and realizing one's personal potential.

11. During the 1994 genocide, bodies of Tutsi victims were famously thrown in this river, because the infamous genocide propagandist, Léon Mugesera, incited the Hutu population to send Tutsi "back" up the river to Ethiopia. This was an invocation of the well-known Hamitic hypothesis, which suggested that Tutsi were foreign invaders from Ethiopia who had conquered the Hutu population in the distant past.

12. Charles was referring to the regime of President Juvénal Habyarimana, which was famous for favoring Habyarimana's natal region of northern Rwanda, especially Gisenyi and Ruhengeri (Guichaoua 2005).

Chapter 5

MAKING PEACE BY REMAKING PERSONS

∽∾

The meeting room at the Groupe Scolaire in central Butare looked like it had been decorated for a party, but one that had long since come to an end. The bright green, blue, and yellow streamers in the colors of the Rwandan flag drooped and dangled loosely where the masking tape holding them in place had come free from the stained, off-white plaster walls. Twelve wooden tables had been pushed to the back of the room to make space for a semi-circle of twenty-four straight-backed wooden chairs that faced a single table at the front with four chairs behind it. Of those seats, nineteen were occupied by men and women each grasping worn bundles of paper—lists of goods that had been stolen or destroyed during the genocide, identity papers, and other relevant documents. The problem of unpaid goods is a consequence of the *gacaca* process in which perpetrators were sentenced to repay livestock, money, bicycles, corrugated metal roofing, and other goods that they took from their victims in 1994. The seven women present were all claimants seeking payment for goods owed to them. All wore the colorful wrap skirts paired with second-hand T-shirts typical of rural Rwandan women. Of the twelve men, all of whom were dressed in mismatched blazers and pants much too large for their slender frames, two were claimants, and the rest owed goods they had stolen in 1994. The room was unnervingly silent until Xavier, one of the meeting facilitators and the coordinator of the Kigali office of an organization I call the Association rwandaise pour la paix et la réconciliation (ARPR, Rwandan Association for Peace and Reconciliation[1]), joked that they were acting like they were waiting for a priest. He encouraged them to chat while we waited for officials from a governmental working group charged with the payment problem to arrive.

When Xavier convened the meeting, he began by asking each person to introduce her or himself and to state whether they were there to be paid or to pay. Xavier explained that his role was to facilitate payments, and he emphasized his impartial position. "I am on neither the side of payees nor payers," he assured the group. "To make people pay by force cannot foster peace. We seek payments through consent, not force, because otherwise there can be no coexistence." As Xavier spoke, a colleague of his filmed the meeting on his mobile phone; another snapped photos on an iPad.

> We know there are problems in your two groups [payers and payees], but you need to talk to each other to understand each other's problems. Some of you are asking, why have I not been paid? It has been twenty years. Others are asking, how can I pay when I have nothing to give? The most important thing is to seek the path to the positive. Look where you want to go and choose a path that will not hurt either party. We need to see both sides of the problem. That is why we are here today. (Butare, June 2014)

At this point, a flip chart was rolled out, and the participants were divided into small groups, each with a facilitator from ARPR, to discuss the obstacles to payment and to brainstorm solutions. The groups were not mixed—payers were grouped with payers, payees with other payees. After forty-five minutes, we all reconvened so they could share their results. Each group posted its chart paper on the wall, showing the responses they had written. Obstacles to payment included poverty, shame, refusal to pay on behalf of now-deceased family members, lack of will to pay, poor record keeping on debts, and fears that payment will not set things right with victims. Possible solutions included decreasing amounts owed, more education, and pooling resources to make payments. These solutions were articulated only in general terms, and at no point during the meeting did the facilitators call on payers to take action to settle their debts. In fact, the only money that changed hands was between the facilitators and the participants, who all received round-trip bus fare and a small payment to offset the missed day of work in their fields. In the end, Xavier announced that the solution must be to lobby the state to pay on behalf of debtors, which numerous audience members contested as unrealistic. But for Xavier, the main purpose of the meeting had been served. Each group had heard the other's point of view. The meeting, in other words, had aimed to build mutual understanding more than anything else. A shared meal in a small dining hall next to the meeting room at which mixed tables of payers and payees ate and talked together further convinced Xavier that good work had been accomplished that day.

This emphasis on mutual understanding emerged as a guiding framework for the work that civil society-based peace-building organizations like ARPR do in post-genocide Rwanda. What became apparent during my fieldwork was that the activities of these organizations were not directed toward effecting change at the level of political or legal reform. Rather, their mandate aimed at transformations in the capacities of "normal" persons through the encouragement of new forms of sociality and consensus building (de Lame 2005: 303; Doughty 2014; Ingelaere 2010: 53). In the case of the Groupe Scolaire meeting, the objective was to build agreement about the reasons for obstacles to payment. But there is a deeper purpose to these practices of manufacturing consensus and peace-building practice more generally. As the interviews and conversations in this chapter demonstrate, organization staff point to the shortcomings of *persons* as the conditions of possibility for political violence and other social problems from which they say the violence is inseparable, especially poverty. They captured these personal shortcomings with a term whose vagueness and polysemy are what make it a useful catchall: poor "mentality" [*mentalité*]. The basic—and virtually unquestioned— assumption in the world of peace building in Rwanda is that helping people overcome their "mentality problems" is the path to peace. Indeed, parallel to the discussion in Chapter 4 on self-making through work and entrepreneurship, peace-building organizations aim to produce a Rwandan person engaged in a different kind of self-development project. Here, the self must be worked on until it is capable of building agreement about the nature of conflicts *and* capable of withstanding "negative" influences and calls to violence in the future. One by one, these "mentality" transformations, peace builders say, are what will effect a new era of stability and prosperity for Rwanda.

Readers familiar with contemporary political rhetoric in Rwanda will remark that the language of changing "mentalities" thoroughly expresses the core of RPF development discourse and its acutely controversial unity and reconciliation effort (Pottier 2002; Thomson 2013). It is a statement par excellence of the onus that the RPF places on individuals to do their part for the new, "improved" Rwanda (e.g. Kagame 2015), one shot through with the RPF's open contempt for the peasantry, whom peace builders principally target for mentality transformations. Peace building (*la construction de la paix*) and reconciliation are words that staff used as synonyms, and so I do the same. The debates are vast and nuanced on the meaning of "reconciliation," how or whether it is possible in societies divided by violent pasts, or if it is even desirable to those who live in the wake of violence (Clark 2008; Gibson 2004; Minow 1998; Pankhurst 1999; Parent 2010; Sarkin 2001; Shaw 2007; Wilson 2001). In the context of Rwanda, debates on reconciliation pivot primarily around whether the state unity campaign is a good-faith effort to mend social relations or a politically convenient strategy of silencing political dissent (Buckley-Zistel 2006; Eltringham 2004; Thomson 2013; Zorbas 2009). Scholars have also pondered what measures might be taken—either by state agencies or non-state actors—to better effect post-genocide reconciliation in Rwanda (Clark 2010; Zorbas 2004).

My aim in this chapter is to develop an ethnographic perspective on everyday peace-building practices. "Peace," from an anthropological perspective, is a difficult category (Malkki 2015: 92) in that it relies on a view of harmony as the "normal" state of society. In Rwanda, the significance of reconciliation and peace building is that they are open, amorphous signifiers (Zorbas 2009: 128). My interest lies in how civil society-level peace-building organizations, whose moral authority rests on direct, regular contact with the population, make use of these inherently flexible terms. The linkage between changing mentalities and making peace points precisely to the core issues surrounding personhood and the moral basis of post-genocide social belonging. In this chapter, I argue that peace-building practice seeks to transform the basis of "normal" Rwandan personhood. Indeed, changing "mentalities" is a matter of changing the capacities that normal persons should have in the post-conflict moment—especially capacities for resisting calls to commit violence. When the architects of peace building locate the causes of the genocide in the shortcomings of persons, they also locate possibilities for peace in the transformative power of therapeutic interventions to promote self-mastery, openness, and empathy. However, the logic of these interventions in the end gives rise to old and new forms of social boundary production and accusations of ill-gotten gains against local peace-building industry insiders.

Portraits of Two Rwandan Peace-Building Organizations

What drew me to investigate the workings of peace building in Butare in 2014 was the observation during my 2008–2009 fieldwork that many of my research participants were connected to these organizations, whether as staff, disciples, collaborators, or resistors to their teachings. Jean-Claude, the student who appeared in Chapter 2, was working for ARPR when I met him, and Simbi had done some work for the same organization. Charles has presented research talks to ARPR staff members, and they occasionally cite his ideas. Meanwhile, genocide survivors, like Odette and Rose, debated the virtues and shortcomings of their interventions and sometimes acted as reluctant participants in or denouncers of their work. Organization staff members were acquainted with many of my NUR contacts and attended conferences that the university organized. Hence, these organizations seemed to have a presence in the lives of many of the Butare residents I had been working with over the years.

The fieldwork I undertook with peace-building organizations aimed to get at the questions of what one does in practical, everyday terms when one is "building peace," and what meanings and justifications peace-building organization personnel give to their work. My aim was to investigate the range of activities that fell under the rubric of peace building and how disparate, perhaps even contradictory threads of post-genocide reconciliation interventions might expose cracks in the RPF's unified veneer (cf. Abrams 1988). There are many different types of organizations in Rwanda that work under the broad rubric of "peace building," but I focused on those conceived and founded by Rwandans rather than international NGOs. While these local organizations' guiding ideas are drawn from a range of Rwandan and Euro-American knowledge systems, I was interested in how Rwandans put those diverse ideas to work in practical contexts.

I initially set out to begin my research on peace building with a single organization, one that I call the Institut pour la construction de la paix durable (ICPD, Institute for Sustainable Peace Building). It was founded in 2001 at a moment when staff explained there was a growing need for peace-building expertise in Rwanda. It not only conducts community-level peace-building activities, but also trains peace-building personnel through a number of certificate programs. The central office is located in Kigali, but it has smaller satellite offices in other towns, including Gitarama and Butare. ICPD is considered a state organization, but it depends primarily for its funds on a European NGO. Nonetheless, an organ of the Rwandan state is responsible for channeling those funds to ICPD. Staff complained that this state broker was responsible for their financial woes, because the firm control it maintains on the purse strings prevented them from pursuing their agendas autonomously. During my fieldwork, ICPD was a struggling organization. Its Butare office is housed in a spacious state building, but it has fallen into disrepair. A rusted sign on the front lawn announces the presence of the organization, and a dilapidated chain link fence surrounds the property. Inside, offices contain a hodgepodge of worn tables, chairs, and desks. Panes of glass are missing in some of the windows, so during the torrential downpours of the wet season, rain pools on the cracked concrete floor. Of the three computers in the office, only one had a reliable internet connection. The computers were virus-ridden and regularly malfunctioned; coaxing a technician in to work on them was one of the main tasks that preoccupied the office support staff. The employment contracts of the support staff had also been reduced from six months to three shortly before my arrival, and new administrative problems were plaguing the office. In particular, ICPD's parent organization cut off the institutional email addresses of secretarial staff at the end of each three-month contract. Even though most staff members were simply rolled into a new three-month term, they still had to personally visit the state office of their parent organization to get their email addresses reinstated. Staff members were well aware of their "organizational disorder." Internal ICPD documents frequently cited limited staff and internet problems as key challenges facing the organization. Once in June 2014, the office was even left unlocked overnight, because the last staff member to leave was not provided with a key. That nothing was stolen might have been a happy accident, but it may also speak to the low value and obsolescence of most of ICPD's equipment.

Upon arrival at ICPD in the spring of 2014, staff warned me that their organization is very small, so I may have difficulty learning much of anything. In part, I wondered if this was not a strategy of keeping me at arm's length and trying to convince me that there was not much about their work that was worthy of my interest. While ICPD proved to be a fruitful site of study *because* it was a struggling organization, high rates of office absenteeism did emerge as an obstacle roughly a month into my fieldwork. Staff complained that the state does not pay sufficient wages on which to support families, and so most employees sought out private contracts on the side to round out their livelihoods. The practical result was that, at both the Kigali and Butare offices, it was often only the receptionist who was present. Jackie, the Butare receptionist and a new mother in her late twenties, often spent her days reading parenting advice online to pass the time. On especially quiet days, I would become the de facto receptionist when she would announce that she was popping into town to do an errand. If people came looking for her, she advised me to give them her mobile number. Needless to say, it is hard to do ethnographic fieldwork when the researcher is the sole occupant of the field site.

To supplement my work at ICPD, I contacted another organization, the aforementioned Association rwandaise pour la paix et la réconciliation (ARPR), founded in 1997. A true civil society organization with no ties to state organs, its donors are roughly an even split between secular and faith-based European NGOs. While ARPR is not a religious organization, staff members were adamant that they are "believers" (*croyants*), which is to be expected given the overwhelmingly Catholic population of Rwanda. Most ARPR personnel were Catholic, but two practiced Pentecostalism. Nonetheless, prayer is not a part of ARPR's teachings, and the organization does not explicitly ground its approach in any faith.

I had loose ties to ARPR, because of Simbi's brief employment at its Kigali office for a time in 2009. ARPR also has an office in Butare, and this is where I primarily worked in 2014. The Butare office is easy to miss; it is located in a house converted to an office in a quiet residential neighborhood. ARPR's office also shows signs of disrepair, including shredded window screens, peeling paint, flickering fluorescent lighting, and a sewage problem that necessitated tearing up the front lawn halfway through my stay. Nonetheless, in contrast to the ICPD offices, ARPR's offices were lively and bustling. Their director, Olivier—a charismatic man in his early forties—made it his mission to ensure that ARPR had a reputation as a "dynamic" organization.

While there are two spacious, but sparsely furnished private offices occupied by Olivier and the vice-director, Tharcisse, the central common office space is small and cramped. It houses the receptionist's desk in one corner, and the rest of the room is full of chairs, benches, and storage boxes that are haphazardly arranged around a worn wooden table that dominates the room. This table functions as a gathering, meeting, and work space, which lends a buzz to the atmosphere in contrast to ICPD's large, yet largely uninhabited space. ARPR's office walls are cluttered with awards and certificates for its peace-building accomplishments. Framed photo collages commemorate ARPR events and ceremonies. The organization's founder—a man named Jean-Paul whom I never met and who was living abroad at the time of my fieldwork—is pictured prominently. One image in particular stood out to me in which his photo is superimposed onto an ethereal cloud motif. Staff spoke of him as a spiritual leader, not simply as an employer. It was common for them to defer to his knowledge of the organization when I asked if I could interview them about their perspectives on their work. A typical remark came from Alphonse, a yoga instructor employed by ARPR, when I asked him to sit down with me to discuss his work: "Have you met our founder, Jean-Paul? If only you could speak to him—then you would truly understand the ideas and the force of what ARPR does!" (Butare, June 2014).

In spite of their marked differences, the objectives of ICPD and ARPR are much the same. The central focus of both organizations' community peace-building activities is the formation of reconciliation associations known as *groupes de rapprochement* or *groupes mixtes*, "mixed" in the sense of comprised of Tutsi genocide survivors and convicted and released Hutu perpetrators. When ICPD or ARPR staff talk about peace building or reconciliation work, they mean the establishment and education [*formation*] of these groups. Organizations seek to bring survivors together in these *groupes* with the same perpetrators who harmed them. This approach is in part a response to the patterns of the massacres in 1994 in which local authorities called on people to attack the neighbors in their midst (Fujii 2009), and it is also a crucial part of organizations' objectives of building personal capacities for peace among those who are bitterly divided. At the time of my fieldwork, ICPD was working with eight *groupes*, and ARPR had fifteen in its charge. They are based throughout the country and almost always in rural areas, since peace-building practice does not challenge general Rwandan elite attitudes toward rural people that range from paternalism to contempt (Thomson 2013). The assumption is that the rural peasantry is "uneducated" about peace and needs the most guidance to overcome their "mentality" problems (an idea that is by no means intuitive, since those who planned and oversaw the massacres in 1994 were the educated elite rather than ordinary rural people). Moreover, because of scarce land and high population density, rural people are thought to have the least choice about living next door to their foes, so organizations frame the work of peace building as especially pressing in the hills.

The principal conceptual pillars on which these organizations base their work with *groupes de rapprochement* are "open dialogue," "mutual understanding," "education," and in the case of ARPR, "self-confidence" and "non-exclusion." They draw on the North American therapeutic ethos in which open dialogue, communication, and empathy are the basis of desirable forms of sociality (Illouz 2008: 88). The defining quality of peace building in ICPD and ARPR is a consensus-building model (cf. Doughty 2014) in which the objective is less forgiveness or dispute resolution than building mutual understanding between survivors and perpetrators. Both organizations work to settle cases of unpaid goods stolen or destroyed during the 1994 genocide. However, as I described in the opening vignette of this chapter, "settling" cases is usually not a matter of brokering repayment because most perpetrators lack the financial wherewithal to do so. Rather, it means building mutual understanding between the victim and the perpetrator, or reaching consensus about why the perpetrator is justified in claiming inability to pay and why the victim is justified in seeking reparations. Peace builders explain this practice on the basis that mediation and consensus are inherent to Rwandan culture—capacities for consensus being upheld as more "civilized" than capacities for conflict (Doughty 2014: 783–84, 788). Further, to foster consensus is to make strides to return to the idealized precolonial past of official RPF histories (see Pottier 2002). The glaring paradox is that peace builders take most Rwandans to be *incapable* of the mutual understanding on which consensus is built. Rather than an inherent, shared feature of Rwandan sociality, achieving consensus requires the expertise and guidance of trained staff. Building peace is about building capacities in *groupe* members for mutual understanding rather than conflict, which raises the question, just who is staking a claim to be the guardians of "Rwandan culture" and its inherent consensus-building attributes?

Upon formation, each *groupe* is provided with start-up funds ranging from 100,000 RWF to 500,000 RWF (roughly US$145 to roughly US$725) to undertake a collective project. The options are either cultivating common fields or raising livestock such as pigs or goats together. The purpose of these projects is twofold: it gives survivors and perpetrators a way to improve their livelihoods, and the thinking is that collaborative work will build trust, mutual confidence, and reconciliation. As Julie, the de facto head of the Kigali ICPD office explained:

We bring together a type of association aimed at improving everyday life, but after a certain amount of time, we start to see a social impact. For example, there were women who are genocide widows; they were unhappy—they were without life [*sans vie*]. But after bringing them together [with former perpetrators], after providing them with training sessions, after some time those women began to see that they could do something in society; they could produce something. They could make money. But before [the association was created] it was not like that. The association gave them a way to create new relations of mutual confidence and mistrust began to decline. (Butare, June 2014)

Julie framed the act of joining a *groupe* as a path to personal growth, prosperity, and the mending of social relations. But beneath these manifest objectives of reconciliation and mutual livelihood improvements, I contend that peace-building practices are ultimately directed toward changing persons. At issue is how ARPR and ICPD understand the legacy of the 1994 genocide and the obstacles to building peace and stability in post-genocide Rwanda.

Political Conflict and Peace Building: Personal Trouble or Public Issue?

When C. Wright Mills (1959) wrote that personal troubles are public issues, he wanted to demonstrate the power of sociological analysis for making connections between personal biographies and the broader social forces that shape them. In the case of peace building, however, the dynamic is turned on its head: the difficulties Rwandans experience in the post-genocide period are configured as first and foremost *personal*, and their resolution at that level is thought to bring about positive effects at the level of public issues—here, "peace" and the making of the New Rwanda. ARPR and ICPD combine the "naturally Rwandan" propensity for consensus (Doughty 2014; see also de Lame 2004: 300) with another set of powerful, globally appealing solutions to the burdens of living in the wake of genocide. They have taken up what Pupavac (2004: 149–50) calls "an Anglo-American therapeutic ethos," one that sees emotional rehabilitation and personal transformation as the solutions to the distress left behind by violence and as the building blocks for more peaceful futures (see also Neocleous 2012). As Rieff (1966: 13) writes, the "triumph of the therapeutic" lies in a framing of social problems in which what is mainly at stake is a "manipulatable sense of wellbeing." The public issues that ARPR and ICPD say are intertwined with the legacy of the genocide—from socioeconomic inequality, to land conflicts, to access to education, to joblessness, to ongoing interethnic enmity (Newbury 2011; Sommers 2012)—are configured as personal troubles produced by emotional dysfunctionalism and individual shortcomings (Pupavac 2004: 150). Resolving these personal troubles is as preventative as it is corrective in the logic of peace building in Rwanda. Organization rhetoric is shot through with the emergent discourse of "resilience" (ARPR training manual, n.d.).[2] It aims to make persons who can both find the wherewithal to build relations with former enemies and resist future calls to violence. Conversations and interviews with staff as well as their training literature indicate that they see emotional states of hopelessness, vengeance, and jealousy as the main obstacles to building peace and resisting calls to future violence. Indeed, they see redressing feelings of vengeance or distress in victims and changing the "mentality" of former perpetrators as essentially the same activity—both rely on a transformation of the self. For example, a training brochure from ARPR frames peace building as a matter of building "self-confidence," "self-mastery," and an ethic of openness, empathy, and acceptance. It explains:

> The person who has achieved "inner power" knows how to reject negative forces. This is why she sees the good in those around her. Her relations are compassionate and based on empathy. The man or the woman who achieves "inner power" no longer knows the logic of war; they do not fight or struggle anymore, and instead they dance their way through life ... They can deflect negative energy and transform forces of destruction into forces of life. They can exist in a context in which violence is all around them but without being contaminated by it and without losing their initiative for good thought and action. (ARPR training manual, n.d., my translation from the original French)

The ideas contained in ARPR's peace-building approach sound remarkably like the understandings of power and self-mastery that come out of psychological approaches to wellbeing and conflict management. As Illouz writes, "for psychologists 'real' power is established precisely by not engaging in power struggles and by keeping one's emotions in check ... Not reacting becomes the mark of self-control, which in turn signals a hidden and subtle psychological power that can in fact bypass hierarchical status and power" (Illouz 2008: 83). And just like this, ARPR says that the person who is capable of peace is one who no longer engages in struggles, who is capable of not reacting to conflict, and who can transform "negative energy" into "forces of life" (ARPR training manual, n.d.). Crucially, it is a person who is capable of withstanding the "contaminating" influence (Fujii 2009) of violence that ARPR seeks to produce.

With respect to the psychologization of war making and peace making, ICPD and ARPR are not unique. Globally speaking, there is a long tradition of peace-building practices zeroing in on the individual as a site of transformation (Ilcan and Phillips 2006). Vanessa Pupavac (2004) traces a decades-long history of therapeutic interventions aimed at the level of the individual in international conflict management and peace-building processes. She argues that the psychologization of conflict takes as a fundamental assumption that people who commit violence are driven by emotion rather than reason (Pupavac 2004: 152). She shows that these approaches have their roots in 1960s studies in the United States that aimed to understand how "frustration" and "low self-esteem" of disaffected, disenfranchised populations are linked to the potential for violent action. Summerfield (1999) echoes Pupavac's critical approach to therapeutic conflict management interventions in his critique of the idea that war and political conflict are, more than anything, mental health emergencies.

ARPR's and ICPD's work bears a particular expression of these guiding ideas of global peace-building agendas in the Rwandan context. It is important to note that not only peace-building personnel purvey the idea that the suffering born of legacies of violence is a personal trouble rather than a public issue. Genocide survivors, too, see something attractive in the idea that they can—in contravention to their experience of powerlessness and victimization in 1994—assert control over their past and possibilities for their futures. As Donata, a middle-aged genocide survivor in Butare explained:

> After the genocide, *mon Dieu*, I simply did not know how I would go on. And for years, I guess I didn't. I couldn't get out of bed. We had nothing. People used to bring me things—food, clothing—because I still had my two surviving sons to care for, but I couldn't do it myself. And then I realized that I had to go on—for them and for myself. Because if I didn't, then in a certain way, they would have succeeded in killing me, too. (Butare, February 2009)

Here, Donata expresses how she experienced the legacy of the genocide as a personal trouble, one that it was up to her to overcome, lest she and her children suffer the consequences. Interestingly, she stridently opposed the work that ARPR does when I asked her about it. As a genocide survivor, she knows the local networks of experts who try to draw people like her into reconciliation associations. "I don't trust these *histoires* [tales] of Jean-Paul [the ARPR founder]. He thinks that by opening you up and laying bare all of your pain, this will heal you. This is something I just can't bear [*supporter*]" (Butare, February 2009). And yet Donata's framing of the personal challenges she faced since 1994 is in no way incompatible with peace builders' teachings about self-mastery, resilience, and personal development to overcome the problems of the past. These ideas strike a chord with the contemporary ethic of positive thinking and determination not to "let the killers win," as Odette put it in Chapter 4. But strikingly, this emphasis on transforming selves means that the grievances and misery of the genocide's legacy—problems produced by complex pasts and politics bigger than any individual—are effectively transformed from public issues into personal troubles. Indeed, ARPR and ICPD locate the sources of conflict in persons, not in structural conditions that give rise to social inequality, disenfranchisement, or hopelessness. Hence, they aim to transform how people *see and feel about* those conditions and their own position within them. Indeed, changing "mentalities," and with them normal capacities, is the focal point of peace builders' interventions.

The "Mentality" Problem

Peace building, in its broadest sense, is a question of how to forge the path to the "good life" in the wake of war and conflict (Pugh 2005: 38). However, the questions of what makes for a "good life" and what obstacles stand in its way are always shaped by local histories and social relations in addition to "travelling universals" (Tsing 2005) of peace building, development, and reconciliation. When ICPD and ARPR staff say that Rwandans are blocked from realizing a peaceful "good life" by the problem of "mentality," they articulate a worldview in which mentality problems are not just detrimental to individuals; they are also dangerous on the social level.

I interviewed Olivier, the director of ARPR, at his Butare office. His characterization of ARPR's work and vision is perhaps the purest expression of the spirit of peace-building interventions by both ICPD and ARPR. After some warm-up questions in which I inquired about how many years he had been at ARPR, previous work experience, and his education and training, the first question I put to him (and all of my interviewees) was what he thought were the main objectives of his organization. Olivier's response was instructive, so I quote him at length here:

> Overall, ARPR aims to contribute to the creation of a society in equilibrium. That's why we say here that we aim to promote [the growth of] all persons and the whole person.[3] So it's quite holistic: all persons in the sense of non-exclusion, because we are in a country where exclusion has been promoted for a long time, and that leads to [*débouche au*] genocide, as you know. So, as a lesson, we think it is necessary to work to cultivate non-exclusion, for the unconditional welcome of the other. We try to promote this mentality, not just verbally, but also concretely in the field when we work with the population. And then, we also try to create a person here in Rwanda who is capable of working for peace. And that is in our philosophy, the person must be understood in the sense of body, heart, intelligence, and spirit [*l'âme*]. These are the four elementary planes of the human being—the body, the heart, the intelligence, and the spirit. And we think that in order to be able to genuinely work for peace, and for peace to be reflected in real contexts, we must go into

the field to try to create this kind of person. And it's for that that we say we want to promote all persons and the whole person. *Voilà*.

... We analyze the history of our country to search for theories, but we believe that at the root of what we lived here is a spiritual problem. Why did people take up machetes to kill their neighbors? It was to seize their land, to seize their goods. It was to hold on to power. It was to keep a monopoly on knowledge. All that. And then there is the role of the colonizer. But we [ARPR] think that all of these things are merely pretexts. The real problem is spiritual. Often we focus on secondary causes—on pretexts, in reality. We forget the real cause. We relieve symptoms, but the real illness remains. The work that we do aims to heal the real illness. Our work aims at a change in mentality ... And I have seen these shifts; I can say this from experience. Personal development is something that takes time. There are exercises one must do to achieve self-mastery—I have seen the changes. Because me, I think that peace begins with the interior [of the person]. And then, when it bubbles up and overflows [*bouillonner*] from the interior, then it's reflected on the exterior. (Butare, May 2014)

According to Olivier, personal development, building capacities for "thinking for oneself" and "self-mastery," and for resistance to genocidal propaganda are central features of ARPR practice. They aim to produce a kind of person who is impervious to group influences, who is autonomous, bounded, and the very antithesis of the porous, composite, relational person now seen as dangerously susceptible to the influences of others. As he spoke about the work and guiding ideas of ARPR's approach to building peace, Olivier took on the tone of a preacher in the cadence of his speech. He became increasingly fervent in his claims, and he testified to having personally witnessed dramatic changes in persons who have been transformed by ARPR's teachings. What is especially striking, however, is Olivier's suggestion that there are persons who are capable of peace and those who are not, at least not without expert intervention. The task, from his perspective, is to guide Rwandans to become the kinds of persons who have *capacities* for peace—a change in the basis of what a human being is and ought to be and the capacities of normal personhood.

Olivier is by no means the only peace-building professional who framed the challenges of building peace in terms of "mentality." Bernard, the director of the secular, state-based ICPD, underscored the "mentality problem" during an interview in June 2014 when I asked him what he sees as the main obstacles to building peace in Rwanda.

Obstacles? There are a lot of them. First, peace in the country is also a function of peace in the region. So, if things aren't going well in the region, we have anxieties that things could blow up again. Our country is very populated, and our agricultural sector is still very... traditional in its methods. There are problems we know will take a while to resolve relative to the war and genocide.

LE: So problems with regional politics and populated land are the main obstacles to peace?

Bernard: No, no, the problem is what's in people's heads! Because the land, we can transform the land. Land doesn't cause massacres. It's the ideas that have conditioned people's attitudes and behaviors and that inspire politics. It's not the land. When you go to visit the masses in the hills, the rice fields, you find that these are places where people don't do anything to help themselves. They could be producing tons and tons of rice. Their poverty isn't an insurmountable problem, but it is a challenge. It's a question of changing what's in people's heads.

LE: And how do you try to change these ideas?

Bernard: All of the work of ICPD is about educating, building awareness [*sensibilisation, conscientisation*] of what is wrong with the mentality today. It's true, equal distribution of resources, an equitable society—these are issues that have some weight. But I think that it's really education that is essential. Because it's through education that we create new mentalities.

LE: New mentalities?

Bernard: Yes, new molds, new ways of thinking that will prevent injustices. It's a new mentality that we try to create. I think that this is the key. ... Personally, I think we need a new kind of Rwandan citizen. Yes, a Rwandan who isn't easily manipulated, who is capable of making any judgment that needs to be made, who grasps the limits placed on their lives, who is sociable, who knows how to find solutions with others. ... We need a citizen who won't tumble [*basculer*] into the crowd and follow along blindly. Ignorance is the problem. People are ignorant about a lot of things in our society. They're ignorant of how to fight against exclusion, how to have communities that function well. Ignorance of laws, of how to cultivate better, how to draw water during the dry season, of information technology, so ignorance of all sorts. Also how to read and write. Ignorance of basic tasks. (Butare, June 2014)

Bernard's discussion seamlessly links the causes of the genocide, of poor harvests, and of rural poverty to the core problem of "mentality" and the ideas that shape people's conduct and outlooks. He briefly acknowledges the importance of distributive justice and equality for peaceful social relations, but quickly downplays their significance to highlight once again the centrality of education and new mentalities. In Bernard's framing of the "mentality" problem, he indicts rural people and the kinds of selves who are built out of relations with others, because they are too susceptible to the crowd. Like many agents of the state, he points to the failures of the (Hutu) people for their willingness to buy into anti-Tutsi propaganda—in other words, the ease with which they were apparently persuaded to follow orders (Burnet 2009: 89).

In an interview with Julie, she echoed the "mentality" problem, albeit with a more sympathetic tenor than Olivier or Bernard. She spoke about these issues when I asked her what she likes best about her job at ICPD.

> I like doing community outreach, because when you're with people, you understand their ideas. You understand their challenges and how they live in the country [à la campagne]—what's different from how we live here [in the city]. If you're with them, you put yourself in their place—how they live, which can be different from what people say about them and what we read in the newspapers. ... The authorities don't listen to the *paysans*, and they oblige them to follow orders—no discussion. If the authorities say it's time to stop growing bananas and switch to rice, well, that's the end of it—rural people don't discuss; they just take orders. With our open dialogue sessions to build peace, we try to encourage rural people to talk and to ask questions. But the problem is, even if this little group learns the culture of open dialogue and asking questions, it's still just a small group—it's not everyone in the whole region. So life remains very different in the hills. It's not easy. (Kigali, July 2014)

While Julie did not make explicit reference to the "mentality" problem, her words nonetheless convey that rural people require the assistance of experts to refrain from simply following orders, and to start asking questions. The irony, of course, is that urban people are also constrained in their ability to engage in "open dialogue" with state authorities, and these claims to doing so are much less an accurate description of social relations than a claim to being a particular kind of self. Indeed, Julie frames peace-building personnel as modern persons who are capable of open dialogue and who think for themselves instead of following orders—the cardinal sin leveled at those who were embroiled in the massacres in 1994. Mentality, as I have suggested, is a vague word, and peace builders use it to capture all that they see as wrong with (rural) Rwandan persons, practices, and life ways. The question is by what techniques do ICPD and ARPR design interventions aimed at changing mentality and forging new foundations and capacities of "normal" personhood?

Changing "Mentalities" through Education: ICPD

As a state organization, ICPD's approach (and their affiliate organizations) relied on "educating" people in the official version of history of the day— the one that is purveyed at *ingando* camps, the one that romanticizes the precolonial past and blames the genocide on colonization and postcolonial "bad (Hutu) governance" (Pottier 2002; Purdeková 2015; Thomson 2013). Since formal education has been so inseparable from power in (post)colonial Rwanda (Chapter 1; see also Turner 2005), it seems as though education is the magical factor that transforms a person from a rural subsistence cultivator into a civil servant, entrepreneur, or urban professional. While careful analysis shows that the (post)colonial elite become powerful not just through formal training, but also by exposure to sources of cultural and social capital (Bourdieu [1986] 2011; Comaroff and Comaroff 1997), what remains alive and well in contemporary Butare is the idea that education can miraculously transform a person. Éric, the head of a youth reconciliation organization in Butare that is partnered with the local ICPD office, explained the role of education in changing persons and building reconciliation. He and his family are post-1994 returnees to Rwanda, and he has wholeheartedly embraced the new state discourse of good citizenship through leadership in reconciliation.

> You see, the best tool to reach people, in Rwanda specifically, is the history of the nation. You have to show them, one at a time, that the people of Rwanda were one. You show them that we were one people—same beliefs, same culture, same understandings. Everything. So after showing them something positive, *it changes them.* Once they know how it used to be, you don't even have to try to convince them—they can draw the right conclusions themselves ... So I'm showing them where we want to be. If anyone feels that they want a bright future for the nation, we cannot have a bright future when people are divided. (Butare, June 2014)[4]

In my interview with Éric, I was keenly aware of his conscious efforts at self-presentation as a "good Rwandan." Indeed, being well versed in the state discourse of unity and reconciliation is today a path to power, especially for those in leadership positions like Éric. What must be borne in mind is that a carefully managed impression in an interview does not render it false or produce invalid data. Rather, those managed impressions are precisely of interest to grasp the techniques by which peace-building organizations make their interventions. Becoming educated in the "right" version of history—which of course is the highly contested, politicized RPF narrative that has been subject to scathing criticism (Pottier 2002)—is what "changes" people in Éric's view. As part of its educational outreach work for community peace building, ICPD engages in focus groups with the population. Any methodologist would take issue with naming these sessions focus groups, because they are not directed at eliciting collective understandings of an issue. Rather, they are re-education workshops in which facilitators "correct" the population's view of history. It is this process that, as Éric explained, produces educated persons who are not only capable of peaceful, united coexistence, but who will also choose it themselves without convincing once they are shown a "positive" view of the past. A glossy, colorful report published on ICPD's focus group sessions is telling. It describes how they begin by asking the population about their impressions of the causes of the genocide, the meaning of citizenship today, and effective conflict resolution strategies. After participants expressed their views, the report explained that the facilitators intervened to "give a sense of direction" (*donner une orientation*) to the debate. The facilitators then provided the RPF-approved account of history, in which colonialism divided the formerly unified population and in which genocide was prepared under the "bad governance" of the first and second republics. What followed this education session was an evaluation phase, in which facilitators asked participants the same questions with which they began about the causes of the genocide. They measured the changes in responses to see how closely they adhered to the history taught in the "focus group," which of course showed remarkable "improvement" in participants' understandings. Indeed, on this basis, the report concluded that education is an effective way of building peace and creating persons who are "capable of becoming new types of citizens" who can "live and resolve conflicts peacefully" (ICPD report, 2013). It closes with a description of how participants thanked ICPD for the knowledge they had acquired from them and assured facilitators that the conversations they had shared would have positive effects on their everyday lives. What this report lays bare is that, for ICPD, fostering capacities for conflict resolution and consensus building is fundamentally a matter of educating people, which will then produce people who are enlightened and capable of peace.

Changing "Mentalities" through Personal Development: ARPR

ARPR's approach to changing mentalities and personhood relies less on teaching state history than personal development and self-mastery. Still, like the teaching of state history, these guiding precepts dovetail with broader RPF reconciliation directives, especially the idea that reconciliation both produces and is produced by a rediscovery of Rwandans' "self-worth and confidence" (Kagame 2012b). In workshop meetings with *groupes de rapprochement*, Olivier, Tharcisse, and other personnel always began by positioning themselves as neutral facilitators of "dialogue" between former perpetrators and their victims. Many of the staff members at ICPD and ARPR are well read in continental philosophy and popular self-help literature. Staff quoted the teachings of French author Olivier Clouzot (2000) and his "levels of consciousness" through which individuals must pass to achieve "awakening" (*l'éveil*) and enlightenment. They cited these as preconditions for the making of persons capable of living peacefully and not succumbing to the negative influences of those who incite violence. I quote Olivier, the ARPR director, at length from an interview in which he explained the "levels of consciousness" in ARPR's peace-building teachings, adapted from Clouzot, through which all Rwandans must rise if peace is to be lasting and durable:

Inspired by a number of authors [Clouzot; David R. Hawkins], we try to categorize persons in four categories. We call these "levels of consciousness" [*niveaux de conscience*], or levels of maturity in *ubuntu*.[5] Yes, yes—levels of maturity, according to one's level of maturity and humanity. So for us, the lowest level is the "sociocultural being" [*rukurikirizindi* in Kinyarwanda]—here one cannot even speak of the individual yet. At this level, people there, they never speak in the first person. They're always in the crowd, easily manipulated, blinded by the emotions of the collective. *And the genocide would not have been possible if it weren't for the fact that the majority [of Rwandans] is comprised of these people* [my emphasis]. These people are easily programmed, they blindly obey, and they never question the orders that come down from above—that is to say, the authorities. And unfortunately, humanity is full of these people; Rwanda is full of these people. And that is why they blindly launched themselves into the genocide. I've seen it in *gacaca*—the judge will ask the accused, why did you kill your neighbor? And he will reply, I don't know ... And so that right there, that is lack of consciousness. It's the level of unconsciousness. Second is the level we call individualist [*niveau individualiste*; *babona* in Kinyarwanda]. These people at this level, they're the great manipulators of those who are still at the first level. And unfortunately, the large majority of our leaders, be they political leaders or leaders of multinationals—the people with the real power in the world—they're at this level. Yes, these people know how to manipulate others for their own advantage—these people want to accumulate wealth and power to the detriment of others. I was still very young in 1994, but I could still see it was just a handful of leaders who galvanized the crowd [to commit massacres] because they saw that killing was in their interest to hold on to power ...

The third level is the individualized level [*niveau individualisé*; *umuntu nyirizina* in Kinyarwanda]. In fact, this is the level of consciousness that the doctrine of universal human rights comes from. Because at this level, I know I have rights, but I also know that those rights confer certain duties on me. If I'm going to live, I must also let the other live. If I have rights, I must respect the rights of others. If I have the right to life and aspire to live, I am conscious that the other has this same aspiration. Peace is possible at this level. *Peace only becomes possible at this level* [my emphasis]. Here, I want to live in peace, I want everyone to appreciate and support me, and I am conscious that everyone else has that same aspiration. And finally, the fourth level is the level of the "masters." This is the "transpersonal" level—the transpersonal being [*l'être trans-personnel*; *imana y'i Rwanda* in Kinyarwanda]. It's the theory of Clouzot that we've tried to adopt. It is these persons at the fourth level who enlighten the rest of humanity. And so we work to help people move up these levels, because we know that the real problems of humanity are problems of consciousness. We don't expect everyone to achieve this level, but our main objective is to take all Rwandans at least to the third level. Because it's at that level that peace is possible—it is here that we have a *mentality geared toward peace* [my emphasis]. (Butare, May 2014)

What is so striking about Olivier's account and ARPR philosophy is that it locates the conditions of possibility for the genocide precisely in the shortcomings of persons. Most remarkable of all is how the characterization of the lowest level of consciousness evokes the relational configuration of the person. Like the relational self, those at the lowest level do not identify themselves primarily as bounded, self-governing entities. Olivier captures this in the notion that they never speak in the first person. Likewise, the relational self is porous and comprised of relations with others, which makes it susceptible to influences—positive or negative. Hence, ARPR philosophy disparages the relational self—so fundamental to Rwandan conceptions of the person and experiences of selfhood—as dangerous, easily manipulated, and blindly obedient because of insufficient personal development toward bounded, individuated personhood. The second level is framed as a corrupted, or "stunted" version of the third level. Here, the self is conceptualized in individual rather than relational terms, but it is too individualistic, is incapable of empathy or mutual understanding, and privileges self-interest over all else, including others' rights to freedom from harm and from want. It is at the third level of consciousness that ARPR sees the possibility of "peaceful selves" emerging who will not blindly pursue self-interest or obey orders to kill. In ARPR's peace-building approach, it is the *person* who is in need of improvement. Once persons become "capable" of peace, then, the thinking goes, it does not matter if political leaders remain at the corrupted consciousness of the second level, because the population will have undergone sufficient personal development to resiliently withstand their calls to arms.

Why Remake Selves to Make Peace?

As reductive as it seems, it is not hard to see why the individual is the level at which these organizations intervene. Given the strict hierarchies of Rwanda's governance structure and the tight state controls on the limits of critique and acceptable political discourse (Pottier 2002), the self is a level at which these organizations are capable of intervening and at which it is also politically safe to do so. There is little they can do about the problems people face with respect to land tenure, job opportunities, political and economic disenfranchisement, and certainly not the genocide. However, they can try to change the stories people tell about themselves, about their past, and how they *feel* about those difficulties in their lives. What ICPD and ARPR do in their training, education, and awareness-raising approaches to building peace bears a striking similarity to what Arlie Hochschild (1979, 1983) calls emotion work, that is, actively working to change how one feels about a situation. She argues that emotion work is directed toward adhering to feeling rules (Hochschild 1979: 563–64), social guidelines for emotional responses often framed in terms of how one has a "right" to feel or how one "should (not)" feel. Indeed, peace-building practice aims to enact a new set of feeling rules in survivors and perpetrators with respect to each other and the history of violence. These new feeling rules call on survivors and perpetrators to approach each other with empathy rather than animosity and to work on feelings of enmity to produce capacities for mutual understanding and consensus. The causes of people's emotions are not the main site of intervention; rather it is people's *responses* to those causes that peace builders target for transformation (cf. Hochschild 1983: 25). Being a "good Rwandan" in the post-conflict moment means developing the capacities to work on one's negative feelings with respect to the violent past and the divisions that constitute it. In other words, it is up to the individual to do her part to transform her emotions and move beyond the "negativity" of the past. And according to ARPR, "inner power" is precisely the ability to master one's emotions (cf. Illouz 2008: 83) and to adhere to socially appropriate feeling rules.

I want to push this analysis one step further. What is startling about these peace-building interventions is the fundamental idea that the self who is capable of successful emotion work *is* the self who is capable of peace. Especially for ARPR, peace requires persons who are able to achieve mastery over their emotions. Although their approach does not use these words, the contrast drawn in ARPR's levels of consciousness is between a bounded, autonomous individual capable of successful emotion work versus a relational self who is vulnerable to the contagion and negative influences of others. Indeed, the porous, relational self simply adopts the emotions of the crowd. Left untransformed, these kinds of persons with their collective emotions run amok, blind obedience, and an inability to reason for themselves leave Rwanda vulnerable to further violence. But if persons can be changed into skilled emotion managers through apolitical therapeutic interventions, if peace-building organizations can guide them toward learning to accept their lot in life—whatever it might be—then the thinking is that personal capacities for self-mastery will act as safeguards against recurrent outbreaks of violence.

As well intentioned as the peace builders I knew were, and no matter how much I grew to like some of them personally, I could not shake my ambivalent feelings toward their work. First, to frame the problem of violence as primarily a problem of how people feel about themselves and each other demands critical intervention.[6] But second, it seemed that the self that ARPR aimed to produce, one singularly in control of her or his emotions and impervious to the negative influences of others, is ultimately a caricature of what Hochschild had in mind when she developed the concept of emotion work. Indeed, emotion work is never the exclusive work of the individual, and we always rely on others' influences to assist us with actively changing how we feel (Hochschild 1983: 44). In the end, even as it resonates with Butaréens' modern aspirations, ARPR's vision of making Rwandans who are the sole managers and authors of their emotions and actions gets caught in its own logic. On the one hand, ARPR's teachings negate the fundamentally social nature of the self—whether grasped as individuated or relational (Goffman 1959; Mauss [1938] 1985; Mead 1913)—and they insist that persons can and should be fully autonomous, self-governing subjects. But on the other hand, ARPR relies precisely on persons' porousness and openness to *the organization's* influences—ones that personnel see as positive rather than negative to be sure, but influences that rely on the Rwandan "logic of contagion" (Fujii 2009) nonetheless. Organization staff drew a strict opposition between themselves and the majority of Rwandans who must be coached and guided in order to develop capacities for peace. And yet even ICPD and ARPR staff did not in practice orient to their disciples as fully autonomous, rights-bearing individuals who freely choose the parameters of their interactions with others. Rather, there is implicit in their outlooks a profound sense of obligation—one often couched in paternalistic, disparaging language of "mentality" problems and rural ignorance, but a sense of obligation and duty based on role obligations nonetheless. Organizations' emphasis on re-education and self-transformation suggests a sense of responsibility on the part of staff to distribute the material and symbolic resources to which people expect to have access when they get involved with NGOs (cf. Englund 2006: 38), a duty patterned on longstanding expectations in Rwanda that those with means owe something to others. Hence, in the end, even peace-building personnel—some of the most vocal devotees of the virtues of individuated, autonomous selfhood—find themselves caught in the logic of two competing moral orders and value frameworks when it comes to the questions of who owes what to whom and just how unfettered or "joined up" (Carsten 2004) the self is and ought to be.

As I grew to understand the guiding ideas that underpinned their approaches, I politely, but firmly, pushed staff members on the question of whether the sources of violence and its prevention are really so contained within the self as their interventions presuppose. My questions were never met with outright dismissal, but people quickly shifted the emphasis back to the "root" causes of violence—namely, the shortcomings of persons. As Joseph, an ICPD staff member who splits his time between educational and community outreach functions put it, "It must be admitted that poverty is a problem, that bad governance was a problem in the past. We don't know what the future holds, but if we can make a Rwandan who can withstand negative influences even when they come from the authorities, then we can ensure that peace is still possible" (Butare, July 2014). The refusal to seriously engage with how history and political economy shaped the conditions for the 1994 genocide, and the focus on individuals' failure to cultivate sufficient personal resistance to negative influences never sat well with my anthropological sensibility. Perspectives such as these directly conflict with basic anthropological premises, including the imperative to understand not only people's beliefs and practices but also the larger forces that shape them, as well as the fundamental idea that all selves are inherently porous (e.g. Smith 2012: 53). Likewise, the disparaging assumptions about rural people— and especially about the "mentality" of Hutu who became embroiled in the massacres—suggest that perhaps peace-building organizations have produced an idiom that makes distinctions between people on the basis of their moral qualities in a way distinct from but parallel to the moral languages of the past, including those constitutive of ethnic stereotypes. The final section of the chapter details one more way in which the practice of remaking persons to forge peace produces unplanned outcomes that threaten to destabilize their moral authority, namely the production of a small group who seem to profit from others' suffering.

Reconciliation Celebrities, "Output," and Ill-Gotten Gains

In spite of the educational and therapeutic goals of peace building in Rwanda, there is, of course, a strictly bureaucratic component to their work—one that sits awkwardly alongside the value-rational forms of social action in which peace builders locate and justify their work. On a mundane level, I found that the work of building peace in Rwanda does not differ a great deal from any form of office work. There are activities and staff members to coordinate, forms to fill out to secure and release funds, squabbles between personnel, and reports to draft on organizations' successes and ongoing challenges. Two of the main questions I put to my research participants, both in formal interviews and informal conversation, concerned that final point. First, I asked them to explain to me how they know that their organization is building peace, and second, how they assess the results of their peace-building interventions. Members of both organizations explained that they rely on *groupe* member testimony to measure the results of their work. The more dramatic and convincing the testimony, the better it is for their relationships with donors and for the flow of resources. Each organization had a number of *groupe* members whom I call "reconciliation celebrities"—people whose testimony is especially captivating and who travel around the country with their guiding organization to speak to its power to shepherd people toward peace and personal development. Testimony from survivors and perpetrators in post-genocide Rwanda was by no means a practice limited to these peace-building events; indeed, testimony was also a critical element of the annual genocide commemorations and the *gacaca* tribunals, and I described a form of informal testimony to loss in Chapter 3. However, the tenor of testimony from reconciliation celebrities departed from those other testimonial practices in the emphasis put on redemption, overcoming the schisms of the past, and personal improvement. At least in the formal commemoration and *gacaca* testimonies that I personally witnessed over the course of my fieldwork, commemoration testimony by survivors was overwhelmingly characterized by devastation and grief, while *gacaca* testimony focused primarily on factual matters of establishing who did what to whom as well as where and when the crimes took place. By contrast, reconciliation celebrity testimony was first and foremost directed at establishing the speaker's exceptional capacities for forgiveness, peace, and reconciliation.

At a workshop meeting of three regional peace-building organizations in Butare, reconciliation celebrities were called upon to testify to their personal transformations to "peaceful selfhood." These testimonies are choreographed rather than spontaneous, and reconciliation celebrities are hand-picked in advance and brought all expenses paid to the gatherings at which they speak. A former perpetrator, Jean de Dieu, was called upon to testify to his personal transformation with the assistance of ARPR. He is famous on the local peace-building circuits, and I even saw him featured in international media stories during the twentieth anniversary of the genocide in April 2014. Regrettably, the drama of the delivery of these testimonies is lost on the written page.

> I must confess that I participated in the genocide—it's not a secret, of course. I stole from victims; I killed people … I spent twelve years in prison. When I got out and when ARPR approached us with their *ubuntu* philosophy, this allowed us to overcome what we had been through. *Ubuntu* means that if I committed crimes, to have *ubuntu* means I must give back to the lives of those I have hurt. In our reconciliation group, there were extremists and resistors. But ARPR helped us to form a cooperative group so we could pay back what we owed to people. ARPR helped us to stop fleeing each time we laid eyes on a survivor. During the genocide, high-ranking authorities came and encouraged the people of S——— to kill, but today it's calm because of what ARPR has done. Others on our hill who are not in our group are very interested in what we do—they see us work and prepare sorghum beer together and drink together, and they are astonished at our transformation. We have learned

that the solutions to our problems here in Rwanda—they are in the interior strength of persons. (Butare, June 2014)

At a similar meeting in Kigali in June 2014, Pascaline, another of ARPR's reconciliation celebrities, spoke of her transformations with the help of ARPR's teachings.

> Before ARPR came, I tried to chase away peace. Unlike others here, I never wanted payment [for goods stolen during the genocide]; I told them instead to just send all the perpetrators to prison—I didn't want to look at them. But now I very much want to forgive. I was the head of the unity and reconciliation effort in my sector. ARPR taught us that you can't give what you don't have. I was dead in my heart—I had nothing to give … But today, I've woken up and with even more strength. Now I work with survivors to encourage them to forgive … We learned from ARPR how to find peace in ourselves. I brought together twenty survivors and twenty perpetrators, and no one could understand at first. Everyone in my family was killed—my side and my husband's side. But after I learned ARPR's teachings, then I had power and strength. I was so strong, even the [state] authorities were afraid of me, because I could do something they couldn't. I could bring survivors and perpetrators together.

Peace-building personnel were always eager to talk to me about their "reconciliation celebrities"—their star pupils in the transition to higher levels of personal development. As Olivier explained, his staff always encounter resistance when they first begin working with a new *groupe*. Pascaline, as her testimony suggested, was herself one of these obstinate types. The trope of initial resistance is central to the narrative that ARPR tells about itself and its astounding power to transform even the most vengeful survivors and hate-filled perpetrators into "peaceful selves" who can "understand each other."

Alongside these celebratory moments, there is an undercurrent among outsiders to the local peace-building apparatus that the renown of reconciliation celebrities and the comfortable livings made by peace-building staff are ill-gotten gains, because it is difficult to confirm the degree of sincerity in people's stories of personal transformation. Due to limited resources, peace-building organizations are not able to spend long periods in their field sites to immerse themselves and observe the nature of social relations, and even if they could, it is still not self-evident that reconciliation can or should be read into people's dealings with each other (Ingelaere 2010). Indeed, victims and perpetrators may have a multitude of reasons for interacting, including strategy, necessity, resignation, a heartfelt wish to repair reciprocal ties, or some difficult-to-characterize combination thereof. The reliance on testimony—on *groupe* members' word—is the glaring lacuna in all of this, since testimony about one's inner state that cannot be confirmed by objective evidence is by nature open to disbelief. Impressions are always managed with varying degrees of consciousness and calculation (Goffman 1959), and "absolute transparency" in social interactions is not possible (Jones 2014: 61). I encountered no small number of people who expressed skepticism about *groupe* members' testimonies, especially those from "reconciliation celebrities." I even witnessed an open charge of corruption at the Kigali workshop meeting at which Pascaline spoke, in which an angry genocide survivor accused her of taking bribes to give false testimony to reconciliation (Eramian 2017). In other words, Butare residents—especially genocide survivors who cannot conceive of forgiving those who harmed them—suspect reconciliation celebrities of a particularly contemptible form of surface acting (Hochschild 1983) and have difficulty believing that their testimony is the product of successful emotion work and transformations of feelings. Hence, reconciliation celebrity status does not bring strictly positive forms of renown, because it can make people targets of threats by those who still harbor resentment over the genocide, who see reconciliation celebrities as "ethnic traitors," or who accuse them of immoral profiteering from the legacy of the genocide. Indeed, Pascaline makes her home in a police compound, because the authorities recognize that it is not safe for her to live without protection.

It is not difficult to see where these suspicions of self-interest and ill-gotten gains come from. That *groupes* receive start-up funds for collective projects and that organizations engage with unpaid goods cases invites suspicion that members "pretend peace" for financial gain. Even Olivier, who so earnestly attested to having seen genuine transformations in reconciliation *groupe* members, described to me how peace builders must use people's "thirst to be known" to overcome their resistance and to bring them around to their way of thinking. In this moment, he acknowledged not only that people might have concealed interests for getting involved with peace-building organizations, but also that ARPR actively manipulates them. Finally, some organization personnel, at least at some times, express no special commitment to peace building as a vocation. As Robert explained when I asked him if he thinks he will spend his whole career at ICPD, peace building was not his first choice. He wanted to study law, but he was never admitted to a law program. He said that he likes the stability of his job (he is one of the few ICPD staff members who earns enough to support his family without seeking side contracts), but the work holds no special resonance for him. By his own admission, Robert lacks commitment to his work and is primarily interested in the stable livelihood it provides. Ironically, in producing peace-building "experts" whose guidance is required to show Rwandans the path to peace, and in producing reconciliation celebrities who testify to achieving self-mastery and transcending their old "mentality" problems, the peace-building industry in Rwanda does nothing less than produce figures who might be perceived to occupy ARPR's second, disparaged level of consciousness—the one in which persons are doggedly individualistic and have no moral qualms about making a comfortable living off of an industry made possible by the genocide and to which they feel no special moral commitment.

By contrast—at least for the purposes of bureaucratic tracking of their results—organizations accept *groupe* member testimony to renewed cooperative social relations as hard evidence that peace building is having its intended effects. However, not just any testimony will do. ICPD and ARPR personnel underscored the necessity for "good testimony" (*bons temoignages*), especially for their reports to their donors. The most arresting articulation of the relationships between *groupe* member testimonies, the evaluation of results, and donor funds came from Éric. When I asked him how his organization knows it is contributing to the reconciliation effort, he explained how his organization measures its "output":

> First of all, what I can say about full reconciliation, it can only be a personal issue. It is something within you. So I can pretend, I can be a hypocrite, you see? I can say we are united, that we are reconciled. But then within me there is a big difference. So it is not easy, it's a personal issue, but most of the time, we look at results in terms of the output.
>
> LE: Output?
>
> E: The output, yes. This output is measured from whether people socialize with one another, you see? I might be your neighbor, and maybe there is no big problem when we meet—we shake hands[7]—no problem. But still you find there is no real... can I say intimacy between me and you, as much as we're neighbors. Because I'm from a different—I'm Hutu, Tutsi—that thing. Culturally, in Africa, we visit one another in the evenings—you visit your neighbor, you share, you discuss, you laugh. But now [after 1994], maybe you're my neighbor, but I have a function [party] at my place, and I don't invite you. We don't visit one another. So today we find that people are neighbors, but they have never shared anything—no challenges, no opportunities. So reconciliation—it is a challenge in this context. But after [peace-building organizations intervene], there are people [about] whom you can say, these people are really reconciled. You find they are now like one family. This time I can come and have lunch at your place, and the next time you come and have dinner at my place. If I want something from the market and you're going there, I can say, can you bring me this? After reconciliation, people have great intimacy; they have great relationships, so I think that is how we measure our output... So generally, you can say there has been some great output; there is some great reconciliation. (Butare, June 2014)

From what Éric explained, I first was under the impression that "output" was measured by directly observing whether people were visiting and socializing.

When I pushed him a little further on this matter, it emerged that "output" measurements were instead based on people's *reports* of whether they socialize with their neighbors. Thus, Éric puts faith in people's reports of having rebuilt convivial social ties, even as he acknowledges that there are people who might "hypocritically" claim to be reconciled when they still feel deep enmity. When I asked how one might distinguish a false from a heartfelt testimony, Éric explained that they look for signs of "intimacy" and specific instances in which people "socialize" or "share opportunities and challenges," preferably ones confirmed by the other party in question. In ways not unlike a criminal investigator might ascertain the veracity of a witness statement, peace builders like Éric look for accounts of reconciliation with details that can be "fact-checked" by talking to others. It is those testimonies deemed reliable that he calls "output" for his organization.

Julie also spoke about the importance of testimony at ICPD and put faith in its reliability when I asked her what the hardest part of her job is:

> The hardest thing about my job is reporting results of consultancies for clients [local authorities] who hire us to promote reconciliation in their region. You might find that your client won't accept what the research shows—the results. For example, one could say that in a certain community, reconciliation is at 30 percent, and if this is what the results show, your client is not going to be happy. He won't be happy because he was thinking the results would be more like 80 percent. Because you see, he's invested in these projects, so he doesn't want to accept what the research shows.
>
> LE: And how does one measure reconciliation—how does one evaluate whether it's at 30 percent, 80 percent?
>
> J: We base it on the testimonies people give us. People tell us things like, "Before I was here [in the *groupe de rapprochement*] working together with these people, I couldn't even greet the people who killed my family. But now, we work together, they can come and help me build my house or cultivate my fields." It's on the basis of these testimonies that we measure our success. (Butare, June 2014)

Finally, Tharcisse dramatically illustrated the necessity of compelling *groupe* member testimony to reconciliation and continued financial support from their donors. At an ARPR staff meeting, he impressed on everyone the importance of choosing a "dynamic" *groupe de rapprochement* to visit when their European donors arrived to check on the progress of ARPR's activities the following month:

> There is good testimony coming out of K———. That is one possibility. But there are *groupes* as you know who have no common activities, no common fields to cultivate or projects. These groups may as well not even exist. We need

to work with them so we don't lose them, though. These groups have cost us a lot of money. We've invested in them. We've brought them to meetings where they eat macaroni [a food townspeople say is unknown in the rural hills]; we've paid for them to talk to therapists and professors. Now we need to make sure we can make use of [*exploiter*] them after all we've invested! (Butare, July 2014)

Tharcisse's explanation of ARPR's reliance on testimony to show their donors good results was perhaps the most mercenary of all the ways I heard peace-building staff articulate this issue. What is striking is the faith that organizations put in the evidence by which they measure "true" reconciliation. Indeed, dramatic testimony to being able to work with those who killed one's family, or reports of visits between neighbors, are framed as concrete evidence of reconciliation between *groupe* members. According to Éric, reports of merely shaking hands and greeting are not sufficient to conclude that reconciliation is taking place, but testimonies into which he can read greater "intimacy" are satisfactory criteria for judging his organization's "output." However, Éric did not question the usefulness of testimony as a measure of reconciliation; rather, he suggested that the expertise of peace-building personnel is the crucial factor in distinguishing "good testimony" that can be measured as "output" from mere surface acting (Hochschild 1983). Only Robert, a graduate student with training in qualitative research methods and who teaches for ICPD's certificate programs, expressed skepticism about the use of testimony to measure reconciliation when I asked him how his organization knows that their interventions are contributing to peace in Rwanda:[8]

> I think that's a complicated question. We base it on testimonies from our association members [*groupes de rapprochement*]. If for example we see that the associations we've been working with—the associations of survivors and perpetrators and their families—if we get some testimonies that they are still working together, and if we see that they are still developing in that materialistic way [i.e. cultivating or raising animals together to generate income], that can at least show us that something good is happening. *Which does not mean that we are sure everything is going well between them. It just means they are working together.* (Butare, July 2014, my emphasis)

Robert was the only person I spoke with who was either aware of or willing to discuss the basic differences in the types of qualitative data yielded by interviews with *groupe* members and direct observation of their activities. He distinguished the observable fact that *groupes* are working together—which he says is not a bad thing in itself—from the question of how members feel about each other and whether things are "going well" between them. As interviews involve impression management just like any other social interaction (Portelli 1991), Robert's response demonstrates an understanding that testimony gathered by ICPD interviewers does not provide a direct, unmediated window into the mind of the other, which raises questions in his mind about just what his organization is doing and what it is measuring when it collects testimonies.

Nonetheless, while some peace-building staff grapple with the question of what the testimonies they are gathering mean, these tensions and lacunae in no way interrupt the everyday practices of organizations like ICPD and ARPR. At first I wondered how staff could place faith in a methodologically questionable approach to "measuring" reconciliation, but what eventually became clear to me is that they can do so because testimony is the measure that is accepted by their donors as evidence that peace is advancing. And therein is the crucial point: all organizations like ICPD and ARPR *need* is testimony—preferably "good" testimony, of course, that contains detailed accounts of "intimate" sociality—because reports of reconciliation are the currency that their donors accept. As long as there is no eruption of overt violence between people or any other evidence to suggest that reconciliation is *absent*, then testimony is *as good as* genuine, and so the problem of unknowability does not interrupt the work of peace-building organizations. Éric described signs that ethnic schisms persist, such as tormenting survivors by throwing rocks onto the roofs of their homes at night, or anti-Tutsi/anti-Hutu graffiti on the university campus, which he said has been cleaned up and no longer exists.[9] Hence, so long as these overt signs of conflict are absent, and so long as *groupe* members attest to having reconciled, peace-building organizations and their donors can claim success in their interventions. Whether people still "carry hatred in their hearts," as Alphonse, the ARPR yoga instructor put it, or whether they are "truly reconciled," is in practice immaterial to the ongoing operations of peace-building practice. So long as organizations can produce compelling and convincing stories about conversions from hatred to forgiveness, then donor funds continue to flow. Nonetheless, the question of sincerity is by no means so easily resolved for other Rwandans—a problem to which charges of corruption and ill-gotten gains against "reconciliation celebrities" attest.

Conclusion

In transforming problems of peace and conflict from public issues into personal troubles, civil society-level peace-building organizations in Rwanda offer a thorough expression of the kinds of selves on which the "New Rwanda" should be built. Self-mastery through emotion work and personal development through education and advancing through levels of consciousness is ultimately a matter of working to transform the basis of "normal personhood." What are the qualities and capacities of the "normal person"? In building peace, the "normal" capacities they aim to instill entail efficacy in what Foucault has called the "technologies of the self"—techniques that "permit individuals to effect by their own means or with the help of others a certain number of operations on their own bodies and souls, thoughts, conduct and way of being, so as to transform themselves in order to attain a certain state of happiness, purity, wisdom, perfection, or immortality" (Foucault et al. 1988: 18). It is a matter of instilling both the "will to improve" (Li 2007) and the *capacity* to do so, since ARPR and ICPD locate not only the genocide, but also poverty, jealousy, and other social problems in the singular but multifaceted problem of "mentality." The trouble is that qualities like self-mastery, reason, thinking for oneself, and their opposites in the "mentality" schema—blind obedience, passion, and deference—are not politically neutral in Rwanda. The same moral qualities that have been expressed in ambiguously ethnic idioms are now being reworked in the language and categories of therapeutic selfhood. Like older, ethnic idioms, these new ones are not innocuous, but have an express relationship to power. Indeed, underlying all of these past and present ways of making moral distinctions—ethnicity, class, occupation, rural/urban, north/south, or the new idioms of the enterprise culture or therapeutic personal development—is the fundamental problem of the person and what one is and ought to be. In the end, it is an open question whether peace-building organizations paradoxically continue to enliven the very social boundaries and "mentality problems" they claim to overcome. Coupled with the problem that peace-building staff and reconciliation celebrities are thought to be profiting from the legacy of the genocide, the social relationships and practices constitutive of the Rwandan peace-building industry raise serious questions about its prospects for producing anything that could be called by that vexingly open signifier, "peace." More than anything, the practices of self-development and personal transformation that peace builders aim to instill in the population reveal a profound anxiety about whether violence like the 1994 genocide could once again befall Rwanda. Even if state leaders cannot be trusted not to incite the population to violence again, ICPD's and ARPR's approach aims at personal development as fortification against any possible future calls to take up arms against one's neighbors, friends, and colleagues.

Notes

1. I give both organizations and individual personnel pseudonyms in an effort to better protect people's identities, given the small world of peace building in Rwanda.
2. I avoid providing a full citation for this source and all other organization documents and publications to protect the identities of the organizations and their staff.

3. Olivier used the expression, "*tous hommes et tout l'homme.*" In my translation from French, I opt for the gender-neutral term, person, rather than the direct translation, "man," since it also captures better what he aimed to convey, i.e. "man" as an androcentric synonym for human being or person.

4. This interview was conducted in English.

5. *Ubuntu* is a Bantu philosophy that became especially well known, globally speaking, when Archbishop Desmond Tutu famously invoked its principles in the South African Truth and Reconciliation Commission. It refers to a basic unity of humankind, our humanness itself, and universal human bonds of solidarity and interdependence (Kamwangamalu 1999). For a critical perspective on *ubuntu* as a romanticized, apolitical device of state-sponsored projects of unity and reconciliation, see Wilson 2001.

6. Hochschild (1983) in her discussion of emotion work among flight attendants offers an important critique of this perspective, specifically airlines' reduction of the problems of the workplace to how flight attendants feel about their work.

7. Whenever Rwandans greet each other, there is a requisite handshake. The style of the handshake varies based on the intimacy of the relationship, but to withhold a handshake from a friend, acquaintance, or stranger is read as a profound affront to the rules of sociality. Small children are socialized from a very early age to put out their hands when greeting people, especially adults.

8. At Robert's request, the interview took place in a combination of English and French. Hence, some passages are my translations and some are directly quoted from English.

9. I saw such graffiti at the university during fieldwork in 2004 and 2008, but I have noticed a sharp decline in it, as Éric suggested. For example, in 2004, I found "Hutu Pawa [Power]" graffiti in the university bathrooms and on items in the university library card catalogue.

Conclusion

THE POST-CONFLICT, THE POSTCOLONIAL, AND PEACEFUL SELVES

In the introduction to this book, I suggested that it unfolds the story of a jarring juxtaposition in the selfhood of Butare residents. On the one hand, they expound on the virtues of cultivating individual autonomy, developing their inner resources, and individual success through hard work, all in the service of promoting personal and national wellbeing. On the other hand, the devastation of the genocide lays bare how these urban, educated town residents conceive of the self as deeply relational and dislocated by the loss of kin, friends, and neighbors. It was this sense of discord that was so palpable during my field research but that there is no easy way to render on the written page.

While this book told a story of how these contradictory moral formulations of the person play out in the setting of one Rwandan town, it also tells of the much more general problem of the uneasy coexistence of two ways of doing social relationships, both of which are fundamental to all forms of collective life: (inter)dependence and disconnectedness. In a post-conflict moment characterized by explicit state-driven endeavors of social re-engineering—including the production of new kinds of persons—the relationship between interdependence and disconnectedness carries all the more weight. Lives lived through conflict lay especially bare the stakes—political, personal, social, and moral—of the perennial question, what kind of person should I be? The ways that those who live through violence attempt to respond to that core, moral question uncover how post-conflict suffering collapses and confounds the distinction between private and public life (Chakravarti 2014: 38–39). Even as political violence is by definition a public, not a "personal" problem, its felt effects are perhaps most palpable at the level of the intricacies and trivialities of daily, private life.

As incongruous and incompatible as they seem, the tensions and inconsistencies in "good personhood" in Butare are ultimately artifacts of each other, ones produced by the work of managing the dangers attached to the moral failures of different "kinds" of persons. The contrast in Butare residents' selfhood is a product of their strivings to navigate the overlaps and intersections of individuated and relational moral fields of the self in the post-genocide moment. Does this mean that the relational self represents purely the devastation of the genocide while the individuated self is ruthlessly strategic in the quest for modern selfhood? Of course it does not. The relational self can be profoundly strategic in certain moments, for example in appealing to social ties to make claims on others' resources or personal connections, or making use of flexible, ethnically marked categories to play up or down one's relationally constituted Tutsiness or Hutuness. At the other end of the spectrum, the individuated self is not all-knowing and strategic, but can be deeply vulnerable, especially when the promises of urban cultural capital, education, or entrepreneurial drive fail to deliver the "good life." The aspiration to become a "modern" person—autonomous, self-sufficient, and connected to others by volition rather than necessity—is in no way incompatible with feelings of loss, devastation, or appreciation for the security and opportunities to aid others afforded by patronage obligations.

Most important of all, because Butaréens' enactments of competing forms of personhood never maintain firm or clear boundaries between those types, we could read relational or individuated qualities of selfhood into any single choice, action, or behavior. As Lambek (2015) suggests, individuated and relational views of the person are like the famous drawing from perception studies in which viewers can see either a duck or a rabbit in the same image, but never both simultaneously. So with models of the person, he writes,

> one can see the same image [the person] in two different ways [relational or individuated], but not both at once. In a given cultural or historical setting there may be forces conspiring to bring out one form rather than the other, whether through structural factors, ideological ones, or the cultural idioms available. But this will never preclude the other image revealing itself … Perhaps they can be seen as complementary social processes rather than discrete kinds of persons. (Lambek 2015: 402)

In the context of post-genocide Butare, then, the problem is that the very same action can appear as a sign of either the composite/relational or the bounded/individuated self at work. To become entangled in a patron–client relationship, for instance, could be read on the one hand as a relational self doing what relational selves do, namely embedding themselves in relations with others that make them "someone" in their social worlds. On the other hand, it could be read as the strategic, individuated self who makes the voluntary choice to enter exchange relations in order to later exact services or make claims on others. Aiding and exploiting can look vexingly similar (Sahlins 1972: 134), and depending on how we look at it, we can see one or the other and—*pace* Lambek—perhaps even both at once. That duality is precisely what is apparent in Butare residents' indeterminate evaluations of those who continue to sponsor or depend on others in patronage relations. It is what underpins Butaréens' mapping of the individuated self onto the urban and the relational self onto the rural and their ambiguous assessments of which "kind" of person is morally preferable. While the urban is conducive to personal development and making "modern" bonds of volition rather than necessity, town residents also complain that urban culture undermines basic forms of sociality and mutual aid. The rural is more "convivial," as Charles once put it, a remark that might be best read as a solidarity claim with the poor rather than a factual description of rural social relations. And yet, given the frequency with which town residents denigrate rural people and their "porousness" to others' influences, conviviality and other positive descriptors Butaréens assign to the rural might be read as mere euphemisms for dependency and all its disparaging connotations.

Since distinctions between different "kinds" of persons produce moral hierarchies with consequences for power and inequality, one might wonder: are Butare residents' fluctuations between accounting for their own and others' actions through relational and individuated moral frameworks simply a matter of strategic self-presentation and impression management? Is the capacity to self-present (although never conclusively) as either an individuated or a "joined up" self (Carsten 2004) simply one more mark of urban privilege and connections that straddle "the modern" and the "parochial"? If we follow that line of reasoning, self-presentation in Butare exceeds Goffman's (1959) acts of impression management directed toward living up to or breaking with situational role expectations within a particular cultural framework of what a person is. It would further entail the capacity to situationally define the very *sources* of one's selfhood—externally and relationally defined through connections with others or individuated and internally produced through the work of personal development. And while I would never suggest that strategic considerations are absent from Butaréens' situational invocations of competing moral frameworks of the self, neither self-presentation nor the constitution of the self can be reduced to pure strategy (Goffman 1959). Not only is this a reductive understanding of why people do the things they do, it could also lead to the error of presuming that social actors have virtually perfect knowledge of what forms of impression management are most expedient in any given moment. The problem that Butare residents face is precisely the ambiguity of what it means to be a "good person" in the post-genocide moment. To what degree should I seek to embed myself in relations of mutual obligation and sociality? To what extent should I try to cultivate a self that is not defined by its position in relations of kinship or clientship? And regardless of what I do or how I justify it, how will other people receive my actions? Even as theories of self-presentation and impression management produce a certain view of the person (e.g. Goffman 1959), they are not coterminous with that view.

We would also do well to remember that the very act of writing ethnography—of drawing out how the world looks to our research participants—is what can produce a disproportionately strategic, calculating view of the social actor.[1] In the interpretive endeavor of ethnography, to make sense of why people do what they do and what those things mean to them, we can end up flattening people's practices and outlooks for the purposes of crafting an argument. Even if we take seriously the importance of underscoring contradictions in people's lives and outlooks, nonetheless, we select, we emphasize, and we modulate. Perhaps it is ethnographers who manage impressions for our research participants?

Fanon ([1963] 2004: 2) wrote that it is only upon the creation of "new men" [sic], ones who author themselves instead of being "fabricated" by the colonist and the colonial system, that the process of decolonization will reach completion. Butare residents, too, locate the source of their predicaments, both ordinary and extraordinary, not just in the politics of the genocide or in the post-conflict moment, but in the condition of postcoloniality more generally. Poverty, jealousy of others' successes, dependent dispositions, greed, dissimulation, nepotism, blind obedience to authority, and a lack of creativity—these are all (ethnically marked) qualities of "ordinary Rwandans" that educated Butaréens perceive as obstacles to achieving modern personhood and modern nationhood. Crucially, they conceive of these obstacles as rooted in Rwanda's colonial legacy and the forms of dependency it fostered not only between colonizer and colonized, but also between Tutsi and Hutu. The appeal they see in striving to become "peaceful selves" is not a matter of becoming good Rwandans who conform to superiors' demands. Indeed, as people who claim freedom in their thoughts and actions and who blame blind conformity for the scale of the 1994 genocide, they would vigorously reject this perspective on why they do what they do. What is striking is that when Butare residents do conform to the authorities' expectations—be it eschewing ethnic labels, extolling the virtues of entrepreneurship or personal development, or preaching the gospel of unity and reconciliation—they configure their acquiescence to those calls as a *choice* they freely make because of the kinds of persons they aspire to be. To be sure, social forces much greater than individual preferences shape those aspirations. But it is the fact that Butaréens profess to actively choose them that is compelling in the context of the foregoing analysis. Town residents desire to become the kinds of persons who will not become mired in violence again, who are above ethnic squabbles, who envisage the self as a project in the act of becoming, and who deeply value rootedness in Butare and the social relationships that ground them there. Indeed, peaceful selves are not only those who refrain from violence, but also those who live well with others. And so, upholding expectations of sociality, mutual aid, humble living, and obligations to the dead are all part of becoming the kinds of selves they aspire to be, but so are pursuit of personal development, prosperity, and autonomy. It is not that the peaceful self lacks connections to others, but rather that it disconnects from negative influences in order to better connect and cooperate with others. This is a self who aims to connect and disconnect from others according to a new logic of sociality based on mutual cooperation, understanding, and open communication (Illouz 2008: 104). While the forms of sociality that link people on the basis of ascribed status and role obligations have in no way disappeared from Butaréens' social worlds, they now tell themselves a story about those obligations as ones they have freely chosen. But nonetheless, those stories of free choice never quite manage to quiet the nagging worry that one has not and cannot fully author the self. As Englund (2006: 39) writes, "freedom as a potential to transform oneself can be achieved only through social relationships, not in the unproductive state of abstract individuality. It also follows that freedom is precarious and discontinuous, very different from the permanent condition that neoliberal rhetoric promises."

And yet, in spite of these vexing contradictions, it is not hard to see why Butare residents see a virtue in striving to be new kinds of persons. Self-development is profoundly appealing in Butare today precisely because it suggests that people are still in the act of becoming. If the self is a project, then what they have been or what they are now is not what they are condemned to remain (Illouz 2008: 182). Another life is possible. To be able to transcend categories of victim, bystander, perpetrator, returnee, Tutsi, or Hutu and to become known for something else cannot but be captivating in a social world marred by violence. But the trouble, as Fanon ([1963] 2004) incisively elicits, is the indefinite deferral of this future in postcolonial contexts. Just when will the New Rwandan and New Rwanda definitively emerge? At what point will Rwandans overcome not only the condition of the post-conflict, but also the postcolonial? Even the most ambitious authors of their own selves in Butare are daily confronted with the impossibility of getting over the postcolonial legacy in their lives. Each time they wonder if they should read an ethnic commentary into someone's evaluation of their behaviors, the history of the colonial production of ethnic stereotypes and their political uses and abuses is there. That past is also present each time they think of those lost in the genocide. Even as the genocide cannot be reduced to the effects of colonialism, it would likely never have happened in quite the way it did if a fraught colonial history was not available to be manipulated by political elites. But the question arises, are there social worlds—formerly colonized or otherwise—in which persons ever really freely script who they are? Herein lies the symbolic violence of the impossible standards of "peaceful selfhood" in post-genocide Butare: even as they recognize the condition of the post-conflict and postcolonial as structuring forces in their lives and social worlds, residents nonetheless *experience* the contradictions of self-making as personal failings to live up to competing ideals, to author the self freely and autonomously. Indeed, they experience these tensions in this way even as freely authoring the self in a genuine sense would be tantamount to nothing less than overcoming the social itself.

What of the meaning of the foregoing analysis for "peace" in Rwanda? As I noted in the Introduction, the notion of the "peaceful self" imbues peace with an ironic distance, since Butaréens' endeavors to become "capable" of peace necessarily catch them in social and moral binds and pull them in different directions. The trouble is that all endeavors to be "good Rwandans" by either RPF or popular standards—doing one's part to build the country, aiding those in need, remembering the (Tutsi) victims of 1994, but otherwise eschewing ethnic categories—produce social boundaries that look and feel a great deal like those manipulated in the 1990s. The one who works hard to rebuild Rwanda through entrepreneurship also seems to set herself apart from the majority and is insufficiently "of" the people. The one who aids others might be viewed as either (or both) benevolent or exploitative. To remember genocide victims, especially publicly, easily leads to the suspicion that those who remember harbor a sense that Hutu share collective guilt for 1994. And to self-present as someone who refuses ethnic categories evokes longstanding strategies by which Tutsi political leaders bolstered their legitimacy as Rwanda's "rightful" rulers. What, if anything, can the category of "peace" mean in a social world like this one, where appeals to peace are always suspect because of how they have historically been invoked in projects directed to securing both political legitimacy and personal aggrandizement?

In the end, the question of what kind of person one can and should be remains pressing for urban Rwandans precisely because it is inseparable from questions of what caused the violence, what it means to be modern, and what makes for good social relationships and a just moral order. But there is a difficult question that I have not yet addressed—perhaps it seems that I have assiduously avoided it. Given the competing demands to which Butare residents are subject in the post-conflict moment and the ways they aim to live up to them, does their experience of themselves *feel* fragmented or inconsistent on the experiential level? It is one thing to talk about personhood at the abstract, categorical level of how Butaréens conceptualize what a human being is and ought to be, and quite another how people live out and experience *being* a person in a post-conflict moment. In other words, are the sharp contrasts in their selfhood troubling to them? Do they feel compelled to try to reconcile these disparate senses of who they are and ought to be that emerge from the competing moral orders in which they are caught? In what is now an anthropological truism, Gluckman (1958: 26) argued that people can and do "live coherent lives by situational selection from a medley of contradictory values, ill-assorted beliefs, and varied interests and techniques." Yet something gnaws at Butare residents when it comes to how they live out the dissonance in their selfhood, which makes me wonder just how coherent the lives lived by Butaréens feel on an experiential level. A conversation between Odette and a young Butare doctor, a genocide survivor named Frédéric, stands out in my mind for how their exchange poignantly captured this sense of discord. "It's like I have two Frédérics inside me," he mused one afternoon when Odette and I were visiting him in the shade of his garden. "There is the one who is successful and who has worked hard, who travels and has a good job. And then there is the one who is still wounded and suffering." He lowered his head bashfully. "Maybe it's sort of a silly thought, but this conflict between the two parts of me—it's how I feel every day." No one spoke for several seconds, and then Odette added, tentatively at first:

> I used to have a photo of my old family [before the genocide] hanging in my living room. I had to move it into the bedroom, because people who came to the house were curious about it, and they asked too many questions. I have no peace. Every morning when I wake up, a scene passes before my eyes, and I think about what happened to them. It's true, when you're like us, you always have a second self inside of you. You don't know if it's who you used to be or who you're going to become, but there's always another. Sometimes I've found myself calling my own name out loud to myself—"Odette"—just to see if I was still in there somewhere, to see if it was still me and if I knew myself at all. (Butare, July 2014)

And so, people like Frédéric and Odette locate in their twoness a profound disconnect—between who they used to be and who they are or might become, between their devastation and their successful, high-profile statuses in the town. The stories they tell about their lives and about themselves are hopelessly discordant. For Odette, for Frédéric, and for others too, when they wake up in the morning, when they pass by places haunted by the genocide, and when they are confronted with the stark duality of their own subjectivity, the questions of who they are, how they belong, and what can make for a good life in the shadow of genocide continue to raise disquieting predicaments.

Note

1. I am grateful to Dan Yon for pointing this out to me.

GLOSSARY OF KINYARWANDA TERMS

abakene	the poor
abakire	the rich
abatindi	the vulnerable
abatindi nyakujya	the most vulnerable
Banyarwanda	people of Rwanda; Rwandan people
gacaca	semi-traditional, local-level tribunals revived to try genocide crimes
guterekera	a tradition of honoring and offering gifts to the deceased
ibiteekerezo	historical tales and oral traditions of Rwanda, especially southern and central Rwanda
imfura	those of high status and moral standing; those who have the qualities of *ubupfura*
imihigo	performance contracts
imisozi	hills
impano	a gift between friends
ingando	solidarity camps for civic re-education, part of National Unity and Reconciliation Commission
intara (pl. *intara*)	province
interahamwe	"those who work together," the youth militia responsible for many of the massacres during the 1994 genocide
inyoroshyo	a bribe, an interested gift
Kinyarwanda	the indigenous language of Rwandans; Rwandan culture

maneko	spy
mumujyi	in town
muzungu (pl. *bazungu*)	white person
mwami	traditional ruler of Rwanda; sometimes translated as "king"
ruswa	a bribe, an interested gift
shebuja	*ubuhake* patron
ubuhake	cattle clientship
ubukonde	land clientship
ubuntu	humanity; unity of human beings
ubupfura	dignity; nobility of heart
ubureetwa	form of clientship or corvée reserved only for Hutu clients in which labor or gifts were exacted by Tutsi patrons
ubwoko (pl. *ibwoko*)	clan; category; later, ethnicity
umudugudu (pl. *imidugudu*)	smallest administrative unit in Rwanda; a controversial villagization plan that groups 100–150 houses on collectively held land
umuganda	compulsory nationwide monthly community work
umugaragu	*ubuhake* client
umunyamujyi (pl. *abanyamujyi*)	urban person
umuturage (pl. *abaturage*)	peasant farmer; rural person
uturere	district
wihangane	to try to bear or withstand

BIBLIOGRAPHY

Abramowitz, Sharon. 2014. *Searching for Normal in the Wake of the Liberian War*. Philadelphia, PA: University of Pennsylvania Press.

Abrams, Philip. 1988. "Notes on the Difficulty of Studying the State." *Journal of Historical Sociology* 1(1): 58–89.

African Development Bank. 2014. "Analysis of Gender and Youth Unemployment in Rwanda." Retrieved 20 May 2015 from http://www.afdb.org/fileadmin/uploads/afdb/Documents/Publications/Rwanda_-_Analysis_of_Gender_and_Youth_Employment.pdf.

Agar, Michael H. [1996] 2008. *The Professional Stranger: An Informal Introduction to Ethnography*. Bingley, UK: Emerald Group Publishing.

Alatas, Syed Hussein. 1977. *Intellectuals in Developing Societies*. London: Frank Cass.

Allan, Graham. 1998. "Friendship, Sociology and Social Structure." *Journal of Social and Personal Relationships* 15(5): 685–702.

Anderson, Benedict. [1983] 1991. *Imagined Communities: Reflections on the Origin and Spread of Nationalism*. London: Verso.

Ansoms, An. 2011. "Rwanda's Post-Genocide Economic Reconstruction: The Mismatch between Elite Ambitions and Rural Realities." In *Remaking Rwanda: State Building and Human Rights after Mass Violence*, ed. Scott Straus and Lars Waldorf, 240–51. Madison, WI: University of Wisconsin Press.

Antze, Paul. 1996. "Telling Stories, Making Selves." In *Tense Past: Cultural Essays in Trauma and Memory*, ed. Paul Antze and Michael Lambek, 3–23. New York: Routledge.

Antze, Paul and Michael Lambek. 1996. "Introduction: Forecasting Memory." In *Tense Past: Cultural Essays in Trauma and Memory*, ed. Paul Antze and Michael Lambek, xi–xxxviii. New York: Routledge.

Arendt, Hannah. 1963. *Eichmann in Jerusalem: A Report on the Banality of Evil*. New York: Penguin Books.

Argenti, Nicolas and Katharina Schramm, eds. 2010. *Remembering Violence: Anthropological Perspectives on Intergenerational Transmission*. New York: Berghahn Books.

Asad, Talal. 1993. *Genealogies of Religion: Discipline and Reasons of Power in Christianity and Islam*. Baltimore, MD: The Johns Hopkins University Press.

Austin, John L. 1962. *How to Do Things with Words*. Cambridge, MA: Harvard University Press.

Avruch, Kevin. 1998. *Culture and Conflict Resolution*. Washington, DC: United States Institute of Peace Press.

Barth, Fredrik. 1969. *Ethnic Groups and Boundaries: The Social Organization of Cultural Difference*. Boston, MA: Little, Brown.

Battaglia, Debbora, ed. 1995. *Rhetorics of Self-Making*. Berkeley, CA: University of California Press.

Bauman, Zygmunt. 1989. *Modernity and the Holocaust*. Cambridge: Polity Press.

Bauman, Zygmunt and Rein Raud. 2015. *Practices of Selfhood*. Cambridge: Polity Press.

Bellman, Beryl. 1984. *The Language of Secrecy: Symbols and Metaphors in Poro Ritual*. New Brunswick, NJ: Rutgers University Press.

Biggar, Nigel. 2001. "Making Peace or Doing Justice: Must We Choose?" In *Burying the Past: Making Peace and Doing Justice after Civil Conflict*, ed. Nigel Biggar, 6–22. Washington, DC: Georgetown University Press.

Bolten, Catherine. 2012. *I Did It to Save My Life: Love and Survival in Sierra Leone*. Berkeley, CA: University of California Press.

Booth, W. James. 2001. "The Unforgotten: Memories of Justice." *American Political Science Review* 95(4): 777–91.

Borneman, John. 1997. *Settling Accounts: Violence, Justice, and Accountability in Postsocialist Europe*. Princeton, NJ: Princeton University Press.

Bourdieu, Pierre. 1984. *Distinction: A Social Critique of the Judgment of Taste*, trans. Richard Nice. Cambridge, MA: Harvard University Press.

———. [1986] 2011. "The Forms of Capital." In *Cultural Theory: An Anthology*, ed. Imre Szeman and Timothy Kaposy, 81–93. Malden, MA: Wiley-Blackwell.

Bourdieu, Pierre and Loïc Wacquant. 1992. *Invitation to a Reflexive Sociology*. Cambridge: Polity Press.

Brounéus, Karen. 2010. "Truth-Telling as Talking Cure? Insecurity and Retraumatization in the Rwandan Gacaca Courts." *Security Dialogue* 39(1): 55–76.

Brubaker, Rogers. 2004. *Ethnicity without Groups*. Cambridge, MA: Harvard University Press.

Buckley-Zistel, Susanne. 2006. "Remembering to Forget: Chosen Amnesia as a Strategy for Local Coexistence in Post-Genocide Rwanda." *Journal of the International African Institute* 76(2): 131–50.

Burnet, Jennie E. 2009. "Whose Genocide? Whose Truth? Representations of Victim and Perpetrator in Rwanda." In *Genocide: Truth, Memory, and Representation*, ed. Alexander Laban Hinton and Kevin Lewis O'Neill, 80–110. Durham, NC: Duke University Press.

———. 2012. *Genocide Lives in Us: Women, Memory, and Silence in Rwanda*. Madison, WI: University of Wisconsin Press.

Carney, J.J. 2013. *Rwanda before the Genocide: Catholic Politics and Ethnic Discourse in the Late Colonial Era*. Oxford: Oxford University Press.

Carrier, James. 1999. "People Who Can Be Friends." In *The Anthropology of Friendship*, ed. Sandra Bell and Simon Coleman, 21–38. Oxford: Berg.

Carrithers, Michael. 1985. "An Alternative Social History of the Self." In *The Category of the Person: Anthropology, Philosophy, History*, ed. Michael Carrithers, Steven Collins, and Steven Lukes, 234–56. Cambridge: Cambridge University Press.

Carrithers, Michael, Steven Collins, and Steven Lukes (eds). 1985. *The Category of the Person: Anthropology, Philosophy, History*. Cambridge: Cambridge University Press.

Carsten, Janet, ed. 2000. *Cultures of Relatedness: New Approaches to the Study of Kinship*. Cambridge: Cambridge University Press.

———. 2004. *After Kinship*. Cambridge: Cambridge University Press.

Chakravarti, Sonali. 2014. *Sing the Rage: Listening to Anger after Mass Violence*. Chicago, IL: University of Chicago Press.

Chrétien, Jean-Pierre. 2003. *The Great Lakes Region of Africa: Two Thousand Years of History*, trans. Scott Straus. New York: Zone Books.

Clark, Janine Natalya. 2008. "The Three Rs: Retributive Justice, Restorative Justice, and Reconciliation." *Contemporary Justice Review* 11(4): 331–50.

———. 2010. "National Unity and Reconciliation in Rwanda: A Flawed Approach?" *Journal of Contemporary African Studies* 28(2): 137–54.

Clark-Kazak, Christina R. 2009. "Towards a Working Definition and Application of Social Age in International Development Studies." *Journal of Development Studies* 45(8): 1307–24.

Clouzot, Olivier. 2000. *L'éveil et la verticalité: Essai sur la transcendence et sur le chemin de transformation qui y conduit.* Gap: Éditions le Souffle D'Or.

Codère, Helen. 1962. "Power in Ruanda." *Anthropologica* 4(1): 45–86.

Cohen, Abner. 1969. *Custom and Politics in Urban Africa: A Study of Hausa Migrants in Yoruba Towns.* London: Routledge.

———. 1974. *Urban Ethnicity.* London: Tavistock.

Cohen, Anthony P. 1992. "The Right to Personal Identity." In *The Values of the Enterprise Culture: The Moral Debate,* ed. Paul Heelas and Paul Morris, 179–93. London: Routledge.

———. 1994. *Self Consciousness: An Alternative Anthropology of Identity.* London: Routledge.

Cohen, Ronald. 1978. "Ethnicity: Problem and Focus in Anthropology." *Annual Review of Anthropology* 7: 379–403.

Cohn, Bernard. 1996. *Colonialism and Its Forms of Knowledge: The British in India.* Princeton: Princeton University Press.

Comaroff, John and Jean Comaroff. 1997. *Of Revelation and Revolution Volume 2: Dialectics of Modernity on a South African Frontier.* Chicago, IL: University of Chicago Press.

———. 2001. "On Personhood: An Anthropological Perspective from Africa." *Social Identities* 7(2): 267–83.

Connerton, Paul. 1989. *How Societies Remember.* Cambridge: Cambridge University Press.

Corey, Allison and Sandra Joireman. 2004. "Retributive Justice: The *Gacaca* Courts in Rwanda." *African Affairs* 103(410): 73–89.

Corrigan, Philip. 1981. "Moral Regulation: Some Preliminary Remarks." *Sociological Review* 29(2): 313–37.

Corrigan, Philip and Derek Sayer. 1985. *The Great Arch: English State Formation as Cultural Revolution.* Oxford: Blackwell.

Crenshaw, Kimberlé. 1991. "Mapping the Margins: Intersectionality, Identity Politics, and Violence against Women of Color." *Stanford Law Review* 43(6): 1241–99.

Davis, Kingsley and Wilbert Moore. 1945. "Some Principles of Stratification." *American Sociological Review* 10(2): 242–49.

de Heusch, Luc. 1966. *Le Rwanda et la civilisation interlacustre: Études d'anthropologie historique et structurale.* Brussels: Université Libre de Bruxelles, Institut de Sociologie.

De Lame, Danielle. 2004. "Mighty Secrets, Public Commensality, and the Crisis of Transparency: Rwanda through the Looking Glass." *Canadian Journal of African Studies* 38(2): 279–317.

———. 2005. *A Hill among a Thousand: Transformations and Ruptures in Rural Rwanda,* trans. Helen Arnold. Madison, WI: University of Wisconsin Press.

Des Forges, Alison. 1995. "The Ideology of Genocide." *Issue: A Journal of Opinion.* 23(2): 44-47.

———. 1999. *Leave None to Tell the Story: Genocide in Rwanda.* New York: Human Rights Watch.

Desrosiers, Marie-Eve and Susan Thomson. 2011. "Rhetorical Legacies of Leadership: Projections of 'Benevolent Leadership' in Pre- and Post-Genocide Rwanda." *Journal of Modern African Studies* 49(3): 429–53.

D'Hertefelt, Marcel. 1964. "Mythes et idéologies dans le Rwanda ancien et contemporain." In *The Historian in Tropical Africa: Studies Presented and Discussed at the Fourth International*

African Seminar at the University of Dakar, Senegal 1961, ed. J. Vansina, R. Mauny and L.V. Thomas, 219–35. London: Oxford University Press.

Dieterlen, Germaine. 1973. "L'image du corps et les componsantes de la personne chez les Dogon." In *La Notion de la Personne en Afrique Noire, Actes du Colloque international du Centre national de la Recherche scientifique*, ed. Germaine Dieterlen, 205–29. Paris: L'Harmattan.

Dominus, Susan. 2014. "Portraits of Reconciliation." *New York Times*, 6 April. Retrieved 18 April 2014 from http://www.nytimes.com/interactive/2014/04/06/magazine/06-pieter-hugo-rwanda-portraits.html?_r=0.

Dorsey, Learthen. 1983. "The Rwandan Colonial Economy, 1916–1941." Ph.D. dissertation. East Lansing, MI: Michigan State University.

Doughty, Kristin. 2014. "'Our Goal Is Not to Punish but to Reconcile': Mediation in Post-Genocide Rwanda." *American Anthropologist* 116(40): 780–94.

———. 2015. "Law and the Architecture of Social Repair: Gacaca Days in Post-Genocide Rwanda." *Journal of the Royal Anthropological Institute* 21(2): 419–37.

———. 2016. *Remediation in Rwanda: Grassroots Legal Forums*. Philadelphia, PA: University of Pennsylvania Press.

Douglas, Mary and Steven Ney. 1998. *Missing Persons: A Critique of Personhood in the Social Sciences*. Volume 1. Berkeley, CA: University of California Press.

DuBois, Lindsay. 2005. *The Politics of the Past in an Argentine Working-Class Neighbourhood*. Toronto: University of Toronto Press.

Dumont, Louis. 1992. *Essays on Individualism: Modern Ideology in Anthropological Perspective*. Chicago, IL: University of Chicago Press.

Durkheim, Émile. 1995. *The Elementary Forms of Religious Life*, trans. Karen Fields. New York: The Free Press.

———. 1997. *Suicide: A Study in Sociology*. New York: The Free Press.

Ehrenreich, Barbara. 2009. *Bright-Sided: How the Relentless Promotion of Positive Thinking has Undermined America*. New York: Metropolitan Books.

Eltringham, Nigel. 2004. *Accounting for Horror: Post-Genocide Debates in Rwanda*. London: Pluto Press.

———. 2014. "Bodies of Evidence: Remembering the Rwandan Genocide at Murambi." In *Remembering Genocide*, ed. Nigel Eltringham and Pam Maclean, 200–219.London: Routledge.

Englund, Harri. 2006. *Prisoners of Freedom: Human Rights and the African Poor*. Berkeley, CA: University of California Press.

Englund, Harri and James Leach. 2000. "Ethnography and the Meta-Narratives of Modernity." *Current Anthropology* 41(2): 225–48.

Eramian, Laura. 2014. "Ethnicity without Labels? Ambiguity and Excess in Postethnic Rwanda." *Focaal: Journal of Global and Historical Anthropology* 70: 96–109.

———. 2015. "Ethnic Boundaries in Contemporary Rwanda: Fixity, Flexibility, and Their Limits." *Anthropologica* 57(1): 94–103.

———. 2017. "Testimony, Disbelief, and Opaque Peace Building in Post-Genocide Rwanda." *Political and Legal Anthropology Review* 40(1): 52–66.

Eriksen, Thomas Hylland. 1993. *Ethnicity and Nationalism: Anthropological Perspectives*. London: Pluto Press.

Evans-Pritchard, E.E. 1967. "Introduction to Marcel Mauss." In *The Gift: Forms and Functions of Exchange in Archaic Societies*, v–x. New York: Norton.

Ewing, Katherine. 1990. "The Illusion of Wholeness: Culture, Self, and the Experience of Inconsistency." *Ethos* 18(3): 251–78.

Fanon, Frantz. [1963] 2004. *The Wretched of the Earth*, trans. Richard Philcox. New York: Grove Press.

Feldman, Allen. 2004. "Memory Theaters, Virtual Witnessing and the Trauma Aesthetic." *Biography* 27(1): 163–202.

Felman, Shoshana. 2002. *The Juridical Unconscious: Trials and Traumas in the Twentieth Century*. Cambridge, MA: Harvard University Press.

Ferguson, James. 2013. "Declarations of Dependence: Labor, Personhood, and Welfare in Southern Africa." *Journal of the Royal Anthropological Institute* 19: 223–42.

Fioratta, Susanna. 2015. "Beyond Remittance: Evading Uselessness and Seeking Personhood in Fouta Djallon, Guinea." *American Ethnologist* 42(2): 295–308.

Fisher, Jonathan. 2015. "Writing about Rwanda since the Genocide." *Journal of Intervention and State Building* 9(1): 131–45.

Fortes, Meyer. [1973] 1987. "The Concept of the Person." In *Religion, Morality, and the Person: Essays on Tallensi Religion*, ed. Jack Goody, 247–86. Cambridge: Cambridge University Press.

Foucault, Michel, et al. 1988. *Technologies of the Self: A Seminar with Michel Foucault*. Amherst, MA: University of Massachusetts Press.

Freeman, Carla. 2014. *Entrepreneurial Selves: Neoliberal Respectability and the Making of a Caribbean Middle Class*. Durham, NC: Duke University Press.

Fujii, Lee Ann. 2009. *Killing Neighbors: Webs of Violence in Rwanda*. Ithaca, NY: Cornell University Press.

Geertz, Clifford. 1973. *The Interpretation of Cultures: Selected Essays by Clifford Geertz*. New York: Basic Books.

Gibson, James L. 2004. "Does Truth Lead to Reconciliation? Testing the Causal Assumptions of the South African Truth and Reconciliation Process." *American Journal of Political Science* 48(2): 201–17.

Giddens, Anthony. 1991. *Modernity and Self-Identity: Self and Society in the Late Modern Age*. Stanford, CA: Stanford University Press.

Gifford, Paul. 1998. *African Christianity: Its Public Role*. Bloomington, IN: University of Indiana Press.

Gluckman, Max. 1958. *Analysis of a Social Situation in Modern Zululand*. The Rhodes-Livingstone Papers. Manchester: Manchester University Press.

Goffman, Erving. 1959. *The Presentation of Self in Everyday Life*. New York: Doubleday.

Gravel, Peter Bettez. 1968. *Remera: A Community in Eastern Rwanda*. The Hague and Paris: Mouton.

Guichaoua, André. 2005. *Rwanda 1994: Les politiques du génocide à Butare*. Paris: Karthala.

Hamber, Brandon and Richard A. Wilson. 2002. "Symbolic Closure through Memory, Reparation, and Revenge in Post-Conflict Societies." *Journal of Human Rights* 1(1): 35–53.

Hardt, Michael. 1999. "Affective Labor." *boundary 2* 26(2): 89–100.

Harrison, Faye. 2002. "Unravelling 'Race' for the Twenty-First Century." In *Exotic No More: Anthropology on the Front Lines*, ed. Jeremy MacClancey, 145–66. Chicago, IL: University of Chicago Press.

Hatzfeld, Jean. 2005. *Machete Season: The Killers in Rwanda Speak*, trans. Linda Coverdale. New York: Farrar, Strauss, and Giroux.

Hawkins, David R. 2005. *Pouvoir contre force: Les determinants cachés du comportement humain*. Paris: Guy Trédaniel.

Heelas, Paul and Paul Morris, eds. 1992. *The Values of the Enterprise Culture: The Moral Debate*. London: Routledge.

Heremans, Père Roger. 1973. *Introduction à l'histoire du Rwanda*. Kigali: Éditions Rwandaises.

Herman, Judith. 1992. *Trauma and Recovery*. New York: Basic Books.

Hickman, Jacob. 2014. "Ancestral Personhood and Moral Justification." *Anthropological Theory* 14(3): 317–35.

Hintjens, Helen. 2008. "Post-Genocide Identity Politics in Rwanda." *Ethnicities* 8(1): 5–41.

Hochschild, Arlie R. 1979. "Emotion Work, Feeling Rules, and Social Structure." *American Journal of Sociology* 85(3): 551–75.

———. 1983. *The Managed Heart: The Commercialization of Human Feeling*. Berkeley: University of California Press.

Hollan, Douglas. 1992. "Cross-Cultural Differences in the Self." *Journal of Anthropological Research* 48(4): 283–300.

Human Rights Watch. 2008. "VII: 'Divisionism' and 'Genocide Ideology'." In *Law and Reality: Progress in Judicial Reform in Rwanda*. Retrieved 26 February 2013 from http://www.hrw.org/reports/2008/rwanda0708/7.htm.

Ilcan, Suzan and Lynne Phillips. 2006. "Governing Peace: Global Rationalities of Security and UNESCO's Culture of Peace Campaign." *Anthropologica* 48(1): 59–71.

Illouz, Eva. 2008. *Saving the Modern Soul: Therapy, Emotions, and the Culture of Self-Help*. Berkeley, CA: University of California Press.

Ingelaere, Bert. 2010. "Do We Understand Life after Genocide? Center and Periphery in the Construction of Knowledge in Post-Genocide Rwanda." *African Studies Review* 53(1): 41–59.

Institute of Policy Analysis and Research Rwanda. 2014. *Imihigo Evaluation 2013/2014 Final Report*. Kigali: Republic of Rwanda.

Jackson, Michael and Ivan Karp (eds). 1990. *Personhood and Agency: The Experience of Self and Other in African Cultures*. Uppsala Studies in Cultural Anthropology, 14. Washington, DC: Smithsonian Institution Press.

Jacobson-Widding, Anita. 1990. "The Shadow as an Expression of Individuality in Congolese Conceptions of Personhood." In *Personhood and Agency: The Experience of Self and Other in African Cultures*. Uppsala Studies in Cultural Anthropology, 14, ed. Michael Jackson and Ivan Karp, 31–58. Washington, DC: Smithsonian Institution Press.

Jefremovas, Villia. 1997. "Contested Identities: Power and the Fictions of Ethnicity, Ethnography and History in Rwanda." *Anthropologica* 39: 91–104.

Jones, Graham M. 2014. "Secrecy." *Annual Review of Anthropology* 43: 53–69.

Joseph, Gilbert M. and Daniel Nugent. 1994. "Popular Culture and State Formation in Revolutionary Mexico." In *Everyday Forms of State Formation: Revolution and the Negotiation of Rule in Modern Mexico*, ed. Gilbert M. Joseph and Daniel Nugent, 3–23. Durham, NC: Duke University Press.

Kagame, Alexis. 1972. *Un abrégé de l'ethno-histoire du Rwanda*. Collection "Muntu," 3–4. Butare: Éditions universitaires du Rwanda.

Kagame, Paul. 2012a. Remarks by H.E. Paul Kagame, President of the Republic of Rwanda, at an Agaciro Fundraising Event Organised by Umurinzi Young Professionals. Retrieved 13 May 2017 from http://presidency.gov.rw/index.php?id=23&tx_ttnews%5Btt_news%5D=623&cHash=c0723478308dd97f057756473f871707.

———. 2012b. Speech delivered by H.E. Paul Kagame at the Official Closing of Gacaca Courts, Kigali, 18 June 2012. Retrieved 28 October 2016 from http://www.paulkagame.com/index.php/speeches/691-speech-by-he-paul-kagame-president-of-the-republic-of-rwanda-at-the-official-closing-of-gacaca-courts.

———. 2013. Speech Delivered by H.E. Paul Kagame, President of Rwanda on the Occasion of Rwanda Day in London, May 18, 2013. Retrieved 12 May 2017 from http://www.paulkagame.com/index.php/speeches/1080-speech-delivered-by-he-president-paul-kagame-president-of-rwanda-on-the-occasion-of-rwanda-day

———. 2015. Speech in Huye District, 12 April. Retrieved 28 April 2015 from http://www.paulkagame.com/index.php/speeches/official-visits/1523-president-kagame-s-speech-in-huye-district.

Kalibwami, Justin. 1991. *Le catholicisme et la société rwandaise: 1900–1962.* Paris: Éditions Présence Africaine.

Kamwangamalu, Nkonko M. 1999 "Ubuntu in South Africa: A Sociolinguistic Perspective to a Pan-African Concept." *Critical Arts: A North-South Journal of Cultural and Media Studies* 13(2): 24–41.

Kanimba, Célestin M. 2005. "Préservation de la mémoire du génocide: Rôles, actions, et stratégies." In *Le génocide de 1994: Idéologie et mémoire.* Études rwandaises 9, Série lettres et sciences humaines, 128–47. Butare, Rwanda: Éditions de l'Université nationale du Rwanda.

Kermode, Frank. 1979. *The Genesis of Secrecy: On the Interpretation of Narrative.* Cambridge, MA: Harvard University Press.

Keza Gara, Akaliza. 2012. "Rwanda: Unemployed = Self-Employed." *The New Times*, 29 May. Retrieved 19 April 2013 from http://allafrica.com/stories/201205290188.html.

Kinzer, Stephen. 2008. *A Thousand Hills: Rwanda's Rebirth and the Man Who Dreamed It.* Hoboken, NJ: Wiley.

Lambek, Michael. 1996. "The Past Imperfect: Remembering as Moral Practice." In *Tense Past: Cultural Essays in Trauma and Memory*, ed. Paul Antze and Michael Lambek, 235–54. New York: Routledge.

———. 2006. "Memory in a Maussian Universe." In *Memory Cultures: Memory, Subjectivity, and Recognition*, ed. Susannah Radstone and Katharine Hodgkin, 202–16. Piscataway, NJ: Transaction Publishers.

———. 2008. "Value and Virtue." *Anthropological Theory* 8(2): 133–57.

———. 2015. "Afterword: What's Love Got to Do with It?" *Hau: Journal of Ethnographic Theory* 5(1): 395–404.

Langer, Lawrence. 1991. *Holocaust Testimonies: The Ruins of Memory.* New Haven, CT: Yale University Press.

Lemarchand, René. 1970. *Rwanda and Burundi.* New York: Praeger.

———. 1995. "The Rationality of Genocide." *Issue: A Journal of Opinion* 23(2): 8-11.

———. 2002. "The Tunnel at the End of the Light." *Review of African Political Economy* 29(93–94): 389–98.

Lester, Rebecca J. 2011. "Review of *Abject Relations: Everyday Worlds of Anorexia*, by Megan Warin." *American Anthropologist* 113(1): 189–90.

———. 2017. "Self-Governance, Psychotherapy, and the Subject of Managed Care: Internal Family Systems Therapy and the Multiple Self in a US Eating-Disorders Treatment Center." *American Ethnologist* 44(1): 1–13.

Levi, Primo. 1988. *The Drowned and the Saved.* New York: Simon and Schuster.

Li, Tania Murray. 2007. *The Will to Improve: Governmentality, Development, and the Practice of Politics.* Durham, NC: Duke University Press.

Liebow, Elliot. 1967. *Tally's Corner: A Study of Negro Streetcorner Men.* Boston, MA: Little, Brown.

Lienhardt, Godfrey. 1985. "Self: Public, Private: Some African Representations." In *The Category of the Person: Anthropology, Philosophy, History*, ed. Michael Carrithers, Steven Collins and Steven Lukes, 141–55. Cambridge: Cambridge University Press.

Linden, Ian, with Jane Linden. 1977. *Church and Revolution in Rwanda*. New York: Africana Publishing Company.

Longman, Timothy. 2001. "Church Politics and the Genocide in Rwanda." *Journal of Religion in Africa* 31(2): 163–86.

———. 2010a. *Christianity and Genocide in Rwanda*. Cambridge: Cambridge University Press.

———. 2010b. "Trying Times for Rwanda: Reevaluating Gacaca Courts in Post-Genocide Reconciliation." *Harvard International Review* 32(2): 48–52.

Longman, Timothy and Theonest Rutagengwa. 2006. "Memory and Violence in Post-Genocide Rwanda." In *States of Violence: Politics, Youth, and Memory in Contemporary Africa*, ed. Edna G. Bay and Donald L. Donham, 236–60. Charlottesville, VA: University of Virginia Press.

Louis, W.M. Roger. 1963. *Ruanda-Urundi: 1884–1919*. Oxford: Clarendon Press.

Luft, Aliza. 2015. "Toward a Dynamic Theory of Action at the Micro Level of Genocide: Killing, Desistance, and Saving in 1994 Rwanda." *Sociological Theory* 33: 148–72.

Malkki, Liisa H. 1995. *Purity and Exile: Violence, Memory, and National Cosmology among Hutu Refugees in Tanzania*. Chicago, IL: University of Chicago Press.

———. 2015. *The Need to Help: The Domestic Arts of International Humanitarianism*. Durham, NC: Duke University Press.

Mamdani, Mahmood. 2001. *When Victims Become Killers: Colonialism, Nativism, and the Genocide in Rwanda*. Princeton, NJ: Princeton University Press.

Maquet, Jacques J. 1961. *The Premise of Inequality in Ruanda: A Study of Political Relations in a Central African Kingdom*. London: Published for the International African Institute by the Oxford University Press.

Marriott, McKim. 1976. "Hindu Transactions: Diversity without Dualism." In *Transactions in Meaning: The Anthropology of Exchange and Symbolic Behavior*. ASA Essays in Social Anthropology, 1, ed. Bruce Kapferer, 109–42. Philadelphia, PA: Institute for the Study of Human Issues.

Maslow, Abraham. 1943. "A Theory of Human Motivation." *Psychological Review* 50(4): 370–96.

———. 1993. *The Farther Reaches of Human Nature*. New York: Penguin Books.

Mauss, Marcel. [1925] 1967. *The Gift: Forms and Functions of Exchange in Archaic Societies*, trans. Ian Cunnison. London: Cohen & West.

———. [1938] 1985. "A Category of the Human Mind: The Notion of Person, the Notion of Self." In *The Category of the Person: Anthropology, Philosophy, History*, ed. Michael Carrithers, Steven Collins and Steven Lukes, 1–25. Cambridge: Cambridge University Press.

Mazlish, Bruce. 1989. *A New Science: The Breakdown of Connections and the Birth of Sociology*. University Park, PA: Pennsylvania State University Press.

McAllister, Carlota. 2013. "Testimonial Truths and Revolutionary Mysteries." In *War by Other Means: Aftermath in Post-Genocide Guatemala*, ed. Carlota McAllister and Diane M. Nelson, 93–115. Durham, NC: Duke University Press.

McLean Hilker, Lyndsay. 2009. "Everyday Ethnicities: Identity and Reconciliation among Rwandan Youth." *Journal of Genocide Research* 11(1): 81–100.

———. 2014. "Navigating Adolescence and Young Adulthood in Rwanda during and after the Genocide: Intersections of Ethnicity, Gender, and Age." *Childhood Geographies* 12(3): 354–68.

Mead, George Herbert. 1913. "The Social Self." *The Journal of Philosophy, Psychology and Scientific Methods* 10(14): 374–80.

Meierhenrich, Jens. 2011. "Topographies of Remembering and Forgetting: The Transformation of *Lieux de Mémoire* in Rwanda." In *Remaking Rwanda: State Building and Human Rights after Mass Violence*, ed. Scott Straus and Lars Waldorf, 283–96. Madison, WI: University of Wisconsin Press.

Merry, Sally Engle. 1997. "Rethinking Gossip and Scandal." In *Reputation: Rethinking Studies on the Voluntary Elicitation of Good Conduct*, ed. Daniel Bruce Klein, 47–74. Ann Arbor, MI: University of Michigan Press.

Mgbako, Chi. 2005. "Ingando Solidarity Camps: Reconciliation and Political Indoctrination in Post-Genocide Rwanda." *Harvard Human Rights Journal* 18: 201–24.

Mills, C. Wright. 1959. *The Sociological Imagination*. New York: Oxford University Press.

Ministry of Youth, Culture, and Sports. 2005. *The Republic of Rwanda Ministry of Youth, Culture, and Sports National Youth Policy*. Kigali: Republic of Rwanda.

Minow, Martha. 1998. *Between Vengeance and Forgiveness: Facing History after Genocide and Mass Violence*. Boston, MA: Beacon Press.

Mitchell, J. Clyde. 1974. "Perceptions of Ethnicity and Ethnic Behaviour: An Empirical Exploration." In *Urban Ethnicity*, ed. Abner Cohen, 1–35. London: Tavistock.

Nagata, Judith A. 1974. "What is a Malay? Situational Selection of Ethnic Identity in a Plural Society." *American Ethnologist* 1(2): 331–50.

National Institute of Statistics of Rwanda. n.d. *EICV3 District Profile: South-Huye*. Kigali: Republic of Rwanda.

National Service of Gacaca Jurisdictions. 2004. *Process of Collecting Information Required in Gacaca Courts*. Kigali: Republic of Rwanda.

Neocleous, Mark. 2012. "'Don't Be Scared, Be Prepared': Trauma-Anxiety Resilience." *Alternatives: Global, Local, Political* 37(3): 188–98.

Newbury, Catharine. 1988. *The Cohesion of Oppression: Clientship and Ethnicity in Rwanda, 1860–1960*. New York: Columbia University Press.

———. 1995. "Background to Genocide: Rwanda." *Issue: A Journal of Opinion* 23(2): 12–17.

———. 1998. "Ethnicity and the Politics of History." *Africa Today* 45(1): 7–24.

———. 2011. "High Modernism at the Ground Level: The Imidugudu Policy in Rwanda." In *Remaking Rwanda: State Building and Human Rights after Mass Violence*, ed. Scott Straus and Lars Waldorf, 223–39. Madison, WI: University of Wisconsin Press.

Newbury, David. 1980. "The Clans of Rwanda: An Historical Hypothesis." *Africa: Journal of the International African Institute* 50(4): 389–403.

———. 1998. "Understanding Genocide." *African Studies Review* 41(1): 73–97.

Ntakirutimana, Évariste and Josias Semujanga. 2010. "Le manifeste des bahutu et la naissance des idéologies de la haine." In *Le manifeste des bahutu et la diffusion de l'idéologie de la haine au Rwanda (1957–2007)*, ed. Josias Semujanga, Faustin Rutembesa, Évariste Ntakirutimana and Isaïe Nzeyimana, 33–84. Butare: Éditions de l'Université nationale du Rwanda.

Okamura, Jonathan. 1981. "Situational Ethnicity." *Ethnic and Racial Studies* 4(4): 452–65.

Olick, Jeffrey. 1999. "Collective Memory: The Two Cultures." *Sociological Theory* 17(3): 333–48.

Pankhurst, Donna. 1999. "Issues of Justice and Reconciliation in Complex Political Emergencies: Conceptualising Reconciliation, Justice and Peace." *Third World Quarterly* 20(1): 239–55.

Parent, Genevieve. 2010. "Reconciliation and Justice after Genocide: A Theoretical Exploration." *Genocide Studies and Prevention* 5(3): 277–92.

Peale, Norman Vincent. [1956] 2012. *The Power of Positive Thinking: A Practical Guide to Mastering the Problems of Everyday Living*. New York: Random House.

Piot, Charles D. 1993. "Secrecy, Ambiguity, and the Everyday in Kabre Culture." *American Anthropologist* 95(2): 353–70.

Pitt-Rivers, Julian. 1961. *The People of the Sierra*. Chicago, IL: University of Chicago Press.

———. 2016. "The Paradox of Friendship." *Hau: Journal of Ethnographic Theory* 6(3): 443–52.

Portelli, Alessandro. 1991. *The Death of Luigi Trastulli and Other Stories: Form and Meaning in Oral History*. New York: SUNY Press.

Pottier, Johan. 2002. *Re-imagining Rwanda: Conflict, Survival and Disinformation in the Late Twentieth Century*. Cambridge: Cambridge University Press.

Prunier, Gérard. 1995. *The Rwanda Crisis: History of a Genocide*. New York: Columbia University Press.

Pugh, Michael. 2005. "The Political Economy of Peacebuilding: A Critical Theory Perspective." *International Journal of Peace Studies* 10(2): 23–42.

Pupavac, Vanessa. 2004. "War on the Couch: The Emotionology of the New International Security Paradigm." *European Journal of Social Theory* 7(2): 149–70.

Purdeková, Andrea. 2012. "Civic Education and Social Transformation in Post-Genocide Rwanda: Forging the Perfect Development Subjects." In *Rwanda Fast Forward: Social, Economic, Military and Reconciliation Prospects*, ed. Maddalena Campioni, Patrick Noack, 192–212. London: Palgrave McMillan.

———. 2015. *Making Ubumwe: Power, State, and Camps in Rwanda's Unity-Building Project*. New York: Berghahn Books.

Rawlins, William K. 2008. *The Compass of Friendship: Narratives, Identities, and Dialogues*. Thousand Oaks, CA: Sage Publications.

Reckwitz, Andreas. 2002. "Toward a Theory of Social Practices: A Development in Culturalist Theorizing." *European Journal of Social Theory* 5(2): 243–63.

Rettig, Max. 2008. "Gacaca: Truth, Justice, and Reconciliation in Postconflict Rwanda?" *African Studies Review* 51(3): 25–50.

Reyntjens, Filip. 2004. "Rwanda, Ten Years On: From Genocide to Dictatorship." *African Affairs* 103(411): 177–210.

———. 2011. "Constructing the Truth, Dealing with Dissent, Domesticating the World: Governance in Post-Genocide Rwanda." *African Affairs* 110(438): 1–34.

———. 2015a. *Political Governance in Post-Genocide Rwanda*. Cambridge: Cambridge University Press.

———. 2015b. "Briefing the Struggle over the Truth: Rwanda and the BBC." *African Affairs* 114(457): 637–48.

Richters, Annemiek. 2010. "Suffering and Healing in the Aftermath of War and Genocide in Rwanda: Mediations through Community Based Sociotherapy." In *Mediations of Violence in Africa: Fashioning New Futures from Contested Pasts*, ed. Liedwin Kapeitjns and Annemiek Richters, 173–210. Leiden: Brill.

Ricoeur, Paul. 2004. *Memory, History, Forgetting*. Chicago, IL: University of Chicago Press.

Rieff, Philip. 1966. *The Triumph of the Therapeutic: Uses of Faith after Freud*. Chicago, IL: Chicago University Press.

Riesman, Paul. 1977. *Freedom in Fulani Social Life: An Introspective Ethnography*. Chicago, IL: University of Chicago Press.

———. 1986. "The Person and the Life Cycle in African Social Life and Thought." *African Studies Review* 29(2): 71–138

Roht-Arriaza, Naomi. 2006. *Transitional Justice in the Twenty-First Century: Beyond Truth versus Justice*. Cambridge: Cambridge University Press.

Rose, Nikolas. 1992. "Governing the Enterprising Self." In *The Values of the Enterprise Culture: The Moral Debate*, ed. Paul Heelas and Paul Morris, 141–64. London: Routledge.

———. 1996. *Inventing Ourselves: Psychology, Power, and Personhood.* Cambridge: Cambridge University Press.

Roseberry, William. 1994. "Hegemony and the Language of Contention." In *Everyday Forms of State Formation: Revolution and the Negotiation of Rule in Modern Mexico*, ed. Gilbert M. Joseph and Daniel Nugent, 355–66. Durham, NC: Duke University Press.

Ross, Fiona. 2003. *Bearing Witness: Women and the Truth and Reconciliation Commission in South Africa.* London: Pluto Press.

Rumiya, Jean. 1992. *Le Rwanda sous le régime du mandat belge (1916–1931).* Paris: L'Harmattan.

Rwabukumba, Joseph and Vincent Mudandagizi. 1974. "Les formes historiques de la dependence personnelle dans l'état rwandais." *Cahiers d'Études Africaines* 14(53): 6–25.

Rwanda Revenue Authority. n.d. Corporate Income Tax. Retrieved 12 May 2017 from http://www.rra.gov.rw/index.php?id=30

Sahlins, Marshall. 1972. *Stone Age Economics.* Chicago, IL: Aldine-Atherton.

Sarkin, Jeremy. 2001. "The Tension between Justice and Reconciliation in Rwanda: Politics, Human Rights, Due Process, and the Role of Gacaca Courts in Dealing with the Genocide." *Journal of African Law* 45(2): 143–72.

Semujanga, Josias. 2003. *Origins of the Rwandan Genocide.* Amherst, NY: Humanity Books.

Sennett, Richard and Jonathan Cobb. 1972. *The Hidden Injuries of Class.* New York: W.W. Norton and Company.

Shaw, Rosalind. 2007. "Memory Frictions: Localizing the Truth and Reconciliation Commission in Sierra Leone." *Transitional Justice* 1(2): 183–207.

Shils, Edward. 1961. *The Intellectual between Tradition and Modernity: The Indian Situation.* Comparative Studies in Society and History Supplement I. The Hague: Mouton.

———. [1960] 1972. *The Intellectuals and the Powers and Other Essays.* Chicago, IL: University of Chicago Press.

Silver, Allan. 1990. "Friendship in Commercial Society: Eighteenth-Century Social Theory and Modern Sociology." *American Journal of Sociology* 95(6): 1474–504.

Simpson, Anthony. 2003. "Personhood and Self in Catholic Formation in Zambia." *Journal of Religion on Africa* 33(4): 377–400.

Sirven, Pierre. 1984. "La sous-urbanisation et les villes du Rwanda et du Burundi." Ph.D. thesis. Pessac, France: Université de Bordeaux III.

Smith, Adam. 1982. *The Wealth of Nations.* London: Penguin Classics.

Smith, Karl. 2012. "From Dividual and Individual Selves to Porous Subjects." *TAJA: The Australian Journal of Anthropology* 23: 50–64.

Sommers, Marc. 2012. *Stuck: Rwandan Youth and the Struggle for Adulthood.* Athens, GA: University of Georgia Press.

Statistics Rwanda. 2014. *The 2014 Statistical Yearbook.* Kigali: Republic of Rwanda.

Staub, Ervin. 2003. "Preventing Violence and Generating Humane Values: Healing and Reconciliation in Rwanda." *International Review of the Red Cross* 85(852): 791–806.

Steflja, Izabela. 2012. "The High Costs and Consequences of Rwanda's Shift in Language Policy Reform from French to English." Africa Portal, Centre for International Governance Innovation. Retrieved 13 July 2015 from https://www.africaportal.org/dspace/articles/high-costs-and-consequences-rwandas-shift-language-policy-reform-french-english.

Steward, John. 2008. "Only Healing Heals: Concepts and Methods of Psycho-Social Healing in Post-Genocide Rwanda." In *After Genocide: Transitional Justice, Post-Conflict*

Reconstruction, and Reconciliation in Rwanda and Beyond, ed. Phil Clark and Zachary D. Kaufman, 171–90. New York: Columbia University Press.

Stover, Eric and Harvey M. Weinstein. 2004. "Introduction: Conflict, Justice and Reclamation." In *My Neighbor, My Enemy: Justice and Community in the Aftermath of Mass Atrocity*, ed. Eric Stover and Harvey M. Weinstein, 1–26. Cambridge and New York: Cambridge University Press.

Strathern, Marilyn. 1988. *The Gender of the Gift: Problems with Women and Problems with Society in Melanesia*. Berkeley, CA: University of California Press.

———. 1992. *Reproducing the Future: Essays on Anthropology, Kinship, and New Reproductive Technologies*. New York: Routledge.

Straus, Scott and Lars Waldorf. 2011. "Introduction: Seeing Like a Post-Conflict State." In *Remaking Rwanda: State Building and Human Rights after Mass Violence*, ed. Scott Straus and Lars Waldorf, 3–21. Madison, WI: University of Wisconsin Press.

Summerfield, Derek. 1999. "A Critique of Seven Assumptions behind Psychological Trauma Programmes in War-Affected Areas." *Social Science and Medicine* 48: 1449–62.

———. 2001. "The Invention of Post-Traumatic Stress Disorder and the Social Usefulness of a Psychiatric Category." *British Medical Journal* 322(7278): 95–98.

Taylor, Charles. 1985. *Human Agency and Language*. London: Cambridge University Press.

———. 1989. *Sources of the Self: The Making of the Modern Identity*. Cambridge, MA: Harvard University Press.

———. 1993. "To Follow a Rule…". In *Bourdieu: Critical Perspectives*, ed. Craig Calhoun, Edward LiPuma and Moishe Postone, 45–60. Chicago, IL: University of Chicago Press.

Taylor, Christopher C. 1992. *Milk, Honey, and Money: Changing Concepts in Rwandan Healing*. Washington, DC: Smithsonian Institution Press.

———. 2005. "Fluids and Fractals in Rwanda: Order and Chaos." In *On the Order of 'Chaos': Social Anthropology and the Science of Chaos*, ed. Mark Mosko and Frederick Damon, 136–65. New York: Berghahn Books.

Theidon, Kimberly and Lisa J. Laplante. 2007. "Truth with Consequences: Justice and Reparations in Post-Truth Commission Peru." *Human Rights Quarterly* 29: 228–50.

Thomson, Susan. 2010. "Getting Close to Rwandans since the Genocide: Studying Everyday Life in Highly Politicized Research Settings." *African Studies Review* 53(3): 19–34.

———. 2013. *Whispering Truth to Power: The Everyday Resistance of Rwandan Peasants to Post-Genocide Reconciliation*. Madison, WI: University of Wisconsin Press.

Tsing, Anna Lowenhaupt. 2005. *Friction: An Ethnography of Global Connection*. Princeton, NJ: Princeton University Press.

Turner, Simon. 2005. "'The Tutsi Are Afraid We will Discover Their Secrets': On Secrecy and Sovereign Power in Burundi." *Social Identities* 11(1): 37–54.

Uvin, Peter. 1998. *Aiding Violence: The Development Enterprise in Rwanda*. West Hartford, CT: Kumarian Press.

Vansina, Jan. 1962. *L'Évolution du Royaume Rwanda des Origines à 1900*. Brussels: ARSOM.

———. 1998. "The Politics of History and the Crisis in the Great Lakes." *Africa Today* 45(1): 37–44.

———. 2000. "Historical Tales (Ibiteekerezo) and the History of Rwanda." *History in Africa* 27: 375–414.

———. 2004. *Antecedents to Modern Rwanda: The Nyiginya Kingdom*, trans. Jan Vansina. Madison, WI: University of Wisconsin Press.

Van't Spijker, Gerard. 1990. "Les usages funéraires et la mission de l'église: Une étude anthropologique et théologique des rites funéraires au Rwanda." Ph.D. dissertation. Amsterdam: Free University of Amsterdam.

Vidal, Claudine. 1969. "Le Rwanda des Anthropologues ou le Fétichisme de la Vache." *Cahiers d'Études Africaines* 35: 384–401.

———. [1985] 1999. "Situations ethniques au Rwanda." In *Au Coeur de l'Ethnie: Ethnies, tribalisme et état en Afrique*, ed. J.-L. Amselle and E. M'Bokolo, 167–84. Paris: La Decouverte.

———. 2001. "Les commémorations du génocide au Rwanda." *Les Temps Modernes* 56(613): 1–46.

———. 2004. "La commémoration du génocide au Rwanda: Violence symbolique, mémorisation forcée et histoire officielle." *Cahier d'Études Africaines* 175: 575–92.

Wagner, Roy. 1991. "The Fractal Person." In *Big Men and Great Men: Personifications of Power in Melanesia*, ed. M. Godelier and M. Strathern, 159–73. Cambridge: Cambridge University Press.

Weber, Max. 2002. *The Protestant Ethic and the Spirit of Capitalism and Other Writings*. New York: Penguin.

Werbner, Richard (ed.). 1998. *Memory and the Postcolony: African Anthropology and the Critique of Power*. London: Zed Books.

Werner, Cynthia. 2000. "Gifts, Bribes, and Development in Post-Soviet Kazakstan." *Human Organization* 59(1): 11–22.

Wertsch, James V. and Henry L. Roediger. 2008. "Collective Memory: Conceptual Foundations and Theoretical Approaches." *Memory* 16(3): 318–26.

Williams, Brackette F. 1989. "A Class Act: Anthropology and the Race to Nation across Ethnic Terrain." *Annual Review of Anthropology* 18: 401–44.

———. 1991. *Stains on My Name, War in My Veins: Guyana and the Politics of Cultural Struggle*. Durham, NC: Duke University Press.

Williams, James. 2015. "Poor Men with Money: On the Politics of Not Studying the Poorest of the Poor in Urban South Africa." *Current Anthropology* 56(11): 24–32.

Williams, Raymond. 1977. *Marxism and Literature*. Oxford: Oxford University Press.

Wilmsen, Edwin N. and Patrick McAllister (eds). 1996. *The Politics of Difference: Ethnic Premises in a World of Power*. Chicago, IL: University of Chicago Press.

Wilson, Richard. 2001. *The Politics of Truth and Reconciliation in South Africa: Legitimizing the Post-Apartheid State*. Cambridge: Cambridge University Press.

World Bank. 2015. Rwanda Country Overview. Retrieved 15 July 2015 from http://www.worldbank.org/en/country/rwanda/overview.

Youll, Jackie and Helen Meekosha. 2011. "Always Look on the Bright Side of Life: Cancer and Positive Thinking." *Journal of Sociology* 49(1): 22–40.

Young, Allan. 1995. *The Harmony of Illusions: Inventing Posttraumatic Stress Disorder*. Princeton, NJ: Princeton University Press.

Young, James E. 1993. *The Texture of Memory: Holocaust Memorials and Meaning*. New Haven, CT: Yale University Press.

———. 1998. "The Counter-Monument: Memory against Itself in Germany Today." *Critical Inquiry* 18(2): 267–96.

Zorbas, Eugenia. 2004. "Reconciliation in Post-Genocide Rwanda." *African Journal of Legal Studies* 1(1): 29–52.

———. 2009. "What Does Reconciliation after Genocide Mean? Public Transcripts and Hidden Transcripts in Post-Genocide Rwanda." *Journal of Genocide Research* 11(1): 127–47.

INDEX

Institute for Sustainable Peace Building
(ICPD), 132–6, 137–9, 140–41, 147,
148, 152, 153, 154, 155–6, 157
changing "mentalities" through
education, 142–4
knowledge systems, 132
legacies of genocide and mass violence,
136, 138–9, 152, 157
making peace by remaking persons, 130,
132, 135m 143–4, 146–9
mediation, Rwandan culture and, 135
"mentalities," problem of, 134–5, 137,
139–46, 148, 152–3
mutual understanding, peace-building
and promotion of, 130
openness, promotion of, 131, 135, 137
organizations, 16–17, 19, 91, 130–6
peace and modern nationhood, visions
of, 3
personal development and, 138, 140,
144–6, 150, 151, 156–7
personal problems and process of, 136–7,
138
practices of
ethnographic perspective on, 131
political conflict and, 136–9
remaking selves 146–9
staff and, 151, 152–3, 156, 157
psychologization of, 137–8
reconciliation and, 130–31
good citizenship through leadership
in, 143
reconciliation celebrities, 149–56, 157
reconciliation groups (groupes de
rapprochement or groupes mixtes), 134,
135–6, 144, 149–50, 151, 152–3,
154–5, 156
reparations at payer/payee level, 128–9
resilience, discourse of, 137
Rwandan Association for Peace and
Reconciliation (ARPR), 128–9, 130,
131, 133–4, 135, 139–40, 142, 147–8,
157
changing "mentalities" by personal
development, 144–6
consciousness levels in teachings,
144–6

group testimony, 154–6
self-confidence building, 136–9
transformative experiences with help
of, 150–51, 152–3
self-mastery and, 131, 137, 147
social problems 136–7, 138, 157
testimonies, importance of, 149–50,
151–2, 153, 154, 155–6
therapeutic interventions, transformative
power of, 131
victimization, powerlessness and, 138
peaceful selfhood, 9–13, 44, 58, 76, 101,
102, 121, 125, 146, 164
appeal of striving for, 162–3
composite personhood and, 12
dependent relationships and, 10–11
dispositions within, range of, 9
genocide, "contagion" explanation for, 10
ideals of, 11–12
relational personhood, violence and, 9, 12
social hierarchies, popular explanations of
genocide and, 9–10
striving in post-genocide moment to be, 58
symbolic violence within, 164
testimonies of personal transformations
to, 150–53
voluntary social relationships and, 11
"Western" selfhood and 9, 11
peasantry
contempt for, 124, 130, 134
paysans ("peasants") in Rwanda, 25–6, 29,
71, 104, 142
"peasants" (abaturage) and "urban people"
(abanyamujyi) in Butare, 25–6
personal development, 8, 161, 162–3
peace-building and, 138, 140, 144–6,
150, 151, 156–7
promotion of entrepreneurship and,
116–17
pursuit of, 163
personal problems, peace-building process
and, 136–7, 138
personhood, 22, 125–6
absence of relations and, 84–91
competing forms of 160
composite personhood, peaceful selfhood
and, 12